VIRGIN TIME

VIRGIN TIME

PATRICIA HAMPL

Farrar, Straus and Giroux

New York

Library of Congress Cataloging-in-Publication Data
Hampl, Patricia.
Virgin time / Patricia Hampl. — 1st ed.
1. Apologetics—20th century. I. Title.
BT1102.H32   1992   230—dc20   92-5465 CIP

Excerpts from The Asian Journal of Thomas Merton by Thomas
Merton, copyright © 1968, 1970,1973 by the Trustees of the Merton
Legacy Trust. Reprinted by permission of New Directions Publishing
Corporation. Excerpt from Conjectures of a Guilty Bystander by
Thomas Merton, copyright © 1965, 1966 by The Abbey of Gethse-
mani. Reprinted by permission of Doubleday, a division of Bantam,
Doubleday, Dell Publishing Group, Inc. Excerpt from An Introduc-
tion to Buddhism by the Dalai Lama, copyright © 1965 by the Dalai
Lama. Published by Tibet House, New Delhi.

for Terence

and

for Jo

Acknowledgments

For grants and fellowships awarded over the years, abiding thanks to the Bush Foundation, the Guggenheim Foundation, the Ingram-Merrill Foundation, the John D. and Catherine T. MacArthur Foundation, the National Endowment for the Arts, the University of Minnesota Graduate School and College of Liberal Arts, and the Villa Serbelloni Bellagio Study and Conference Center of the Rockefeller Foundation.

Thanks to readers of the early pages: the late Terrence DesPres, Deborah Keenan, Rebecca Hill, Judith Guest, Christina Baldwin, and Scott Walker. A fond and grateful salute, as well, to those who read later versions or in various ways offered insight and help along the way: Phebe Hanson, Marly Rusoff, Carol Conroy, Maureen McAvey, Gail Godwin, Pamela Holt, David Konstan, Antonia Hamilton, Marisha Chamberlain, Charles Baxter, Terence Williams, and my agent, Rhoda Weyr. To Rose Johnstone for her daily help, and to Mary LaChapelle and my editor, Jonathan Galassi, for their meticulous responses to the final ms., my deepest bow.

Wonder is not precisely Knowing
And not precisely Knowing not—
A beautiful but bleak condition
He has not lived who has not felt . . .

—EMILY DICKINSON
poem #1331

FAITH

1

There is nothing to be afraid of. But the plane lifts, and here I go again, crashing down fathoms of dread. God (whom I usually have no trouble cutting out of the picture) doesn't want us to fly. I know this.

To fly: such presumption. Didn't the nuns tell us *human pride* was the one sin that couldn't be forgiven, the worst of the Seven Deadly, inviting the vengeance of the Most High? Phrases like this slither up, smiting from their Old Testament ambush. Wrinkles of terror run along the soles of my feet. My toes curl toward Earth. Then the baleful *thunk thunk* of the landing wheels retracting.

"I've never been on an airplane before," the boy next to me says, startling me out of a deal I'm trying to cut with the Almighty. A fresh haircut has laid bare his skull. It's hard to tell if he's handsome; he looks skinned. And happy, wildly happy.

"I'm from Eveleth," he says, naming one of the hard-luck towns on the Minnesota Iron Range. "I'm on my way to West Point." The jubilant voice of travel—of escape—is unmistakable. "We get two days in New York City first. Never been to New York City. That's a lot of firsts for this kid. This time tomorrow I'll be on top of the Empire State Building."

Death

fear

Worldliness

"The World Trade Towers are taller," I say, roused from terror by this stray fact, but it's a pedant's mean-spirited remark.

It barely grazes him. "Yeah," he says, grinning, "I'll be there, too."

We both look out his window ("I said, give me the window seat, I don't care smoking or no smoking, but I've got to have a window seat"). St. Paul, sweet bluffy town of every age of my life, tilts away. Below us, the Minnesota River knots itself onto the Mississippi's muddy ribbon. There's the green dome of the cathedral where my mother (she *likes* to fly) and my father (he just wants to go fishing up north at Leech Lake) were married a million years ago in 1940.

The world isn't just disappearing; it's becoming anonymous. The dome's oxidized copper looks like a patch of lichen spreading on an outcrop of gray rock. We all die. Why not me, right here, like this. Later, an anchorwoman will say, "Luckily, the plane was only half full."

No one else seems to be facing death, all these strangers reading *USA Today*, entranced as children deep in comic books. The stewardess recites the oxygen mask demo and makes her appalling suggestion about using the orange seat cushion "as a flotation device in the unlikely event of . . ."

It's always like this. Barely controlled terror. Not so bad I can't fly; I wish it were that decisive. I read with admiration about celebrities, sportscasters—some of them big tough guys —who refuse to fly. They take trains or hire a whole bus to get them around. I'm not quite scared enough. I go ahead. Get the non-refundable ticket, chatter about my trip with both feet planted on the ground, my heart ticking like a set bomb. Lucky me, going here, going there. Going, this time, to Italy.

In my pocket, my damp hand closes on the gold airplane brooch my husband gave me as a lucky charm. He has also given me a magazine article outlining the extreme statistical unlikelihood of an airplane crash. But what about terrorists? Those bombs soft as chewed gum lurking in cassette recorders? What about evil? Numbers are cold comfort to someone fed from girlhood on the corrupting Catholic sweets of being *special*, chosen, outside the proletariat of statistics. Not for me the consolations of probability. I stuff the magazine article in the pocket of the seat back in front of me, and go for the totem.

The brooch is a cunningly exact replica of a DC-3. The tiny propellers can be twirled, and the landing wheels, tinier still, spin in their mountings. Windows are etched on the slanting flank of the plane's body. The entire spirit of the thing is brave and buoyant.

The pin once belonged to my husband's Aunt Leah, who was a flapper, went to Paris, had an affair with a French (or Romanian?) prince, then married a rich American (for love). Later, she lived in Las Vegas, a hard-drinking divorcée (love never lasts), and hobnobbed with Names. She played golf with Betty Grable. Somewhere along the line she was given this solid gold airplane by Howard Hughes as a souvenir—of what? A memento from the launching of one of his fleet? Or (love never ends) a trophy of romance? The facts, if there ever were any, are lost.

I rub Howard Hughes's plane in a rhythm of safety known only to my terror. I repeat silently, in a brainless mantra, *Played golf with Grable, golf with Grable, golf with Grable.* The green dome of the toy cathedral is gone. The river is a flick of light, and we are just piercing the cloud cover, entering our climb.

"We may be experiencing a little turbulence, ladies and gentlemen," the captain is saying in that commander-of-the-ship drawl they all seem to have. He advises us to keep our seatbelts secured, as he does. "We'll get above this stuff, and find us a nice smooth ride on out to the New York area." Smooth, smooth, the drawl of doom. St. Paul is gone, all my life in its streets, and we are experiencing turbulence. The West Point cadet has his face up against the window. I rub the DC-3 and repeat my mantra silently, *Golf, golf, golf.*

I must be praying. Proving once again, without meaning to, that there's no stopping the mind's grab for salvation, o ye of little faith, o all of us on the go who hardly know what we believe in anymore. Most of the time I'm so removed from belief I confuse it with having an opinion. As if God were a candidate who may or may not get the vote of my focus group. Then this other thing lunges from its corner, not fear, but the stunning acuity born of fear. How keen the terrified mind is. Its cry is prayer. Planes are my foxhole, I'm always on my knees in them.

But just yesterday I was sitting in the cool, shadowy parlor of San Damiano Monastery outside Minneapolis, visiting Donnie (Sister Mary Madonna, but we're beyond that after my months—years now—of weekly visits). I was trying to explain to her why I was going on this trip. Looking for something, couldn't explain.

"You're going on a pilgrimage," she said, meaning to be helpful.

"No," I said, bristling, "I'm just going." Something about the word set my teeth on edge. *Pilgrimage.* I wince at the eau-de-cologne language of spirituality, but the whole world as I first understood it comes rushing back on the merest scent. I still want to embrace it—so, of course, when it dares to draw close, I slap it clean across the mouth. Love and loathing, those old partners.

Mine was a Catholic girlhood spent gorging on metaphor—Mystical Body, transubstantiation, dark night of the soul, the little martyrdom of everyday life. And remember, girls, life is a journey. Your own life is a pilgrimage. Maybe we had too much meaning too early. It was like having too much money. The quirkiness of life was betrayed, given inflated significance by our rich symbology. We powered around our ordinary lives in the Cadillac language of Catholic spirituality, looking on with pity as the Protestants pedaled their stripped-down bicycles.

Even the spring flowers of that Catholic past—window-box tulips, hyacinths the dog rooted up and pissed on, the alleys of lilac cloaking the garbage cans—were not just our improbable spring after the savage Minnesota winter. They belonged to Mary, our Mother. The public-school children carried nosegays for their teachers' desks, but in May we walked down Summit Avenue to St. Luke's grade school, lugging bouquets almost as big as ourselves to their true owner, the Queen of the May.

6

Nothing was just itself, nothing was left alone. We were clasped, suffocating and yet happy, to the great bosom of Meaning. Which doesn't let me off the hook for snapping at Donnie. She carries it all lightly, as in a day pack, while I can barely lift my trunkful of Catholic memorabilia. "I don't know why I'm going," I told her finally.

"Yes," she said, in that interested way of hers. "Not knowing—that's the spiritual part."

Donnie is over fifty, looks younger (except for the eyes). Her hair is shaped in what used to be called a pixie cut, a sort of monastic tonsure without the bald spot. It suits her. There is an elfin quality to her—tough elf. She's been a contemplative nun since she was seventeen. Not a woman easily rattled. No doubt she sees my grouchiness as "the spiritual part." I can't figure her. Yet I keep going back to visit her, to sort out what I thought was the past, my dead Catholic past, only to find it isn't dead at all.

"It's called 'spiritual direction,' what we're doing," she said one day. "Do you mind?" She's sympathetic to my language foibles. What could I say? Whatever we were doing, I found I required it, though I frown at the terms—spiritual direction, _Paradox_ pilgrimage.

The plane heaves and climbs. It's struggling, doesn't anyone else sense this? I'm being asked what I want to drink. I'm taking the foil packet of peanuts. I'm the only one dying. Beads of water sweat across the window. I can't see a thing. _Golf, golf. God, God._

"Don't worry," Donnie said yesterday. "I'll be in the chapel, praying for you. I'll hold you up there all the way across the ocean." She laughed, a nutty Druid laugh, Irish and ironic. The laugh made me almost believe her. Maybe that's faith: the smart little laugh that holds the world up.

The plane lurches and seethes. I'm a goner, and Donnie is safe on the ground, praying into the sky.

"Look!" The skinhead cadet has turned his moon-face to me, and now he points out the window. We're still tipped slightly upward, still laboring through the wads of wet gray cotton. The plane, surging and unsettled, penetrates the cloud-batten in awful lurches. And there, just crowning, the blue arc of the sky emerges, brittle with the sun's gold. The cadet is gleaming, too, blind with wonder, as we hurtle into heaven.

I got on the plane, against the better judgment of my terror, because I'd come to the conviction that I had to see the old world of Catholicism. More than see—had to touch it. Was it still breathing? Making its low murmur over the votive flames in the dark?

But I also knew that the "old world of Catholicism" was right at home. In me. I was born there, under the wide eye of postwar American Catholicism. Forget Vatican II: ours was the Church triumphant, not the Church reforming and defensive. Going to that world was just a matter of remembering. That's what I thought at first. I would roll out the memories, wrapping them up like a wedding dress bundled in tissue and put absolutely away. Remembering was the only roaming I needed to do. I could do even better. I'm a writer: I would write it up. I would write it away.

But reminiscence is a nag deep in its nosebag of memory. The grass of remembrance is never quite green, having been trod so often. And how many more rages and dumb jokes about the nuns, poor penguins, does the Catholic memory need to tramp to dust? The past is no destination anyway, though it seems so utterly a *place*. The trouble is, there are no humans there. All the figures have turned to wax—nuns in their Renaissance garments, the oracular voices of immigrant priests poised above us in bronze pulpits, the clairvoyant bridal froth of First Communion dresses, the Saturday-night confession buzz of all the wrong sins. You can only get so much story out of these statues.

As a result, people like me, fused by fascination to their past, find themselves taking planes to distant places, boarding with an urgency that suggests a family emergency is calling us home. Looking for our roots, we say. But roots are buried: they're supposed to be. And the past isn't alive. Only our urgency is.

Maybe this urgency *is* the past, the only juice still spurting from the source that made us. It must be this urgency, a peculiar form of desire, that makes us zoom around, looking for what time has put back in its breast pocket.

The cadet touches my arm with his moth finger. " 'Scuse me, ma'am." My eyes are shut, reverent with fear. "I was just wondering if you were going to use those peanuts."

I hand him the packet.

"Thanks. This is great." He has three cans of Coke lined up on his tray table.

I look at his profile, the military tonsure, the happiness. It suddenly hits me: *he's* not going to crash. The plane is still thudding around, searching for a smooth lane of air, but he's all right. He glows with future. I smile at him. Safety courses through me, all sea breezes. I go limp with reassurance, and the little gold plane drops to the bottom of my pocket.

He's off to his future. Never mind if it's somebody's war, or the floating crap game called peace. He'll fly with it.

And I'm off to the past, is that it? Donnie is down there on the ground, keeping us aloft. She got the last word on what I'm up to, after all. As I left the monastery yesterday, she said, "Well, it was good enough for Chaucer."

"What was?"

"Your trip," Donnie said. "It's springtime. Remember?

> *"Whan that Aprille with hise shoures sote*
> *The droghte of March hath percèd to the rote . . .*
> *Thanne longen folk to goon on pilgrimages."*

I don't think there are holy places, but in Assissi I felt as if I were in one.

9

2

I had signed up for a walking tour—"The Road to Assisi" the color brochure called it, showing people in shorts and funny hats hiking through masses of wildflowers, smiling. There were also several photographs of a picnic: a blue-and-white cloth spread on dark grass, liters of wine propped against a still life of bread and hunks of cheese and fat red salamis. An apple tree bent obligingly over the scene. A close-up showed fresh figs cut open, laid alongside a green triangle of grapes.

The picnic shots decided me. Those figs. Something of the graciousness and simplicity, the splendor I imagined Italy to be, was lying on that blue-and-white cloth in light and shade. Something remembered—though I couldn't remember it. The language of the brochure would have satisfied anyone's travel snobbery. It practically discouraged people from signing on. "We are a small, privately held firm, with offices in Cambridge, England. We design and lead walking tours for small groups along little-known trails here and abroad. Those interested in a more standard group tour of 'sites' or those concerned about 'nightlife' would no doubt be happier with other holiday plans." I envisioned a band of hearty spinsters.

Now, getting off the plane at Leonardo Da Vinci airport after the long night flight, nobody I saw looked very hearty. The Roman morning was already puffy with clouds and moist heat. Soldiers stood here and there along the corridor, their shoulder-strap AK-47s at the ready. Some of them had dogs on leads. The dogs looked down, deeply abstracted, but the men stared us right in the eyes as we filed off the plane toward Passport Control. Not the famous Italian flirtatiousness—the look was plain carbon.

A handsome young man (a tenor's military mustache, eyes dark as the inside of a cow, lovely mouth but set hard, on duty) checked me out. Behind him a big sign advertised the Banco di Santo Spirito. His glance stapled me like a memo crossing his desk, and passed on: American tourist, no dope, no bomb, no interest. My first Italian moment, brief and dismissive. It made me feel not innocent but empty. I was free, though, to enter and exchange my currency with the Holy Spirit.

I wandered around the area by the car rental counter, looking for my group. I checked currency exchange, watching for wiry middle-aged women in culottes. I had a friend who had walked "The Road to Assisi" a year before; she had assured me that the grown-up Girl Guides were there in force, with their encyclopedic knowledge of wildflowers and an ability to point out constellations in the night sky.

I wanted the spinsters as travel companions as much as I wanted the fresh figs—sane women without interesting erotic histories, women who had given themselves over to something other than men. But it's wrong to call what I wished to escape "men." It was the tangled histories with men I'd come to dread, my own and everyone else's. The stories women settle down to tell when they begin to be friends. The exhibition of battle scars. The swapping of titles of self-help books. And an ironic laugh bred of frequent recitation of these tales which does not heal the teller, perhaps, but is meant to soothe the wound.

My antipathy was from the finely tuned renditions of those romantic histories, delivered (post-therapy) with heavily analyzed subplots leading back to the Family of Origin, as mother

11

and father are now called, according them the fateful giantism of characters in a novel. *And of course I understand now that because his mother (who was thwarted—one of those really thwarted women) never managed to . . . And naturally, given where I was coming from* (rich pause, empathetic nod from audience of one), *there was no way I could . . .*

I was sick with insight, fed up with *versions*. The need to impose pattern on these baroque tales of sexual liberation, which seemed to send everyone I knew into therapy, had squeezed the very life out of the stories that had appalled everyone enough to require therapy in the first place. Even the phrase *sexual liberation* seemed antique, comic.

People wished to name things now, instead of living them. Intended to be less painful, but it was curiously bloodless, this capacity to label whole episodes, years, loves: passive-aggressive, alcoholic, co-dependent, dysfunctional, all the *terms*.

I had always secretly imagined my life as a story, a movie. Even as a child I felt at home in the third person and the narrative past tense. I scripted effortlessly—always had—as I went through the idiot aspects of life and the grand moments: *She was walking down the corridor to her first day in third grade. She was a little scared, but she opened the door of the classroom and went in. Everyone looked up for a second. Just another third-grader, but if you looked more closely, you would see . . .*

I was used to being a heroine, privately. I was not happy with the (pretty accurate, I thought) batch of labels I used to tidy up the litter of my history. All this analyzing of the past took the story away. I wasn't a heroine—and where were my usual villains? We were all reduced to literary criticism.

I began to wonder if I had jumped from the breathtaking innocence of a girlhood where everything was a cliff-hanger, down to a plain of parched cynicism where the world had become exquisite insight. Maybe I'd missed entirely the mid-stroke of maturity with its moxie of a life being lived.

I married late in life, as the women in my mother's family say of anyone who marries after thirty. I was past forty. Plenty of time before that to mix it up. And I took plenty of time to sort it out.

But the night before my wedding I dreamed not of old loves and friendships lost or eluded. Nothing of the indecisiveness and lush betrayals I had come to see as my history ever since, on a day in May 1966, I left my gynecologist's office, sat alone at the Brothers Deli in downtown Minneapolis, and ate with elation a Reuben sandwich and a piece of seven-layer chocolate cake, polishing off the whole thing with the first birth control pill of my life.

In my wedding dream no one appeared whom I knew in this world. Yet it was the dream of my life. A group of nuns was gathering wheat in golden bundles, singing and smiling in soft focus. The nuns appeared to have been sent over from Central Casting; the habits were graceful, the faces winsome. Very *Sound of Music* nuns, costumes and set design by Cecil Beaton. They exchanged radiant smiles as they trundled up their sheaves.

Bells began ringing, and I saw a monastery, low, made of adobe, off to the side. Of one accord, the nuns put down their wheat, still smiling, and formed two lines. Not military lines, but natural parallels, wavering like melody written on a staff. The bells kept ringing and now I heard a firm, lofting line of Gregorian chant as they moved—still so happy—toward the monastery door for prayer. They entered, disappearing within the abode's dark interior.

I moved toward the door, too. I was practically running through the golden field to catch up. But the monastery was farther away than it appeared, the way a mountain on the horizon is. The door swung shut behind the last of them before I got there. I could no longer hear them, though I knew they were in there, singing the Divine Office. I stopped to catch my breath.

That's when it hit me—*I can't go in there, I'm getting married.*

Grief, as at the death of a true love, shot through me. I felt that utter devastation of dreams, a sorrow so intense it breaks the fierce tension of attachment. Maybe that's why, after nightmares, a person often feels light, carefree. Death is not the end, it is the release.

That's how it was.

When I told the dream, however, I found it brought frowns. "Heavy," said a friend given to Jungian analysis of such things, "heavy dream."

Light or Heavy

No, I wanted to shout, light dream, light dream! Only Donnie understood. "Great dream!" she said, almost crowing. She understood: I had finally saluted the first passion of my life. The passion was not simply to be a nun—though is there a Catholic girl who has not paused, for a longer or shorter fantasy, over that possibility? There was never a question of becoming a nun: no sex. Then, too, I was always a shopgirl at heart, crazy for a pretty dress, ready to spend the last of my paycheck on fancy French food. I was born with a deep dread of missing a treat. "Giving up" something was for Lent, not for life.

The other, richer passion, rooted early, was for the mystery of a dedicated life. Somewhere along the years, it passed beyond the allure of consecration to the mystery of living itself. That mystery, elusive even in its presence in every breath we take, was represented to me as the life of contemplation. The monastery was the hive, the laboratory of life's mystery. And it was the bower of bliss, the place where love reigns for the All, the Creator, in the limitless household. The sweetness of domestic life without the diminishment of becoming a housewife.

This, apparently, was what I secretly cleaved to while I spun the prayer wheel of the month's birth control pills, allowing the years to roll over me, careful never to marry, though I suffered loudly over the rejections I endured and doled out in the toils of romance. I wanted a vocation.

"You've got one," Donnie said. "You're a writer."

"That's a job," I said. "Work."

"So is this," she said. "And if I'm wrong about what I've staked my life on, I'll be the crazy one. You'll just be 'minor.' "

The monastery dream broke a spell, or was the signal that the spell was broken. I married with a light heart. "She's finally settled down," my mother could tell her friends, as if she'd managed at last to get her hyperactive child to take an afternoon nap like everybody else.

With the nice inconsistency of dreams, the happy nuns in the adobe monastery left me free not only to marry but to pursue —from a safe distance—this first love. The one I would have winced to call the love of God. But what else is it?

I began going to Mass again. I sought out a monastery— Donnie's. I prayed. I read the Psalms every day, marveling as if I'd never read a poem before in my life. "Do you know Psalm 89?" I would ask an astonished friend. "The one about 'taking to heart the taunts of the nation'?"

Blank looks.

"What about number 88?" I would say, unfazed.

"You're just doing research, aren't you?" an old friend asked dubiously. "I mean, you don't believe all that stuff, do you?"

"What stuff?"

"All that Catholic stuff," she said.

I didn't know. I had left the Church (lavish theatrical phrase of my university days) twenty years before in a blaze of contempt for just that "stuff." In language still more theatrical, my mother had grieved over me all those years: I had *fallen away*, a figure of speech utterly Catholic in its cosmic reach, obliterating the notion of personal choice. To have fallen away suggested you were not a person but a dislodged fragment of a larger eternal structure. You were a particle which had teetered off the edge of the universe and dropped into limitless black space, where you drifted aimlessly in the thin air of your own vain disbelief.

But now, my big floppy New Jerusalem Bible on my lap, the six-point footnotes taking up half of each page, the legalisms of the Church fell away from me. In a sense, the Church decon-ﬁ structed. It ceased to be the imprisoning cell of catechized thought and repressive habit, with its egregious insults to com- *key !* mon sense. It became, simply, my most intimate past. It re- turned to its initial state, it became poetry.

I ducked into religious gift shops, dodging the plastic statu- ettes of Mary and the clearance sales on mother-of-pearl crucifixes, and made a beeline for the rows of books. I stocked up on studies of the Gospels, personal accounts of prayer life by writers whose names I'd never heard of, and yet another volume by Thomas Merton to add to the yard-long shelf of his books I was accumulating.

I wasn't fallen away anymore; now, magically, the Church had fallen away. What remained of its colossal architecture was a frail structure of wonder, long forgotten. Hence, the return to Mass, the visits to Donnie. And now, the Road to Assisi, which I had difficulty calling a pilgrimage but which certainly felt like an act of fascination.

This was the idea: I would work my way up to the loneliness of the monasteries. I'd start out with this package tour with the English spinsters, women carrying field guides to the birds of Western Europe in their packs, and plastic jars of wheat germ and brewer's yeast in their purses. Maybe one of them would be a convert, given to daily Mass and ducking into wayside shrines. Fine with me. I'd packed *The Cloud of Unknowing* and a book on the mystical visions of Julian of Norwich in my suitcase.

They would take me in, an honorary spinster. We would hike together through the gauzy air of Umbria, from hill town to hill town, into Assisi, the hometown of St. Francis.

He was my first stop, the nut case at the heart of Western mysticism, pulsing from the cusp of the twelfth century, preaching the Word to the birds. Still crazy after all these years. Still beckoning from the golden light of the misty hills, across the sweep of gorgeous landscape he called his cloister.

Donnie's opinion: Don't get complicated, quit trying to figure out what you *believe*, just follow your instinct. I felt, in fact, I was following my instinct for wonder.

This habit of wonder came forward from the girlhood I thought I had ground to cinder with my burning scorn. It rose like mist from the grassy boulevards of the old neighborhood. Everything that mattered was back there. My father, for instance. A Sunday morning in 1968, he is standing on the dining room table on a piece of newspaper, screwing a new light bulb into the ceiling fixture. "What Mass you going to?" he asks casually when I come downstairs. St. Luke's ran them on the hour, like trains, in those years.

"I'm not going," I say. "I'm not going to Mass anymore." I can't believe I've said it, this thing that has gnawed at me for months, years.

There is a god-like silence. He's way up there, above me; I can't see his face. The only indication is a slight pause in his turning the light bulb. Then he gives it a final sharp twist. The sudden glare hurts my eyes.

"Your choice," he says, managing to say the two bitter words without leaving a fingerprint of emotion on them.

We never speak of it again. Though my mother, the voice of the marriage, says a week later in the kitchen, "You broke your father's heart."

Good. That rotten killer instinct of the young which also happens to be the life instinct. The strange thing was, my heart was broken, too. But I was glad it was broken. I was expressing myself. Self-expression had become my true faith.

And now, all these years later, I stopped home to tell my father I'm going to visit some Catholic pilgrimage sites in Europe and will be spending time in a monastery or two. "Why you doing that?" he says, genuinely mystified, but used to me by now. The Twins are on the TV and he doesn't turn it off. I'm watching the game, too, and don't want him to switch it off. Viola is pitching, there are rumors of a trade. We're worried— New York eventually gets all the talent, my father says.

Anyway, his question doesn't require an answer. *Why you doing that?*

"I got a grant," I say.

Appreciative snort of laughter. "You and your grants," he says, shaking his head. The man who worked in a greenhouse six days a week ("and most Sundays") speaking from the superior elevation of a BarcaLounger paid for by honest wages.

Later in the kitchen, the Voice gives me the word: "Your father is so proud of you."

3

No one was lingering by the airport *cambio*. I went upstairs, past the ticket counters, and wandered into the carpeted lounge area near the restaurant. People were sitting at small tables, drinking cups of espresso, twists of lemon curled on the saucers. No group answering to my description. I was about to turn back when a voice stopped me.

"Where the devil is Diana?" This was the name of our guide, given on the instruction sheet for the tour. I turned in the direction of the rich BBC voice. "They've given me a plate of *white beans*, for God's sake. I ordered *strawberries*. Didn't I order strawberries, Lollie?"

He had the face of an aging foreign correspondent, an Eric Sevareid face, and big slouchy height to go with the voice. Next to him sat a delicate woman with a small, once beautiful face.

In a low voice she suggested that he might have used the wrong word in Italian. She spoke with the detached forbearance of one who has endured much melodrama over many hills of beans.

He maintained he'd said something very close, he was sure of it. "Who would order *beans* at bloody eight o'clock in the morning?"

I stepped forward and asked if they were taking The Road to Assisi.

"The road to perdition," someone said behind me. "Going to hell in a hand basket, that's us."

"Ce-ci-il!" The hefty woman sitting with him dragged the name into long naughty-boy syllables.

"Strawberries are *fragole*," said yet another man, sitting at the next table. He peered past me (I did not exist) to Eric Sevareid. "I heard you to say *fagioli*. That's beans. I wondered at the time. Rather heavy, I should have thought. Gas."

The woman sitting with this little man nodded in agreement from the first word he uttered and continued nodding until he stopped. She looked so like him they formed a matched set, little and dry and lean. Their dark hair was thin, laid frugally over their small skulls. They looked permanently displeased.

These three couples had been sitting at separate tables, near each other but maintaining a certain distance. My arrival seemed to draw them into a union that radiated a border. Standing in the middle of their enclave I felt awkward, too tall, too *present*. A human weed. I had crossed over—over what?—with an invalid passport.

"Where is Diana?" Eric Sevareid asked again. Diana could fix the problem, he was sure she could. "She has quite a lot of Italian, hasn't she, Lollie?"

Only Lollie seemed aware of me. "Would you like to join us?" she asked vaguely, the way a cat might extend an invitation. "Can you hand round that chair, Ian?"

"Thanks so much." I sank down by the plate of beans.

As usual I led with my sticky schoolgirl gratitude. *Thanks so much; oh, thanks, thanks, thanks.* They don't *own* the chairs, I scolded myself. But in the eternal convent school of my mind somebody else always owns the chairs. I had strayed into an impersonality more unnerving than open hostility would have been. It was oddly familiar. I was back in high school. Unpopularity oozed from me; it was my essence. I sat there, holding the zero of myself up to the safety of their numbers.

Blocks

19

Introductions followed: Ian and Lollie, retired, from Surrey (he rose slightly from his chair and bowed, more to the plate of beans than to me); Lloyd and Louise, also retired, from "the banks of the River Wye—do you know it?—lovely place, paradise really, Welsh really. I don't know why we ever leave it, even on holiday"; and Cecil and Alma, who didn't give their geography.

"I'm an agent," Cecil said. "I believe you say a 'sales representative'—don't Americans say 'sales representative'?—for Lego toys. Remarkable product, endless possibilities."

The three couples had never met before, but they all had taken other walking tours with the Cambridge firm. They were waiting for Diana, who, Ian said, had got the bloody Land Rover impounded somehow or other. She was off sweet-talking the *carabinieri*. Nothing to do but sit and wait.

"Nigel and Jill have gone to help Diana sort it out," Ian said.

"They're both physicians," Louise said. "We'll be quite safe that way. Two doctors in case anything happens. Although one doesn't think of a woman being a doctor, does one? Of course they *are*."

"Would you care to order something?" Lloyd asked. There it was again, in spite of the courtesy of the words: a voice both cold and intrusive, a tone used with gate-crashers. I was being managed.

Louise said she and Lloyd were having beer. "It can be quite refreshing in the morning."

"Americans won't drink our beer, Louise," Lloyd said to her with a bitterness out of all proportion to the subject. "They want it frosted. Ice cold. They won't drink it any other way." He gave me a frank look of disapproval.

"You lose the flavor that way," Louise murmured.

Ian ordered a beer in his lush radio voice. "Warm, of course. Have to prove my loyalty to the Home Counties, don't you know." He grinned at the others, adjusting with noble ease the slight imbalance caused by the abrasively bourgeois Lloyd/Louise axis in a world otherwise humming along quite nicely, thank you.

"You can take the strawberries," he said in English to the waiter. He sounded like Lord Peter Wimsey, patrician and cheery, purposely silly. "I've finished with the strawberries."

The man looked at him uncertainly, but took the plate of beans. "And for you, my dear?" Ian said, turning to me.

I ordered a beer. Oh, the everlasting schoolgirl urge to placate, to be invited to the senior prom, to fit in with people you don't even care for. I wanted a cup of tea. But the center of social gravity lay flat, with the warm English beer, and I rolled down to it like a smooth stone. The scriptwriter scrolled up: *She'd done it again, let herself be pushed around. Spineless! Hopeless! But inside she saw it all, inside she was free; she had them all pegged inside, inside, inside . . .* $Bloch$

"You must be quite brave," Cecil said, leaning forward from his table. He had a beer, too, and his face was red. "We've been quite surprised, astonished really, at the cowardice of the Americans," he said pleasantly.

I let it lie there.

"Tourism from the States has quite fallen off." He brought his face closer, across his table. "Afraid to fly abroad, they say. Bombs, terrorists, all that. I must say, we thought you had more starch in you, didn't we, darling?"

"Oh, I don't know, darling," Alma said nervously. "We have to stick together, don't we?" she said, turning to me.

I looked at her blankly.

"Those of us from the colonies," she explained. It was her little joke. And a shy invitation, one outsider to another.

Alma, it turned out, was from Australia originally. Her accent separated itself from the others; it was rangier, less skimpy, but too eager. Another unpopular girl trying to edge in.

Cecil said he'd have another beer.

Lloyd and Louise pursed their lips. Over the primer coat of their displeasure a thin stain of satisfaction in being right about something—about Alma? red-faced Cecil? or tractable me caving in to their warm beer?—spread across their small faces.

Ian looked away from us all, far off to an aristocratic middle distance: bored, bored, bored.

Lollie moved even farther afield; she had opened a map of Umbria and was peering at it, tracing her finger along a crease, smiling to herself as she worked her nail up the province, touching lightly the names of the towns we would walk to: Todi, Bevagna, Montefalco, Spello, Assisi. A happy woman, way ahead of the rest of us, already bending her head over the wildflowers.

4

There were no spinsters. Just four marriages and me, plus Diana
and her helper, Will. All week, Diana led us through tangled
woods posted against truffle poachers, and up steep hills where
olive trees and grapevines hung on the slant of terraced ground.
In some places the ancient planting method described by
Virgil—grapevines trained up the olive trees—was still the
habit. "Very bad," Lloyd said. "Outmoded method, saps the
olive trees." "Lovely," Lollie said, smiling at the ancient moment, passing along with her wildflower book.

We walked long hours every day, with a lazy two hours for *Pilgram*
lunch, moving in and out, back and forth across the Umbrian
antiphon of light and shade. Sheets of poppies, Chinese red,
papered the shallow dishes of meadows. In the early mornings,
birds started up like ink flicked against the white sky.

Diana clumped through the hot days in khaki shorts and dingy
T-shirts. Her hiking boots looked as if they weighed ten pounds
each. She lacked only a machete strapped in a holster at her
side to complete the image: intrepid girl explorer.

At night, she appeared, reincarnated in a brief slither of a
black dress and spike heels, her washed hair swinging free to
her shoulders like poured honey. She wore narrow chains of

gold at her neck and wrists, and had a gold signet ring and gleaming hoop earrings. She was a dazzler, and easy with it.

Her great breasts swung free above the sheer fall of her leggy height. Cecil had the habit of addressing himself directly to her chest. "I say, Diana," he would begin, transfixed by the double oracle veiled by her T-shirt, "when are you thinking we might stop for a bite?"

She took it in stride, dipping her head to catch his glance. She drew him up like a fish hooked in the eye until he was looking her in the face. He didn't seem to register the casual, almost friendly, contempt that met him there.

We gathered after the day's march for elegant dinners at the small restaurants Diana ferreted out. We ate, in many courses and with much wine, the food she ordered. She always managed to get herself into the kitchen to do her choosing, then returned to our table with the appeased look of a shrewd interrogator who has her ways of getting information from the prisoner. "They *did* have truffles," she would say, vindicated by her kitchen reconnaissance after correctly mistrusting the false intelligence of a perfidious waiter, "and *we're* getting them."

Diana hiked with us; Will drove the Land Rover, hell-bent for election, billowing dust, to our lunch stop, where he laid out the picnic. After lunch, he careened off to the night's hotel, and lugged the suitcases to our rooms, just as the tour brochure had promised someone would do. Then he took himself off to a corner where he read Petrarch (in Italian) from a ratty paperback, and bit his fingernails raw while the rest of us ordered Cinzano *bianco*.

Will was not Diana's lover, though Cecil did what he could to fan his own projected flames. "I say, Will, pretty close quarters for you and Diana on third. Sharing the bath up there?" Cecil encouraged Will to pursue romance with Diana based, it seemed, on their age difference. "Get yourself an older gal, my lad, that's what I did," he said, jerking his head toward Alma, who blushed. "Didn't I, darling?"

"*Ce-ci-il*," cried Alma hopelessly.

24

Diana's Amazon to Will's boy Mr. Peepers: stranger things under the sun, of course, but they were clearly unsmitten. It was not entirely certain that Diana understood Will to be a person, even. He was a fluent-in-Italian kid, her gofer. She let it be known she was the girlfriend of the firm's owner. An older lover: his slightly disdainful face looked out from the firm's brochure, whose arch prose he had no doubt written. On the trail, though, Diana was the boss, wielding her invisible machete.

Will was afraid of her. Actually, Will was afraid of *everything*, of which Diana was only the most immediate manifestation. He jumped if you spoke his name, and his egg-beater-styled hair stood out from his head in permanent alarm. He scribbled covertly in a notebook. That we had in common.

If truth be told, I thought maybe he was a little smitten with me—I qualified as an older woman (he was just past twenty), and I was an even more manic notetaker than he. We sat across from each other in the gilt salon of our hotel after the first day's hike, before the others gathered for dinner. We were both writing away in our notebooks, sweeping the day's bits and pieces into our ruled dustpans.

Journals
artists
way

We happened to pause and look up, into each other's faces, at the same moment. I had the uncanny, sure sensation that we had each been caught in mid-description of the other. I, for one, bent head to notebook and went right back to it shamelessly: *Skinny and jumpy. He looks thoughtful in repose—or no, I guess he looks hurt. But mostly, just young.*

He sought me out during the siesta the next day after lunch. The lunches were true to the brochure picture: the blue-and-white checked tablecloth, the cheese and leathery sausage, the liters of wine. Only the figs were missing—wrong season. The hike was offered twice a year. "In May you get the wildflowers," Diana said, "in September you get the figs." In the brochure we had gotten both, as you do in fantasy, where travel most truly occurs.

The pages of my notebook were damp with pressed flowers, as if no written word could do justice to the trembling light and mist of the place. I tried and gave up, speechless with the fullness of the floating world. In my frustration, I imposed on the lines of my notebook pages, where all the words were supposed to be, the souvenirs I snatched from the landscape. Lollie named, and I reverently copied, a whole page of wildflowers, listed in ranks as she pronounced them for me: star-of-Bethlehem, wild gladiolus, love-in-a-mist, and convolvulus and forget-me-not, the grape hyacinth and buttercup and wild rose, which I could identify myself, cistus that looked like a rose but wasn't, and the oddly named Christmas rose, which bloomed in May. There were orchids and iris hidden in the sedgy parts of woods where truffles were supposed to be, and simple starry flowers identical in petal and leaf but washed in a range of blue and pink, depending on the soil they leached their color from. Even Lollie couldn't tell their name, and stood before them confounded, thumbing her flower book to no avail.

Will tended to eat his lunch furtively, removed from the rest of us, who were grabbing and reaching around the blue-and-white cloth. Some days he drank only *acqua minerale*, and frowned as our empty liters of wine fell on their sides off the cloth onto the grass, where he parsimoniously retrieved them. Other days he poured himself a tumblerful of Orvieto white wine and gulped it down like milk with cookies, and then sloshed himself another of red warmed in the sun.

Whatever he did—or in those things he refrained from doing (engaging in small talk, for instance)—there was a subtext written in invisible ink, an inchoate message he seemed to be guarding but also displaying for someone, anyone, to decode. Though he made much of carrying himself off to be alone with his Petrarch or his notebook, he stayed within view, and he rarely turned a page. He sat across a room as if across a desert, his pale eyes searching us as we sat in our oasis of Cinzano and chitchat, a mirage he could only rarely bring himself to join.

He had the look of a lost soul, waiting for someone to divine his thirst, to come forward with a cut lemon to rub across his lips so his invisible ink would reveal its message at last, liberated and open for all the world to read. Meanwhile, he held to Petrarch in the original. I asked him, pointing to the book, what it was.

"Love poems," he said in his startled way, as if I'd wormed an addiction to pornography out of him. He stood there twisting the soft cover and flimsy pages of the book as he spoke. "I—I was wondering if I could speak with you. I mean, if I'm not interrupting . . ."

I was writing in my notebook, trying to describe the hill color *Words* . . . *some kind of gray scrim over the green, but not muddy, not depressing* . . . The notebook was bulging with pressed flowers, and I wrote over a bumpy terrain like the one we had walked up that morning. Everyone else was napping. After the morning's walk, we threw ourselves on the picnic lunch in a frenzy of bread-ripping and wine-gulping. Then people curled up on the grass while the spring leaves shushed softly above, and they napped like good children on kindergarten rugs.

Ian slept nobly, like a statue, propped in a seated position against a rock, his burl walking stick straight as a rod next to him; Lollie lay nearby on her side, her hands clasped together, prayerlike, serving as a pillow for her small, high-boned cheek. Cecil hurled himself into the sun as if to defy it with his meat-red face; with an irritated gesture, he knocked off the straw hat Alma crept up and placed gently on his head to protect him before she took herself off to a shady spot, where she lay down, tugging at her culottes to be sure they covered the backs of her dimpled thighs.

Lloyd and Louise had found separate facing trees, like twin beds at an economy hotel. "I say, all of you," Lloyd had called to the rest of us while we were still sipping the last of our wine, "I've found the best tree. Too bad for you."

"And I've found the next best," sang out Louise.

Nigel and Jill lay in dappled light, their arms around each other, Jill's face tilted into Nigel's chest. They were smiling faintly. They looked so simply intimate they might have been at home, in the house attached to their clinic in Devon, rescuing a sweet moment in their own double bed, floating on the afterward of love. As for Diana, she had taken off in the Land Rover to settle arrangements at the next hotel and would be back to lead us there on foot after the siesta. Will had been reading until he braved the distance between us and stood there, wringing Petrarch by the neck.

I got up to follow him and closed my notebook where I'd intended to chart my journey over the hills and dales of St. Francis, spinning out my thoughts along the way about his quirky contemplative life, which refused to remain medieval, refused to disintegrate into mere oddity. His life that called me somehow. Had called me here, I thought.

But only my list of wildflowers and the squashed blossoms pressed between the pages showed I'd been to Umbria at all. My journal displayed the inner life of a score-settler and a hand-wringer. St. Francis was nowhere. And where was the contemplative mind he had staked his life on—and I this trip? I was filling the pages with a documentation of the English on holiday, licking my wounds, unable to detach from the social scene and float as the milky landscape did, into the life of the mind—or into the life beyond the mind which, I'd thought, was my goal, my desire. Instead, I was tracking my companions:

So Ian (who's okay most of the time, one of those guys who hums under his breath when other people are talking: he's chronically bored but tries to be polite about it), anyway he ambushes me! Asks sweetly, "So, Trish, are you much of a walker?" I think I have the right answer (that was my first mistake, right there: why do I always try to figure out what the other person wants to hear? Think about this).

So I say, "You bet I am, Ian, I love to walk, I walk a lot at home." This isn't even true, but I'm bursting with athletic good intentions and some misguided patriotic zeal to convince them all that Americans aren't a nation of slugs.

"Oh," he says, and he's frowning. And he tells me about another hike he and Lollie took a couple of years ago when four Americans, Californians, came along and ruined everything,

walking too fast. "They didn't even stop to look at the flowers,"
he says. Disapproval. I've given the wrong answer—the reply
of a potential non-stopper for the flowers.

And then Cecil comes forward with that Porterhouse face of
his and . . .

So the pages were filling, not with Francis and Clare, but
with Lollie's faded beauty and vague sweetness of mind, with
Ian's lost-the-empire-but-not-our-honor manners. I took up my
ballpoint to rage at Cecil for Alma's ineffectual sake, as if after
all I'd accepted her initial invitation to stick together, two lost
colonials. *He has the nerve to say, "Better watch those sweets,*
Trish. You don't want to lose your figure. Wouldn't want to
thicken the way Alma has now, would she, darling?" Thicken
—as if she's a gravy. And Alma just says, "Ce-ci-il." And I order
the tiramisu, lapping up the cream to revenge us both.

I wasted whole pages tracking the twin minds of Lloyd and
Louise, marveling at the quantities of complacency they managed to cram into those tidy heads. Lloyd, I took a page to note,
was troubled that I spoke a different English from his, one that
must be wrong because his was so patently right—and my being
an American was no excuse.

"I say, Trish," he had piped up at dinner, "why *do* you say
'driver's license' instead of 'driving license'?" He had noticed
my use of the phrase the day before and had been brooding ever
since. "I can't see the logic of it," he said. "One is not licensed
to *be* a driver; one is licensed to *go* driving. Surely the Americans
see that."

Nor could I let pass without notation the incident with Louise,
who had been all in a false flutter because she had let loose with
a casual anti-Catholic remark at lunch. Her point: The Franciscans were the worst of a bad lot, all the Catholic orders were
positively *rolling* in money they extorted from these poor peasants and had done for generations upon generations.

Someone must have passed her the information that I was a
Catholic. I had been seen lighting a candle in a chapel along the
way. Great flapping at dinner. "I had no idea, Trish, I'm quite

29

contrite. I must say I had no idea *what* you were. Lloyd and I thought perhaps Jewish, it's quite difficult to know with Americans." She was paralyzed with embarrassment, she said. "But I would be less than candid," she said, looking around the table with her pert face, "if I didn't maintain that I do find the Catholic orders to be . . ."

What do you do with such people? I gave myself over to them heart and mind, riven as if by family bonds. I endured them, I reveled in them, I judged them in my little ledger, I forgave them and judged them all over again. I took umbrage, I took revenge. I wrote them up at night in the pitched-roof rooms of old hotels and the monasteries-turned-inns where we stayed.

I suppose I was lonely. They were, for now, my people.

As Will was. "I—I really appreciate your taking the time to talk to me," he said, stuttering over the personal pronoun in his usual way, as if he needed to say it twice to make it stick.

"No problem," I said.

He gave me a startled, thrilled look. "I admire you," he said vehemently. "I just want you to know I really admire you."

My turn to look startled.

"You say, 'No problem,' just like that, and there's the end of it," he said, marveling. His hand jerked out in a stagy flourish to the floating hills below us. The gesture indicated I had given him all this and much more. "You say, 'No problem,'" he repeated, "and there is *no problem*. The English would never say that." He said "the English" as if he were speaking of a foreign power, colonial warlords who had crushed his own soul and that of his native people from time immemorial and whom he intended to avenge. But I knew he hailed from Cornwall; his dad had a store in Penzance.

We walked along the edge of the apron of ground where we had stopped for lunch. It was furled above a steep drop of rock and underbrush to a tumble of lesser hills which finally opened its broad hand of farmland, lined this way and that, like a worker's palm, with irregular fields. The vista was awash in haze, imprecise and lovely.

Will ignored it. He gesticulated to this stage set and walked on with his head down, his unwashed hair sniffed by the sharp breeze. He kicked loose stones off the edge and ran his bitten fingers through his hair in a defiant, James Dean movement.

"You're someone a person could talk to," he said, scuffing along.

I took this compliment to heart, maybe because after several days of booby-trapped conversations with Lloyd and Cecil, I was glad of plain friendliness. Or maybe I struck the usual bargain, paying for flattery by calling it insight. Yes, talk to me. Am I not a person of sterling qualities waiting to be tapped?

But Will tapped no further. He seemed alarmed by his own remark; his face became clouded with misgiving, as if I were someone who could not be trusted with the time of day, let alone his inner truth.

"Do you believe in God?" he asked abruptly.

"Is that what you wanted to talk about?" I asked. I sensed he had veered off from his original intention.

"Well, I mean, do you?"

"Do you?" I asked, refusing to be smoked out.

"I asked first," he said. His grin surprised me. It had a lot of charm.

"But why do you ask?" I said, keeping our volley going. Some instinct told me that he was a person more impressed by being denied information than by being given it too easily.

"I don't think the others believe in God," he said, nodding toward the sleepers. "You're interested in St. Francis, but they're just on holiday."

"Does it matter?" I asked.

"It does if you pretend, if you go to church and go along with all of it and nothing means anything," he said, vehement again. "They're all hypocrites."

"So you do believe in God?" I asked.

"Me? No!" he said. "Religion is hypocrisy and lies. I—I"—

31

his trademark stutter again—"I believe in poetry." He looked out at the hazy fields spread below us, not to see them but in order not to be seen. He did not turn back to speak to me. "You write poetry, don't you?" he said.

"Yes," I said.

"So do I," he said. I understood this was a confession. And that I was not, after all, someone a person could talk to. I was someone a person could read to.

"Can I see some of your poems?" I asked.

"I—I don't know," he said, perverse as a girl wishing to be asked to dance and then heading for the powder room in a panic. "I mean, they're all in a mess, the papers and everything. I might have something, I'll have a look. Maybe later."

He turned back toward the picnic site. I trailed after him, oddly let down.

The sun had reached the midday glare. Diana was back and we started the afternoon hike. Will blew off in the Land Rover without another word. Cecil, sweating from his purple face, called to me to hurry up. "Don't you want to be one of the mad dogs and Englishmen out in the noonday sun?" he shouted. "Are you with us or against us, lass?"

5

St. Francis might be in the air of the place, floating in the famous haziness of "mystical Umbria," a mistiness that wrapped hill towns and spreading plains in landscape's version of a soul. But he did not speak to me. I thought of Donnie: "If I'm wrong about what I've staked my life on, I'll be the crazy one."

The contemplative life was crazy. It was far away, maybe nonexistent, a thing I could not locate in this landscape of truffles and flowering fennel. It belonged where I had found it, in Donnie's cinder-block monastery, standing since 1955 in a Minneapolis suburb. "Just take the freeway to the Fremont exit," she'd said the first time I called, "go left at Wally Blatner's Olds dealership, right on Radford. We're the only monastery on the block."

I found it easily, a low sprawl set among the modest bungalows and curbless boulevards of a *Leave It to Beaver* set. There, within walking distance of Ward's and Target, I met the life of prayer. Fifteen women, most of them middle-aged, following the primal cycle of devotion of the Western Church, the Divine Office of psalms and praise.

This daily round, year after year, decade upon decade, means they are never further than a couple of hours away from the

ASSISI

greatest poetry of our tradition. They gather together to recite the Office in an antiphonal choir, passing the ancient words back and forth across the small vault of their chapel, where they, like the words they say or (on certain days) sing, are arranged in two rows.

It was beautiful. But that alone was not what riveted me to the place, not what caused me to return, to be unable not to return. It was not the beauty. Or the beauty only cloaked what drew me. In that chapel, I felt I stood on the ground of a formal balance that was entirely commanding. I felt perfectly *placed*. I did not think as I heard the chant of prayer, Ah, this is beautiful. The statement that came to mind was, This makes sense. But it was a good sense that refused to explain itself, that remained curiously elusive except in the doing. The sensation wasn't even particularly Catholic; it was too fundamental to belong to any single religion. Though part of what grabbed me was a vestigial tribal recognition, the singular voice of *my people* streaming on jets of poetry, still it was not the "Catholic stuff" that made my friends wonder about me.

I had gone to Christmas Mass a few years before at a parish in St. Paul known for its old-style Latin liturgy, where the priests were decked out in satin and brocade like Renaissance princes. They used a heavy hand with the incense; the place was cloudy as an all-night poker game. Much kneeling and bowing and ringing of bells. I hated it, and was surprised that I hated it. I thought I would be swimming in nostalgia, but I gagged on the incense as if on a lie.

At San Damiano the sense of rightness was not merely aesthetic. Nor, as far as I could tell, did it spring from moral probity. It was not an ethical pleasure, though the nuns prayed for the homeless, the poor, the abused, political prisoners, the whole raft of miseries they held in mind. The phone rang all day with calls from troubled people, looking for—and finding—someone to listen. They weren't therapists. They were open ears. Nor did people call for advice: they called for prayers.

The nuns were savvy about world politics. Like most members of religious orders, they have connections everywhere, often in the hot spots of the globe, and are better informed about conditions in places as distant as Korea and El Salvador than many news agencies. Their attachments are firmer and their sources more reliable. A reporter for a local newspaper took this to heart when he went to Poland to cover the Solidarity movement while it was still outlawed. One of the nuns at San Damiano in Minneapolis gave him most of his initial contacts.

But even this political awareness and the ethical intelligence informing it were not the kernel of my attraction to the place, an attraction amounting to trust. The rightness was one of formal balance, of some appropriate gesture which had been missing —badly missing—from my life. And not, I sensed, only from my life but missing from the life around me. It was the instinct to bow the head, to bend the knee.

Will's question—"Do you believe in God?"—was not my question. *Time* magazine, too, had broken the wrong story all those years ago when it published its famous GOD IS DEAD cover. God was not at stake. Prayer was the fatality. Prayer was dead.

This was what I could not accept. Whether God exists or not remains forever a fascination. But God, believed in or not, remains only the elected Official for the colossal job of mystery. To my mind, prayer was the real question. For prayer exists, no question about that. It is the peculiarly human response to the fact of this endless mystery of bliss and brutality, impersonal might and lyric intimacy that composes our experience of life. As the human response to this mystery, prayer, not the existence of God, is the thing to be decided.

But silence was the first prayer I learned to trust when I began my visits to San Damiano. Only later did I begin to let the words in. The silence of the chapel at prayer was broken only by a habit of praise that I came to see was so primal it was not exactly (or not only) human. It was—or it mimicked exactly—the essential utterance of existence. It rose from the raw passion which rules life, an urge which has no voice but craves articulation. This communal prayer voiced a harmony otherwise elusive in all of creation, yet thrumming in the monastic silence.

On the other hand, the self (my own and everyone else's) had always struck me as being nothing *but* voice, all scream and whimper, demand and tease and coax. We want, we want, we want. Most of the time we cannot help but obey the commands of the self: we are human and inevitably remain loyal to ourselves. But the psalms and canticles, I saw, expressed some other allegiance as well:

> *In the scroll of the book it is written of me,*
>   *my delight is to do your will;*
> *your law, my God,*
>   *is deep in my heart.*

The silence and the psalms had equal value for those moments in the chapel. They put things in correct *register*, as printers say of perfect press work, when all the text is lined up straight and true, back and front. The silence was God, the psalms were—us. All of us, it seemed to me.

But now, in the Umbrian landscape that was food and flowers, olives and grapes, roses and poppies, I'd lost this balance, even though I'd thought that was why I had come: to find it even more absolutely than I had on my Sundays at Donnie's Minneapolis monastery, off the freeway past the Olds dealership.

I felt foolish, dipping into the chilly churches along our way to light candles, listening to my coins clatter hideously in the metal box by the ranks of tapers as if into the vacancy of my own soul.

Oddly enough, my churchiness won Cecil's respect as nothing else managed to. He seemed entranced by the apparition of belief—me—in his rationalist midst. "You must be a person of great faith," he said unctuously, his thick brow furrowing with edification. A casual atheist, he had a taste for the divine, and spoke of faith in the pious voice that a man who dislikes women uses to rhapsodize about motherhood.

Whether I was sorry to disappoint God or Cecil, I found myself tongue-tied, unable to tell him the truth, to slice the baloney to a decent thinness for him. I became shy. I even blushed.

Which only convinced him of the depth of my religious experience. The truth was, the closest I'd come to a prayer was Lollie's list of flowers. The rest was gossip and eavesdropping and the lonely comforts of the notebook where I settled my social scores.

Contemplative life eluded me. It was not to be found after all in this place where Francis and his early cohorts had nosed around, looking for caves and aeries where they could listen to the Word of God as it emanated from the utter impersonality at the heart of nature. Inevitably, they found there, too, the human outcasts of their world, the lepers who lived, half maddened by disease and isolation, in the recesses of the woods, holding out their stumps for the alms that rarely came.

But if not here, where? Was I going to become one of those fitful souls, trucking from ashram to monastery, saving up money to make it to India and then jetting back home, disillusioned by an anorectic guru but still plenty hungry for enlightenment, hieing myself off next to a hermitage in the Sinai, followed by a convent in Colorado?

Such people, women usually, turned up from time to time at San Damiano, between spiritual junkets. I became friendly with one, Linda. It was a brief friendship, for she was soon off again, to a Buddhist community she'd heard about in Vermont. She was fortyish, had an M.A. in something, and had worked toward a Ph.D. She made her living (always had, apparently) cleaning people's houses. "It leaves me free," she said.

Donnie pointed her out to me as someone who was going to enter the Benedictines, but when I referred to that, she said, "Oh, that was last week. Things change with me from week to week."

Earlier she had considered joining the San Damiano community, had even begun the long circling-around-each-other process that a candidate and a community engage in when someone declares an interest in becoming a member. But in the end, she had veered off. "It wasn't quite right," she said, looking past me with her absolutely blue eyes, seeing things I could not see.

Was I on the way to being Linda? Or was being Linda the whole point, and I was proving to be too conventional, too much the spiritual coward to cast myself into her dizzy orbit? Yet, no doubt about it, I was giving off religious sparks. Without even speaking about it, I had become marked. My one candle lit in a chapel at Bevagna (where Francis had given his famous sermon to the birds), and Will was asking me to converse on the existence of God. A single genuflection at a chapel in Spello, and Cecil was on his knees to me, treating me gently, like a privileged invalid given to visions.

When they touched on these religious matters, I felt perhaps my only true instant of solidarity with St. Francis: that wild need to get into a cave with all of this, out of sight, out of the social eye. It reminded me of a moment early in my visits to San Damiano in Minneapolis.

A missionary priest had come to say Mass. He worked in Africa and bore an uncanny resemblance to Woody Allen. At the coffee hour after Mass, he was walking around with two giant elephant tusks which Donnie said he was planning to sell—money for his mission. He hoped the tusks would fetch $5,000, whether apiece or for the pair was not clear. He expressed some contempt for the prospective buyer: "You know, one of these people who have to have everything."

He had apparently shot the elephant himself. I wondered why he had shot an elephant; it seemed a very un-Franciscan thing to do. I was about to ask Donnie about this, and whether she agreed that he looked like Woody Allen, when he bounded up to me, bringing his black glasses and his sweet loser face very close. "I understand," he said, a tusk tucked under each arm, "that you praise the Lord with your pen."

I felt massively ashamed. If Donnie hadn't been standing there next to me—smiling from her bottomless reserve of Irish irony that looks so harmless—I would have bolted. She was enjoying the whole thing, but I was dying. Of what?

Of shame.

[handwritten: what is it? Embarrassed?]

38

The white man stood before me smiling, having returned from the heart of darkness with his trophy and his perfectly unquestioned intentions and his label for me. And I, late-twentieth-century woman with a lot stacked against him and his kind, had no voice, no cream pie to smash in his happy-face. *Because*

I just wanted out of there, as I did now, Cecil gazing at me with his rapt face, so like the one he used with Diana. Only he wasn't looking at my breasts. It was my soul he felt he had undressed. Maybe that was the shame: being known without having given permission. Maybe the Woody Allen priest had known me, too? *I understand that you praise the Lord with your pen.*

When I got home from San Damiano that Sunday, I took a long walk through my neighborhood, which is also the neighborhood of my girlhood, and of everything that made me Catholic to begin with.

The scene of the original crime, I thought grimly as I trooped down Summit Avenue, a street punctuated by mansions and churches. I was trying to shake off the fraternal embrace of the comic imperialist dragging his elephant tusks. The long walk—my preferred tonic.

Why did I care so much? What had I been dying of there at San Damiano? Had it been shame? Yes, but shame not merely of that moment. A shame bred much earlier. It belonged to the St. Paul streets, choked with lilacs and dirty slush, this brand of Catholicism burned into the tissue of my mind. I'd never *childhood* succeeded in getting away from it.

And hadn't everybody else escaped? Was I the only diehard left, like one of those aged and confused Japanese soldiers who periodically emerge from some island jungle, bristling with loyalty everyone supposes is for the divine emperor but which might more truly be passion for the war itself.

Let it go, old warrior, the battle is over—and we won. Nobody is making you fight anymore. There's nothing to be loyal to, and nothing to desert from. Nobody cares if you've fallen away or not. You're free to make the usual jokes about the nuns, to take your stand on abortion, to roll your eyes at the latest word from Rome on women and gays.

I spent that Sunday afternoon walking along Summit, my mind muttering. I came around Selby finally, past the giant St. Paul Cathedral, which poised like a Jules Verne spaceship on the prominence of Summit. The place where my mother and father had been married. They started it. Blame them.

But it's been a long time since I had heart for that—or mind either. That was the story of my twenties; I wrote it up a hundred times in the fat notebooks I called, bravely, "my work," which no one ever published. Stories of a sensitive, daring person, misunderstood by a timid Catholic family.

The blaming had leached out of me. It bored me, the way any habitual lie eventually does. I circled around and around the great sphere of the cathedral that Sunday afternoon, pacing like some atavistic pilgrim who has reached the grail but can't stop seeking.

I was trying to think what prompts shame, what is *under* it. I seemed to know instinctively that shame alone was not the end of the story.

6

Lexington, Oxford, Chatsworth, continuing down Grand Avenue to Milton and Avon, as far as St. Albans—the streets of our neighborhood had an English, even an Anglican, ring to them. But we were Catholic. The parishes of the diocese, unmarked and ghostly as they were, posted borders more decisive than the street signs we passed on our way to St. Luke's grade school or, later, walking in the other direction to the girls-only convent high school.

We were like people with dual citizenship. I *lived* on Linwood Avenue, but I *belonged* to St. Luke's. That was the lingo. Mothers spoke of daughters who were going to the junior-senior prom with boys "from Nativity" or "from St. Mark's" as if from fiefdoms across the sea.

"Where you from?" a boy livid with acne asked when we startled each other lurking behind a pillar in the St. Thomas Academy gym at a Friday-night freshman mixer.

"Ladies' choice!" one of the mothers cried from a dim corner where a portable hi-fi was set up. She rasped the needle over the vinyl, and Fats Domino came on, insinuating a heavier pleasure than I yet knew: *I found my thrill . . .*

41

"I'm from Holy Spirit," the boy said, as if he'd been beamed in to stand by the tepid Cokes and tuna sandwiches and the bowls of sweating potato chips on the refreshments table. Parish members did not blush to describe themselves as being "from Immaculate Conception." Somewhere north, near the city line, there was even a parish frankly named Maternity of Mary. But then, in those years, the 1950s and early 1960s, breeding was a low-grade fever pulsing among us unmentioned, like a buzz or hum you get used to and cease to hear. The white noise of matrimonial sex.

On Sundays the gray stone nave of St. Luke's Church, big as a warehouse, was packed with families of eight or ten sitting in the honey-colored pews. The fathers wore brown suits. In memory they appear spectrally thin, wraithlike and spent, like trees hollowed of their pulp. The wives were petite and cheerful, with helmet-like haircuts. Perkiness was their main trait. But what did they say, these small women, how did they talk? Mrs. Healy, mother of fourteen ("They can afford them," my mother said, as if to excuse her paltry two, "he's a doctor"), never uttered a word, as far as I remember. Even pregnant, she was somehow wiry, as if poised for a tennis match. Maybe these women only wore a *look* of perkiness, and like their lean husbands, they were sapped of personal strength. Maybe they were simply tense.

Not everyone around us was Catholic. Mr. Kirby, a widower who was our next-door neighbor, was Methodist—whatever that was. The Nugents across the street, behind their cement retaining wall and double row of giant salvia, were Lutheran, more or less. The Williams family, who subscribed to *The New Yorker* and had a living room outfitted with spare Danish furniture, were Episcopalian. They referred to their minister as a priest —a plagiarism that embarrassed me for them, because I liked them and their light, airy ways.

As for the Bertrams, our nearest neighbors to the west, it could only be said that Mrs. Bertram, dressed in a narrow suit with a peplum jacket and a hat made of the same heathery wool, went *somewhere* via taxi on Sunday mornings. Mr. Bertram went nowhere—on Sunday or on any other day. He was understood, during my entire girlhood, to be indoors, resting.

Weekdays, Mrs. Bertram took the bus to her job downtown. Mr. Bertram stayed home behind their birchwood Venetian blinds in an aquarium half-light, not an invalid (we never thought of him that way), but a man whose occupation it was to rest. Sometimes in the summer he ventured forth with a large wrench-like gadget to root out the masses of dandelions that gave the Bertrams' lawn a temporary brilliance in June. I associated him with the Wizard of Oz. He was small and mild-looking, going bald. He gave the impression of extreme pallor except for small, very dark eyes.

It was a solid neighborhood rumor that Mr. Bertram had been a screenwriter in Hollywood. Yes, that pallor was a writer's pallor; those small dark eyes were writer eyes. They saw, they noted.

He allowed me to assist him in rooting out his dandelions. I wanted to ask him about Hollywood—had he met Audrey Hepburn? I couldn't bring myself to maneuver for information on such an elevated subject. But I did feel something serious was called for here. I introduced religion while he plunged the dandelion gadget deep into the lawn.

No, he said, he did not go to church. "But you do believe in God?" I asked, hardly daring to hope he did not. He paused for a moment and looked up at the sky, where big, spreading clouds streamed by. "God isn't the problem," he said.

Some ancient fissure split open, a fine crack in reality: so there *was* a problem. Just as I'd always felt. Beneath the family solidity, the claustrophobia of mother-father-brother-me, past the emphatic certainties of St. Luke's catechism class, there was a problem that would never go away. Mr. Bertram stood amid his dandelions, a resigned Buddha, looking up at the sky, which gave back nothing but drifting white shapes on the blue.

What alarmed me was my feeling of recognition. Of course there was a problem. It wasn't God. Life itself was a problem. Something was not right, would never be right. I'd sensed it all along, a kind of fishy, vestigial quiver in the spine, way past thought. Life, deep down, lacked the substantiality it *seemed* to display. The physical world, full of detail and interest, was a parched topsoil that could be blown away.

This lack, this blankness akin to chronic disappointment, was everywhere, under the perkiness, lurking even within my own happiness. "What are you going to do today?" my father said when he saw me digging in the back yard on his way to work at the greenhouse.

"I'm digging to China," I said.

"Well, I'll see you at lunch," he said, "if you're still here."

I wouldn't bite. I frowned and went back to work with the bent tablespoon my mother had given me. It wasn't a game. I wanted out. I was on a desperate journey that only looked like play.

The blank disappointment, masked as weariness, played on the faces of people on the St. Clair bus. They looked out the windows, coming home from downtown, unseeing: clearly nothing interested them. What were they thinking of? The passing scene was not beautiful enough—was that it?—to catch their eye. Like the empty clouds Mr. Bertram turned to, their blank looks gave back nothing. There was an unshivered shiver in each of us, a shudder we managed to hold back.

We got off the bus at Oxford Street, where, one spring, in the lime-green house behind the catalpa tree on the corner, Mr. Lenart (whom we didn't know well) had slung a pair of tire chains over a rafter in the basement and hanged himself. Such things happened. Only the tight clutch of family life ("The family that prays together stays together") could keep things rolling along. Step out of the tight, bright circle, and you might find yourself dragging your chains down to the basement.

The perverse insubstantiality of the material world was the problem: reality refused to be real enough. Nothing could keep you steadfastly happy. That was clear. Some people blamed God. But I sensed that Mr. Bertram was right. *God isn't the problem.* The clouds passing in the big sky kept dissipating, changing form. That was the problem—but so what? Such worries resolved nothing, and were best left unworried—the unshivered shiver.

There was no one to blame. You could only retire, like Mr. Bertram, stay indoors behind your birchwood blinds and contemplate the impossibility of things, allowing the Hollywood glitter of reality to fade away and become a vague local rumor.

There were other ways of coping. Mrs. Krueger, several houses down with a big garden rolling with hydrangea bushes, held as her faith a passionate belief in knowledge. She sold World Book Encyclopedias. After trying Christian Science and a stint with the Unitarians, she had settled down as an agnostic. There seemed to be a lot of reading involved with being an agnostic, pamphlets and books, long citations on cultural anthropology in the World Book. It was an abstruse religion, and Mrs. Krueger seemed to belong to some ladies' auxiliary of disbelief.

But it didn't really matter what Mrs. Krueger decided about "the deity idea," as she called God. No matter what they believed, our neighbors lived not just on Linwood Avenue; they were in St. Luke's parish, too, whether they knew it or not. We claimed the territory. And we claimed them—even as we dismissed them. They were all non-Catholics, the term that disposed nicely of spiritual otherness.

Let the Protestants go down their schismatic paths; the Lutherans could splice themselves into synods any which way. Believers, non-believers, even Jews (the Kroners on the corner), or a breed as rare as the Greek Orthodox, whose church was across the street from St. Luke's—they were all non-Catholics, just so much extraneous spiritual matter orbiting the nethersphere.

Or maybe it was more intimate than that, and we dismissed the rest of the world as we would our own serfs. We saw the Lutherans and Presbyterians, even those snobbish Episcopalians, as rude colonials, non-Catholics all, doing the best they could out there in the bush to imitate the ways of the homeland. We were the homeland.

Jimmy Giuliani was a bully. He pulled my hair when he ran by me on Oxford as we all walked home from St. Luke's, the girls like a midget army in navy jumpers and white blouses, the boys with the greater authority of free civilians without uniforms. They all wore pretty much the same thing anyway: corduroy pants worn smooth at the knees and flannel shirts, usually plaid.

I wasn't the only one Jimmy picked on. He pulled Moira Murphy's hair, he punched Tommy Hague. He struck without reason, indiscriminately, so full of violence it may have been pent-up enthusiasm released at random after the long day leashed in school. Catholic kids were alleged, by public school kids, to be mean fighters, dirty fighters. Jimmy Giuliani was the worst, a terror, hated and feared by Sister Julia's entire third-grade class.

So it came as a surprise when, after many weeks of his tyranny, I managed to land a sure kick to his groin and he collapsed in a heap and cried real tears. "You shouldn't *do* that to a boy," he said, whimpering. He was almost primly admonishing. "Do you know how that feels?"

It's not correct to say it was a sure kick. I just kicked. I took no aim and had no idea I'd hit paydirt—or why. Even when the tears started to his eyes and he doubled over clutching himself, I didn't understand.

But I liked it when he asked if I knew how it felt. For a brief, hopeful moment I thought he would tell me, that he would explain. Yes, tell me: how *does* it feel? And what's *there*, anyway? It was the first time the male body imposed itself.

I felt an odd satisfaction. I'd made contact. I wasn't glad I had hurt him, I wasn't even pleased to have taken the group's revenge on the class bully. I hadn't planned to kick him. It all just *happened*—as most physical encounters do. I was more astonished than he that I had succeeded in wounding him, I think. In a simple way, I wanted to say I was sorry. But I liked being taken seriously, and could not forfeit that rare pleasure by making an apology.

For a few weeks after I kicked him, I was in love with Jimmy Giuliani. Not because I'd hurt him, but because he had paused, looked right at me, and implored me to see things from his point of view. *Do you know how that feels?*

I didn't know—and yet I did. As soon as he asked, I realized obscurely that I did know how it felt. I knew what was there between his legs where he hurt. I ceased to be quite so ignorant. And sex began—with a blow.

The surprise of knowing what I hadn't realized I knew seemed beautifully private, but also illicit. That was a problem. I had no desire to be an outlaw. The way I saw it, you were supposed to know what you had been *taught*. This involved being given segments of knowledge by someone (usually a nun) designated to dole out information—strong medicine—in measured drams. Children were clean slates others were meant to write on.

But here was evidence that I was not a blank slate at all. I was scribbled all over with intuitions, premonitions, vague resonances clamoring to give their signals. I had caught Mr. Bertram's skyward look and its implicit promise: Life will be tough. There was no point in blaming God—the Catholic habit. Or even more Catholic, blaming the nuns, which allowed you to blame Mother and God all in one package.

And now, here was Jimmy Giuliani drawing out of me this other knowledge, bred of empathy and a swift kick to his balls. *Yes, I know how it feels.*

The hierarchy we lived in, a great linked chain of religious being, seemed set to control every entrance and exit to and from the mind and heart. The sky-blue Baltimore Catechism, small and square, read like an owner's manual for a very complicated vehicle. There was something pleasant, lulling and rhythmic, like heavily rhymed poetry, about the singsong Q-and-A format. Who would not give over heart, if not mind, to the brisk assurance of the Baltimore prose:

Who made you?
God made me.

Why did God make you?
God made me to know, love and serve Him in this world, in order to be happy with Him forever in the next.

And how harmless our Jesuitical discussions about what, exactly, constituted a meatless spaghetti sauce on Friday. Strict constructionists said no meat of any kind should ever, at any time, have made its way into the tomato sauce; easy liberals held with the notion that meatballs could be lurking around in the sauce, as long as you didn't eat them. My brother lobbied valiantly for the meatball, present but *intactus*. My mother said nothing doing. They raged for years.

Father Flannery, who owned his own airplane and drove a sports car, had given Peter some ammunition when he'd been asked to rule on the meatball question in the confessional. My mother would hear none of it. "I don't want to know what goes on between you and your confessor," she said, taking the high road.

"A priest, Ma, a *priest*," my brother cried. "This is an ordained priest saying right there in the sanctity of the confessional that meatballs are okay."

But we were going to heaven my mother's way.

Life was like that. Full of hair-splitting and odd rituals. We got our throats blessed on St. Blaise's day in February, the priest holding oversized beeswax candles in an X around our necks, to ward off death by choking on fishbones, a problem nobody thought of the rest of the year. There were smudged foreheads on Ash Wednesday, and home May altars with plaster statuettes of the Virgin festooned with lilacs. Advent wreaths and nightly family Rosary vigils during October (Rosary Month), all of us on our knees in the living room in front of the blank Magnavox.

The atmosphere swirled with the beatific visions and heroic martyrdoms of the long dead and the apocryphal. In grade school we were taken to daily Mass during Lent, and we read the bio notes of the saints that preceded the readings in the Daily Missal, learning that St. Agatha had had her breasts cut off by the Romans. We thrilled at the word *breast*, pointing to it and giggling, as if it were a neon lingerie ad flashing from the prayerbook.

Most of the women saints in the Missal had under their names

Background

the designation *Virgin and Martyr*, as if the two categories were somehow a matched set. Occasionally a great female figure canonized for her piety and charitable works received the label *Queen and Widow*. The men were usually *Confessor* or, sometimes, *Martyr*, but none of them was ever *Virgin*.

The lives of the saints were not only edifying stories but cautionary tales. Chief here was St. Maria Goretti, early-twentieth-century *Virgin and Martyr*, who had been stabbed to death by a sex-crazed farmworker. She preserved her honor to the end. Her murderer, "alive to this day," we were told, had gone to her canonization in St. Peter's Square on his knees.

More troubling still was the story of Thomas à Kempis, the great author of *The Imitation of Christ*, one of the treasures of medieval scholasticism. Why, asked someone in Sister Hilaria's fifth-grade class, was Thomas à Kempis not *St. Thomas*?

Ah, Sister Hilaria said, pausing, looking at us to see if we were ready for this truth. We were ready.

Naturally, Sister said, there had been a canonization effort. All the usual procedures had been followed. Thomas was coming down the homestretch of the investigation when "very disturbing evidence was discovered." She paused again.

"The body of Thomas à Kempis was exhumed, children, as all such persons must be," Sister said reasonably. We nodded, we followed the macabre corporate ladder of sainthood without dismay. "When they opened that casket, boys and girls, Thomas à Kempis was lost." For upon opening the moldy box, there he was, the would-be saint, a ghastly look of horror on his wormy face, his hand clawing upward toward the air, madly. "You see, children, he did not die in the peace of the Lord." They shut him up and put him back. "A good man still," Sister said, "and a good writer." But not, we understood, a saint.

There were, as well, snatches of stories about nuns who beat kids with rulers in the coatroom; the priest who had a twenty-year affair with a member of the Altar and Rosary Society; the other priest in love with an altar boy—they'd had to send him away. Not St. Luke's stories—oh no, certainly not—but stories,

49

floating, as stories do, from inner ear to inner ear, respecting no parish boundaries. Part of the ether.

And with it all, a relentless xenophobia about other religions. "It's going to be a mixed marriage, I understand," one of my aunts murmured about a friend's daughter who was marrying an Episcopalian. So what if he called himself High Church? He was a non-Catholic.

And now, educated out of it all, well climbed into the professions, the Catholics find each other at cocktail parties and get going. The nun stories, the first confession traumas—and a tone of rage and dismay that seems to bewilder even the tellers of these tales.

Nobody says, when asked, "I'm Catholic." It's always, "Yes, I was brought up Catholic." Anything to put it at a distance, to diminish the presence of that heritage which is not racial but acts as if it were. "You never get over it, you know," a fortyish lawyer told me a while ago at a party where we found ourselves huddled by the chips and dip, as if at a St. Thomas mixer once again.

He seemed to feel he was speaking to someone with the same hopeless congenital condition. "It's different now, of course," he said. "But when we were growing up back there . . ." There it was again: the past isn't a time. It's a place. A permanent destination: *back there.*

He had a very Jimmy Giuliani look to him. A chastened rascal. "I'm divorced," he said. We both smiled: there's no going to hell anymore. "Do they still have mortal sin?" he asked wistfully.

The love-hate lurch of a Catholic upbringing, like having an extra set of parents to contend with. Or an added national allegiance—not to the Vatican, as we were warned that the Baptists thought during John Kennedy's campaign for President. To a different realm. It was the implacable loyalty of faith, that flawless relation between self and existence into which we were born. A strange country where people prayed and believed impossible things.

The nuns who taught us, rigged up in their bold black habits with the big round wimples stiff as Frisbees, walked along our parish streets, moving from convent to church in twos or threes, dipping in the side door of the huge church "for a little adoration," as they would say. The roly-poly Irish-born monsignor told us to stand straight and proud when he met us slouching toward class along Summit. Fashionable Father Flannery took a companionable walk with the old pastor every night. The two of them took out white handkerchiefs and waved them for safety as they crossed the busy avenue on the way home in the dark, swallowed in their black suits and cassocks, lost in the growing gloom.

But the one I would like most to summon up and to have pass me on Oxford as I head off to St. Luke's in the early-morning mist, one of those mid-May weekdays, the lilacs just starting to spill, the one I want most to materialize from "back there"—I don't know her name, where, exactly, she lived, or who she was. We never spoke. We just passed each other, she coming home from six o'clock daily Mass, I going early to school to practice the piano for an hour before class began.

She was a "parish lady," part of the anonymous population that thickened our world, people who were always there, who were solidly part of us, part of what we were, but who never emerged beyond the bounds of being parishioners to become full-fledged persons.

We met every morning, just past the Healys' low brick wall. She wore a librarian's cardigan sweater. She must have been about forty-five, and I sensed she was not married. Unlike Dr. and Mrs. Harrigan, who walked smartly along Summit holding hands, their bright Irish setter accompanying them as far as the church door, where he waited till Mass was over, his tail thumping like a metronome on the pavement, the lady in the dust-colored cardigan was always alone.

I saw her coming all the way from Grand, where she had to pause for the traffic. She never rushed across the street, zipping past a truck, but waited until the coast was completely clear, and passed across keeping her floating pace. A peaceful gait, no rush to it. When finally we were close enough to make eye contact, she looked up, straight into my face, and smiled. It was such a *complete* smile, so entire, it startled me every time, as if I'd heard my name called out on the street of a foreign city.

She was a homely woman, plain and pale, unnoticeable. Her face seemed made of the same vague stuff as her sweater. But I felt—how to put it—she shed light. The mornings were often frail with mist, the light uncertain and tender. The smile was a brief flood of light. She loved me, I was sure.

I knew what it was about. She was praying. Her hand, stuck in her cardigan pocket, held one of the crystal beads of her rosary. I knew this. I'd once seen her take it out of the left pocket and quickly replace it after she had found the handkerchief she needed.

If I had seen a nun mumbling the Rosary along Summit (and this happened), it would not have meant much to me. But here on Oxford, the side street we used as a sleepy corridor to St. Luke's, it was a different thing. The parish lady was not a nun. She was a person who prayed, who prayed alone, for no reason that I understood. But there was no question that she prayed without ceasing, as the strange scriptural line instructed.

She didn't look up to the blank clouds for a response, as Mr. Bertram did in his stoic way. Her head was bowed, quite unconsciously. When she raised it, keeping her hand in her pocket where the clear beads were, she looked straight into the eyes of the person passing by. It was not an invasive look, but it latched. She had me. Not an intrusive gaze, but one brimming with a secret which, if only she had the words, it was clear she'd want to tell.

7

"Tell me," Alma said, "do you write from your life or from"—
she hesitated, trying to fix on another likely source—"or from
imagination?" Cecil was fascinated by religion, Alma by art. "I've
never met an actual writer before," she said.

It was dusk. We sat alone at a round table on a tiled terrace
cantilevered from the back of our hotel above the broad valley
that spread out below the town of Spello.

Her big rough face with its guileless expectation was beginning
to disappear with the fading light. I looked away, off to the
imprecise landscape below us. We had hiked through that landscape in the afternoon. Then the territory had been steep,
pocked with stinging nettles, a hard hike we had sweated through
with much stopping for swigs out of our plastic liter bottles of
acqua minerale.

Now, from the terrace, it looked like one easy, undulating
plain. Some of the hills still gleamed with shafts of misty light;
the rest of the plain, recessed against the rise of the hills, had
already been pocketed by the slate shadows that soon would be
night.

Off to the side of the terrace, by the iron balcony guard, stood
an alabaster statue of a woman, a Venus turned in profile toward

the same view we had. Her stone hair was done up with a wreath of stone leaves, and the contour of her body was visible under the stone chiffon that draped her. She seemed to get whiter as the light faded.

Alma and I were waiting for the others to come down from their rooms, for Cecil to bound out as he did every evening, rubbing his hands along his still-wet hair, saying, "Time for a drinkie?"

We had been talking about the day's rough hike with the mutual pride of people who are congratulating themselves for having been through something together. We talked, and then fell silent, and talked again, letting the day go. The light slowly left us; we ceased even to look at each other and gazed out at what was left to see—the spreading plain and, nearer, the alabaster goddess.

By the time Alma asked her question, we had entered that anonymous stage of dusk when two people can speak at random, without connecting things, without bothering to make eye contact, reaching that extreme of companionship where it is no longer necessary even to address the other person. We spoke to the valley or to the statue, to whatever was still visible.

Having no answer, I let her question stand.

Alma didn't seem to mind. She picked up her own thread. She was still worried, she said, about something that had happened at Heathrow, before they boarded their plane for Rome. "Why is one so *bothered* by these things?" she said.

She had seen a Nigerian woman, very tall and wearing her native dress (which Alma thought spectacular). A baby was strapped to the woman's back, and she was holding, or trying to hold, several black garbage sacks which were stuffed full. They were obviously her luggage.

Alma wanted to help her. Cecil's attitude: Don't get involved. "That's the English coming out," she says now, as if it were a national or congenital trait, nothing personal.

In the end, they do help the woman. But only until they come to their own gate. Then the English wins out and Cecil says to give the luggage back. The woman struggles on with the baby on her back, dragging the plastic sacks along the floor, Alma watching her until she disappears down another endless corridor.

"I keep thinking, We should have seen her to Gate 36," Alma says fretfully. She has lost sleep over this. "Isn't that foolish? I keep wondering, Did she make it to Gate 36? Did the bags rip open? That sort of thing . . ."

It's quite dark now; even the statue seems to have stopped glowing.

Alma's girlish voice starts up again, rushing from that stolid body. "One wants to help, doesn't one? One wants to make a difference. You'd understand that. Being a writer."

And then Cecil is there, before I can correct her. He's saying there is no *bianco*. He's gotten her *rosso*. He calls her *old girl*.

She turns to me. In the dark, I make out a canny smile, self-knowing, self-forgiving. It startles me, it's so un-Alma. I understand she sees everything and that he is her true love anyway, and that I'm not to mention what she's said about the beautiful, abandoned Nigerian. It's between her and the goddess.

Whether it was from her life or from imagination, the story won't leave her alone. It is entirely of her making. I am just allowed to eavesdrop on the telling, her fellow colonial.

"Darling boy," she says. "Let's try the *rosso*."

I write from my life *and* from imagination. That's what it is to write about—or from—the past. No doubt I write about the past because I want it to *be* the past. Finally. Not because my own past was awful or unbearable. My unremarkable past in the hothouse of family love. Domestic and Midwestern, autobiography's flyover.

What was remarkable "back there" was the endlessness of girlhood, the sheer tenacity of my naïveté. Twenty-five, thirty, thirty-five, still a girl, propelled by a fierce ingenue heart. Which I wished to cut out, I suppose. Innocence gets vicious in the long run.

I didn't want to "recapture the past." And I had nothing to

confess, except of course things I wouldn't admit to. In any case, there's no such thing as *telling all*. No book is as fictional as the one that begins "I remember."

I started with the knowledge, like the "given" at the start of a geometry problem, that there was something Catholic about this virginal self, with its stubborn habit of trust and its taste for finding meaning in everything. Back to the Church to touch the dusty relics.

I knew that I must set out on the trail. That, too, was instinct: I didn't know how to think about the past without *going* somewhere. "You're going on a pilgrimage," Donnie had said. And I had growled at her.

Now Alma, a very manqué Wife of Bath though she has a gap tooth, has asked me to explain myself. No, not myself. She was really asking for an explanation of literature.

And not receiving one, she has done the only other thing, something better, really: told her own troubled tale to the dark.

8

Stories had been there forever. But literature began in high school—except it wasn't called high school. Our school was referred to as "the convent." The students weren't marked to be nuns, but it was the French way of naming things, and our teachers belonged to a French order.

Well before the turn of the century, a band of nuns had come up the Mississippi via steamboat from a community already established in St. Louis. They brought with them, among other things, a brocade chair with gilt woodwork said to have been sat in (how often or for how long was not made clear) by Napoleon. The chair made its way to the school library, where we were asked not to sit on it and where, as a result, when Sister Mary Augustine, the librarian, was not around, we sat. The forbidden tree whose wood we felt compelled to touch.

The group from St. Louis settled into St. Paul, first establishing convent and boarding school on a muddy street in Lower Town. The grainy pictures of this early convent show a large Victorian house made gloomy rather than fanciful by the gingerbread fretwork that festooned its severe structure. Here the nuns made their cloister and set about the task of training the daughters of the city's growing Catholic commercial class. We understood that James J. Hill, the Empire Builder, had sent his daughters to the convent. And more to my taste: F. Scott Fitzgerald's mother, too, had been educated there.

In time, the city's grandees, led by the Empire Builder, moved to a crowning bluff away from the river and the commercial center. High above its rowdy river origin as the whiskey outpost of Pig's Eye, St. Paul made for itself on Summit Avenue a collection of mansions that Scott Fitzgerald, snobbish homeboy, eventually called a "museum of American architectural failures." They weren't failures, really, but colossal improbabilities. These extravaganzas of stone and stucco and brick (only the Weyerhaeusers, the lumber barons, built of wood) were the fevered dreams of an entrepreneurial generation that got its Gothic castles and cathedrals confused with its wholesale warehouses and train stations and Victorian debtors' prisons. Or maybe they intended the confusion. James J. Hill's house lacked only a moat to make its Tennysonian statement: Here, in gloom and grandeur, brooded the bearded Arthur.

The convent, too, moved up from Lower Town and built its monastic dream house on a charming slant of Crocus Hill, where the elms formed cathedral vaults over the cobbled streets. To this enclosure of rosy brick, for over half a century the girls came, passing the torch from generation to generation. The dim hallways of the school were mounted with framed pictures of each class, going back to the pre-history of aught-four, aught-five, aught-six. The gentled, air-brushed girls of each succeeding year had the faces of the departed, their floating heads spiritualized in the milky haze of photographic ovals. They had the mild, hieratic beauty of the Breck shampoo models on the back of *Seventeen* magazine. No human could ever hope to attain it.

At the convent, literature formed the only stable bridge from the fading colonial life of the finishing school to the mainland of modern careerism where, largely unwittingly, we were all being transported into the future. Next to literature, no other discipline seemed quite real or even legitimate. Certainly our chemistry classes did not inspire confidence. They had the feel of historical skits, edifying rather than experimental re-enactments of scientific tableaux from the Renaissance age of Paracelsus and Galileo. We tittered behind our guttering Bunsen burners at the flatulences we concocted—"That's sulphur, girls!"—and we wounded the feelings of the refectory Sisters when we refused to eat the ham salad they unfortunately had made for lunch the morning we dissected pig embryos in biology.

Our science teacher, Sister Celestine, suffered from asthma and had the genuine, if exhausted, humility of one whose frail body always had outwitted her keen mind. She was waxen pale, and appeared to pause thoughtfully between each shallow breath she took, as if breathing required conscious organization. This gave her a benign, preoccupied look.

She knew I wrote poetry behind the physics textbook I propped on my desk, but she said nothing. She would not have presumed to interrupt what, for all she knew, might be a better use of my time. Occasionally, she allowed herself the intrusion of an inquiry. "Patricia dear, excuse me, but did you get this?" she would say shyly, indicating a picket fence of chalky equations she was about to erase from the blackboard. "I'm afraid it might turn up on the mid-term exam," she added apologetically, as if she had no control over these things.

Sister Celestine was assigned to teach chemistry and physics in alternate years: such strong stuff had to be doled out in careful measure. She was gentle and brainy and probably should have been a research chemist with an NIH–funded team under her direction. In time, she was one of the first Sisters to leave the cloister for extended periods in the summer and even during the school year to do advanced work at universities around the country. No doubt she earned her doctorate eventually. But that was much later, after I graduated, after the convent itself had been torn down and our life there had come to seem wholly imaginary.

Even our textbooks were part of a former world order. They had an art deco look to them, physics texts with glossy pages of lean print and grayed photographs of men wearing large, square suits, their dark hair slicked back, their eyes framed by perfectly round glasses, looking deeply foreign. Others, younger and blond, lanky as basketball players, wore plaid shirts, open at the collar: Americans. They stood outside, next to what looked like the white, unadorned dome of a cathedral, coming straight up out of the ground, as if the church structure were a submerged ruin, only the great bulb of its vaulted roof left on the landscape to prove it had ever existed. It was the Livermore Observatory in California. "The most powerful telescope in the world, girls," Sister said. "We can see farther into the heavens here than from any other place on earth." She often said "we" when she spoke of science.

History, too, was oddly out of focus at the convent. Our World History, though it ended with the fact of the Second World War (which we never actually got to in class), was obviously more acutely attuned to the First. The Hapsburgs lived again in our faded green moiré books, and our view of world (that is, European) history made Vienna the capital of a lot more than a minor land-locked state.

History, as it was purveyed to us, was not so much a narrative, not even the detached observation of the rise and fall of fortunes and cultures. It was the litany of loss, attended by inevitable sympathy for the vanquished side. The past was always the underdog, and we sensed it was only right to be on its side against the bully future. We were left with the impression that our own grip was loosening on some essential pediment as one empire after another was swallowed up, and the centuries collapsed into our own.

We were falling, falling—away from the forms that sustained life. Form itself was what kept being smudged out, as if history were a series of clips from an endless Laurel and Hardy movie, crazy guys bumbling into one nicely arranged house after another, reducing each place to a shambles within minutes, leaving the rightful owners in blasted rags on the sidewalk, wringing their hands helplessly as their little world disintegrates not from malice but from sheer idiocy.

Sense of History

History was out of control, a story that stubbornly wrote itself, so that nothing anyone said affected it in the least. As for science—physics and chemistry, even biology formed a future into which we ventured with Sister Celestine on tiptoe. It seemed enough to learn a few menu-card phrases from that exotic place—valence, equation, nucleus, amino acid—never mind the whole language: we were just visitors, passing through.

Our real residence was language itself. Literature was the ancestral estate to which we were natural, unquestioned heirs. We moved with the assurance of royals down the long, echoing corridors of nineteenth-century novels.

We learned the meticulous art of character assessment from class discussions about Jane Eyre and Dorothea Brooke, and we developed a discriminating eye in particular for male behavior. "So," Sister Maria Coeli said, after conducting us through the bloodletting and mangled flesh of Shakespeare's tragedies, "would you say Macbeth was an evil man? Or"—an entirely secular savvy crossed her elegant, high-boned face—"would you say he was a *weak* man?" She cocked an eyebrow, egging us on to the meticulous hair-splitting of the truly judgmental and the truly literary.

As for Hamlet, always a romantic favorite, shouldn't it have been obvious to Ophelia that he was no sure thing? That is, if Ophelia hadn't been such a ninny. A girl should be able to *tell* these things. The lesson of literature: constant vigilance.

In our English class, we spoke of protagonists—Becky Sharpe and Rawdon Crawley, Antony and Cleopatra, Arthur and Guinevere in Tennyson's *Idylls of the King*—as of people in the neighborhood who were up to no good. They were real enough to be gossiped about, and our class discussions had a touch of the whispered kaffeeklatsch to them. Reading was a rarefied form of eavesdropping, breathless and faintly illicit.

The purpose of all this attentiveness was, no doubt, the avoidance of future pain. Observe and elude. Yet literature itself suggested the opposite truth: to live was to get in hot water. Wasn't that the point? The freshets of childhood were brought

61

to the rolling boil of womanhood where something (love, sex?) happened, and then, in time, the heat was brought down to the low simmer of family life, returning at last to the tepid, boiled-away transparency of old age.

We observed the futility of bad Becky Sharpe's manipulative ways, we noted the vacuity of virtue (the good girls of literature—like Becky's gentle schoolmate Amelia Sedley Osborne—got no high marks from Sister Maria Coeli: they lacked *spirit*. Like all religious people, Maria Coeli had a taste for a good sinner). The upshot of literature seemed to be that while evil didn't pay, goodness was notoriously dumb, a lack rather than a radiance. There was no future in being good or in being bad. What was left?

Observation alone, the life of looking. Living was for those who missed this key point, people who dared to be bad or tried to be good. Observing it all, noting it, seeing it—this was the real point not only of literature but of life itself. Life, fundamentally, was neither active nor passive. It was contemplative.

The purpose of a Catholic education for girls was to produce good Catholic wives and mothers. No bones about that pre-feminist intention. The model was—who else?—Mary, the Virgin Mother. But at the convent, Mary was no *Hausfrau*. She was the woman who observed pain and wonder, who "saw all these things, and returned to Nazareth, where she pondered them in her heart."

Pondering was the highest vocation, as if sainthood were a matter of who kept the best notes. Pondering was a special kind of thinking. It was not done in the mind, that chilly place, but in the heart, where the real mystery of intelligence—intuition rather than thought—lay catlike and feminine, ready to pounce. Life was a scurrying mouse, amusing in its way but ultimately helpless before the fixed bead of the contemplative gaze. We took easily to the philosophy of Henri Bergson as it was purveyed to us in Senior Religion: "It is possible to attain to the Absolute by intuition." I imagine; therefore, I am.

"Who sees the parade better, girls?" asked our homeroom teacher, Sister Marie Helene, content as a clam after fifty years in the cloister, "the baton twirler strutting along the middle of the street? Or the person with a balcony view, looking down on it all?"

We did not pursue the idea that being in the parade, hurling the baton into the blue vault of heaven, might provide its own kick, and that flashing your thighs from under a little bolero skirt might be a pleasure unto itself. For all her surface allure, the baton twirler, like Ophelia, was a borderline ninny. She pranced down the middle of a merely personal life.

She might be smug in her skill, which was to fasten attention on herself as she passed by the crowd. But what was she, really? Like the baton she tossed, she amounted to just a momentary glint in the great scheme of things.

Consider, instead, the person with the balcony view. This person, unobserved and virtually hidden, Sister said, possessed the entire event, the baton twirler, the gaudy floats and clowns, the brass of the tuba and the French horn. The balcony dweller possessed even the other people lining the street, watching . . . Which would you rather be?

At intervals during the day, from the cloister side of the second-floor chapel, the choir nuns reeled out a taut line of Gregorian chant into the school corridors as they sang the Divine Office, trolling by hour and season back and forth over the fathomless pools of the Psalms.

I doubt that I was the only one, pausing in study hall over the memorization of irregular French verbs, who heard that music and took the bait, going deep with the beauty of it, seeking whatever lagoon a creature dives for with the lure still bright in the imagination, though the hook has already imbedded itself and any chance of escape is lost.

Faith

But was there dangled bait, a concealed hook? Were the nuns fishing without a license? At Mass we prayed as all Catholics did, in the rote fashion of the day, "for more vocations to the priesthood and to religious life." But this was like hoping for better weather, a harmless wish for the common good.

In fact, the nuns seemed repelled by effusions of zeal or overwrought postures of reverence ("Lorna dear, please just *kneel* in chapel; there's no need to huddle in a heap before the Lord"). A habit of too frequent visits to the chapel by those in the throes of (usually temporary) piety was also frowned upon, as any case of inebriation would be. The Sisters did not court us. True, quite a few of them had been "girls" themselves, had sat at these very desks, had worn these same navy serge uniforms and the white blouses with the Peter Pan collars. Now and then, we caught a glimpse of one of the city's prominent family names peeking out like a silk chemise under the rough alias of a religious name.

"Did you know," someone would whisper in refectory, "Sister Jeanne d'Arc is a *DesVilliers?*" And we would wonder for a moment as this wholesale grocery heiress in a neatly patched habit delivered a tuna casserole to our table, reminding us, as she rushed back to the kitchen, to pass the rolls, please not to toss them to each other.

But beyond their care for us, quilted with motherliness, there was a deeper, unspoken attitude, antithetical to the sentimental seduction associated with nuns netting new recruits but, paradoxically, more alluring. A bracing coolness pervaded the place. It was the essence of aloofness.

The life lived within these red brick walls was so clearly *something*, in distinction to the random snarl of existence littering life in general, life *out there.* Not that the nuns condemned or even disparaged this other life, this parade they regarded with some interest. They were not remote, not dissociated. They were remarkably busy.

It was not uncommon to see Sister St. Sauveur, the French teacher, walking down a dim corridor with a stack of papers, marking accents *grave* and *aigu* in red as she went. There wasn't much spare time, not to mention inclination, to produce PR material for their way of life.

Beyond this absorption in a full day, a full life, something more elusive kept the Sisters at a distance. In spite of their ferocious commitment to education, to the discipline of lesson plans and the tireless perfection-mongering they engaged in as they taught us everything from the Latin subjunctive to the hem stitching of linen, there was a nagging sensation that—I pause as if I'm about to rip a bandage off—we didn't matter to them.

We were not the point. We girls, the students, were—a lot of baton twirlers. We might be bright, lively, requiring instruction in various necessary and some pretty unnecessary skills. But the unstated message remained: No life is dedicated to a baton twirler, not even to the well-behaved baton-twirling daughters of the city's Catholic middle class. Teaching was a profession, and we were a job. We did not provide life's meaning. This was a refreshing wind to have gusting through what was otherwise an oppressively protective environment.

The school itself conveyed the same detachment. The corridors were cool and shadowy; the gray marble floors, buffed to a satin gleam, gave off a visual hush. Light, as if it were a passion, had been subdued. It made its way in jets of clotted color through a bank of stained-glass windows depicting the lives of the order's founders, St. Francis de Sales and St. Jane de Chantal, on the second floor. Elsewhere, the light fell from French windows in great pale lozenges onto the ranks of desks and the winter-white faces of the nuns and the girls. Even this light seemed contemplative.

Perhaps the light streaming into our classrooms was the opposite of a passion subdued; it was light slowed to a voluptuous stretch. It unfurled its endless moment, displaying fine particles of dust like motes of pure sensuality. It seems, looking back, that we often sat, elbows propped on the old walnut desks, staring out the window at nothing, at the gilded light streaming with faint dust. And it also seems that nobody interrupted this vacant staring. It was part of being there. The place was dedicated, perhaps unconsciously, to the imagination. We were left to daydream.

Do I make too much of it? Light is light. Just light. But memory protests: not there—nothing was *just* anything there. The whole place was an injunction to metaphor, to the endless noticing of detail that is rendered into transformation.

How literary the place was! With its formal discipline and its unspoken romance of the detail, the convent's real life of contemplation silently imposed itself on the naïve life of living. The whole fabric of the day from the moment we hefted open the big green door on the street and entered the aquarium light of its corridors was composed of the filmy tissue of the imagination.

The light *was* different there. Not church light. The place displayed the light of the mind, rendered right before us, substantiated. Ordinary things carried a sacred charge. The very dimness of the hallways seemed thoughtful. The stained-glass windows were changeable as a moody person, dark and blank in the morning and then blazing neon when hit by the afternoon sun. The stone steps of the broad staircase were worn into shallow bowls from the generations of girls who had used them. Like everything in the place, those worn steps had a pulse and weren't quite inanimate. Strangely enough, the school perched on the edge of a cloister seemed less inert than most places in spite of its proximity to all that silence. The silence of the cloister acted as an echo chamber for everything within the building. The lives of things became palpable and immediate. They became poetry.

This low rumble of traffic between mind and object invaded everything. The very chairs and desks were steeped in the tea of meaning; so were the old-fashioned casement windows, and the library, that dreamy room with its Napoleonic souvenir and French windows and alcoves where, if you whispered your difficulty to your homeroom teacher, you were allowed to lie down on a brocade daybed and rest. Some girls reported cramps three or four times a month, and took up their odalisque position on the daybed surrounded on three sides by tall bookcases, while Sister Mary Augustine suggested Dickens as a known antidote: "Have you read *Pickwick* lately, dear?" Even the refectory where we ate from unmatched silver embossed with beautiful floral patterns gleamed from another era (each nun was said to bring to the convent a single place setting of silver, part of her dowry).

None of this murmur of significance was spoken. Perhaps it wasn't even thought. It was pure aura and it acted, as a powerful atmosphere always does, as an influence more indelible than the

66

lessons we were taught, far stronger even than the "Catholic values" we were meant to have writ deep in our personalities. In a place like the convent, where the way of life was imported not just over geography (from France) but over time (from the Renaissance), aura counted for a lot. In fact, Catholicism itself came to us as aura, not as dogma. It was a moist air we breathed, composed of incense and altar flowers and soulfulness, refreshed by the cool, refined courtesies of a devout French aristocracy who knew the value of doing things *comme il faut*.

We could be trusted to read more daring contemporary works than the girls at the other (and we believed, lesser) Catholic high schools in the city. The works of Cocteau and Anouilh were too rich for their blood. But in our French class we took on existentialism and had opinions about Camus. The unspoken feeling was: we convent girls were so firmly grounded in the faith, we could take on any of these wild and woolly modernists, and come out of the fray shining and fresh. Not for us the blinkered literary training that denied the present world. After all, we were special.

The atmosphere was not simply pre–Vatican II but pre–French Revolution. Something in the air suggested we might cultivate a certain *noblesse oblige* in relation to—well, to just about anyone. There was a slight, always vague, sense that the girls of Summit School (where the non-Catholic upper middle class sent its daughters) might weigh in as our peers. But so overpowering was the prejudice we held in our own favor that it never quite penetrated our Catholic incense that they might consider themselves superior to us.

Summit School girls were taught by that pallid breed of person, the lay teacher, while we were the charges of women with vocations. Women who had been *called*. Our teachers had taken a good sniff at the world and then turned smartly on their heels. They had chosen a more exalted way of life. There could hardly be a comparison between these women with a calling and the Summit School lay teachers, who arrived every morning with brown-bag lunches, their meters ticking till 3 p.m.

Maybe it all boiled down to a provincial snobbery, the only

snobbery that has real staying power. But that wasn't all there was to it. This dreamy convent atmosphere, parochial and literary, was not much aware of itself. It wasn't social, and some of us definitely did not belong to the ruling class. The school took literature seriously, and harbored the poetic resonance in all things. It invited sensibility. Much was made at the convent of that word which was usually used in the French.

Sensibilité, Sister St. Sauveur would tell us, with the frustration of one who has found her *mot juste* in a language her listeners only dimly understand, was more, oh much more, than mere feeling. Nor was it simply wit—though wit was part of it. Like all the essential things in life, there was no describing it. In this poetic world where nothing was just itself, where everything had a starlet's glittery twinkle of possibility, *sensibilité* was another of those busy footbridges between the humdrum and the spiritual. Welcome once again, girls, to the world of contemplation, where the ineffable is meat and drink.

It was limited and precious, given to strange bursts of intensity, this culture of ours bred in the little petri dish of the cloister, which itself was lodged in the old Crocus Hill neighborhood of St. Paul, a cloistered city of long winters and deep snows and closed habits of mind. We took in the great world of politics and history in our own way, too—personally. The afternoon after John Kennedy had been inaugurated as President (an event we had gathered in the Assembly Hall to watch: the First Catholic President), Sister Dolorosa glided into our history class, carrying several china plates, a soup plate, coffee cup and saucer, a water goblet, three wineglasses, a fistful of silverware, and a napkin and cloth.

These she laid out on her desk in an elaborate place setting as if she were arranging the orbits of the solar system. Then she turned to us, adjusting the black drapery of her habit in that graceful, unconscious way all the nuns had. The habit was a garment designed in the seventeenth century by St. Jane de Chantal, the order's foundress, and it had no buttons, no hooks or zippers. It was held together by straight pins, which the

Sisters maneuvered deftly during the day, tightening a sleeve, fastening the corner of a wimple.

Sister asked us to consider the piece of history-in-the-making which we had just witnessed on the television. What had we noticed of interest?

Someone mentioned the poem read by Robert Frost. Yes, Sister agreed: poetry, clearly a sign of a more cultivated regime. We had all been reminded more than once during the campaign that Mrs. Kennedy spoke *fluent French*. Someone mentioned this fact, though nothing had been said in French on TV.

Sister then drew our attention to a detail she said she could not help finding eloquent. Had we noticed what Mrs. Kennedy and Mrs. Johnson were *wearing*?

Of course we had. Who hadn't taken in that pillbox hat, that *statement*. Yes, Sister persisted, but what about Mrs. Johnson?

A fur coat, someone said from the back of the room.

"A fur coat," Sister said with a little contemptuous tone of finality. "A mink coat," Sister said. "And what did you think of that—in relation to Mrs. Kennedy's ensemble, that is?"

Blank silence. Then, someone trying: "It was maybe warmer."

Pain flits across Sister's face. "Warmer? No doubt her mink coat did keep Mrs. Johnson warmer. No doubt Mrs. Kennedy had to stifle a shiver in her wool. However, girls"—her face is stern with judgment, she is *teaching us*—"Mrs. Johnson was wearing a mink coat at what time of day?"

More blankness. Sister picks up the rhythm. She's dancing on her own. "Mrs. Johnson was wearing a mink coat in broad daylight, at midday. Girls, girls. Never, never wear a mink before five. Do you think Mrs. Kennedy doesn't *have* a mink coat?" Mirthless chuckle at the very thought. "Mrs. Kennedy no doubt has *several* mink coats in her closet for various occasions. But she knows, as Mrs. Johnson so obviously does not, that a lady does not wear a mink coat in the middle of the day."

And then she turned to the place setting on her desk. "And now, girls," she said, her serenity returned, Mrs. Johnson's mink having been disposed of, "I think it's worth taking a moment of class time to discuss how one proceeds at a state dinner with formal service. This," she said, indicating her desk, "is what you would be likely to find before you if you were invited to dine with President and Mrs. Kennedy at the White House." And off she waltzed, preparing us for the invitation that might—who knows?—turn up now that a Catholic had finally won the White House.

We sat rapt before the ridiculous, not yet able to sort it out, though somewhere in our fidgeting there must have been a crazy silence struggling to become a hoot. But for now, we just watched Sister. There she was before us, the plain, regular features, the regal bearing, the graceful, sober, black-and-white habit. The nuns always seemed well dressed. The habit had the definition of couturier clothes, the gravity of drapery in paintings.

I don't think we found it very strange as Sister dined her way on nothing, flourishing the round-bowled spoon through the cream soup course, demonstrating the funny little fish knife requiring a deft turn with the bones ("Though often, at such affairs, the fish will be served to you already boned, girls"), through the astonishing information that it is permissible to eat asparagus with one's fingers.

On and on she went, sipping first an airy white and then, with the metaphysical beef Wellington, an airy red wine, the glass held—please!—by the stem. Salad came at the end—to us a perversion of things, but not something, she insisted, to be surprised about. In France, salad always comes at the end of the meal. Finally, she lifted her champagne flute to toast the new President.

"One does not *clink* glasses when toasting," she admonished. "But it is perfectly correct to call out 'Hear, hear!' in response to the toast."

We raised our ghostly champagne flutes, as she instructed, and cried, "Hear, hear!" to our Catholic President and his bright future. The bright future we understood was now our own.

9

We left Spello early, before sunrise. Breakfast was cheese tucked into hard rolls, which we ate as we walked. We had a long hike ahead of us, all the way up Monte Subasio and down into Assisi. Diana wanted us to get the lion's share done before the heat of the day.

Departing was always difficult. Every morning I had the same regretful sensation: Why are we leaving, this place is perfect, let's stay. I was sure I would never again be able to find any of these little towns we had reached by walking through fields and forests, off any clear path much of the time, occasionally sharing our way with a meditative cow, but often only with bright poppies. In the distance, each hill town seemed to slip down from the top of its peak in a drift of medieval stone like snow caught in pink sunlight capping a mountain.

As we left each town, it seemed to resorb into the mist of the region, and return to its medieval existence, lost in golden haze as if in prayer. Absurd, of course: we were always near the autostrada where the maniacs careened around hairpin turns, taunting one another, tailgating within a millimeter. Still, it seemed that the roads we traveled were strangely carless.

Walking can do that: put one foot in front of the other, day after day, moving across a landscape away from the main thoroughfares, and it doesn't feel like travel; it feels like history. The centuries peel away. The woman in the kerchief who ran out of her house on a dusty road, rushing up to us with two bottles of her homemade wine: she wasn't being friendly in a modern way, she wasn't trying to *connect*. She handed over the black-green bottles to Diana, smiled from a face the color and corrugated texture of the road we stood on, and then ran back into her small, low house guarded by great spears of cypress, and we never saw her again. She met our thirst, not our personalities. The gesture was a million years old, far beyond courtesy, rooted in ancient communion.

It felt better than friendship, this anonymous acknowledgment of human need. We sat in the shade of a plane tree by the side of the road, passed the bottle around, swigging, not wiping the rim, handing it to the next person. Strange, how we fell silent. Even pert Louise put her head back, closed her bright eyes, and drank it in.

Walking allowed such timeless moments, making us slow-moving parts of the landscape we passed through. Maybe the world isn't, at its daily heart, as modern as we tend to think. As we walked, it kept reverting to an ancient, abiding self. We stopped to watch a man working on a small building: the house he was making for his wife and new baby. He pointed to the red roofing tiles. They were curved and fit together in a series of ripples. The shape, he said, was from Roman times: masons took the still-wet clay, cut it in squares, and then shaped it over their own thighs, making the curved form, which then dried in the sun. "Like me," the man said, grinning, putting one of the tiles on his leg, where it fit, "Roman."

I could sit forever, I thought, on the terrace of the Spello hotel, letting one hazy day slough off into the next, the statue of Venus glowing in the dark, Alma worrying her worries by my side, Cecil galumphing in with his tray of drinks. I would be content to watch Lloyd and Louise raising their eyebrows meaningfully to each other when I say something egregiously Amer-

72

ican, and then Will diving into his Petrarch off by himself in a shadow. The days spent walking in this streaming terrain, where light and land refused to divide themselves into separate categories, made even our rough human edges smooth, made us one thing. Analysis had turned to relish, and my notebook bulged with wildflowers and blank pages, which seemed to say it all. The more we walked, the lazier I became.

But the point was to achieve Assisi. We had caught a glimpse of it the day before, perched like a pink cap on a pointed hill. It looked as if we could just march a straight line across a field of red poppies and we'd be there. Once at the base of its hill, however, we would have to shimmy up an almost sheer face to get to the town. That's what it looked like; in fact, it was farther away than it appeared.

"Take a good look," Diana said. "You won't see it again until we're in it." For our route lay by Spello, over and then sharply down Subasio, the mountain where St. Francis first roamed when he began his nomad life.

Now, this last morning of the hike, though we were walking toward it, we could no longer see Assisi. "Take it on faith," Diana said. "Just keep moving."

It was an unusually quiet walk, maybe because we'd started so early. Everyone was sleepy, happy to be left alone. By ten o'clock, the sun was high enough to make trouble, and we were silent just from the effort of climbing. Ian saluted gamely with his walking stick as I passed by; he was leaning against a tree, taking a break, too winded to speak. Lollie, the oldest of the women, was ahead of everyone else, her wiry body and steady pace keeping her out front. But she didn't stop for the flowers today. We were stripped of everything but left, right, left, right.

Even Lloyd had finally fallen silent from the effort. He had started the day by saying loudly as we set off from Spello that he, for one, did not consider cheese with one of last night's buns *breakfast*.

Louise said in her stage whisper that this sort of thing would never happen with the Ramblers, another group to which she and Lloyd gave their hiking business. The Ramblers had always proved to be entirely satisfactory. She wished she could say as much for Diana's firm.

On the other hand, she said, you're contending with Italy, aren't you? And that means Italians. The Ramblers stuck to England—and, mind *you*, plenty to see right there.

Each of us reached the summit alone. We had to give in to our own pace, panting and wheezing along as best we could. I stopped once, disheartened because I had counted on a certain turn leading to a flat stretch, and instead the path had turned even more steeply up. I threw myself flat on the ground and thought I couldn't, wouldn't, mustn't go a step farther. They must have carts to haul people out of here, I thought. I didn't care, I had no pride. Even Cecil, passing by, didn't tease me, but just dragged on, his hand still gripping the invisible rope which I had fatally let go.

Eventually, I got up and, without any will for it, started again: left, right, left, right. I admired my dumb paws as if from a great distance, as they kept making the effort my mind had long ago stopped demanding. My legs felt springy with exhaustion.

Then, just as I'd heard runners claim, I got a sudden burst of buoyancy. It came from nowhere, and it had nothing to do with me. It was not just energy but a kind of intelligence bounding through me. It wasn't left, right, left, right. There was something aerial about it, the left and right giving over to a higher good, moving in an orbit of rhythm I hadn't known existed. I was carried forward by this rhythm. It was a command. I obeyed.

By the time this sensation ended, I wasn't far from the top. The heaven of that rhythm departed without my being aware of exactly when it left. I made it finally, panting, dizzy, the blood pounding in my temples.

St. Francis was there at the summit.

In the wind. The gusts almost knocked me down; it seemed pointless to try to speak because of the loud whacks the wind laid across my ears.

It's not true that a place hallowed by an extraordinary life becomes a husk, that after so many years the meat has been scooped out and fed to the beast of tourism so that nothing is left. Francis was on the top of Subasio, the first time he'd turned up in all my walking of his steep province.

The place itself was bare, a desert at a great height, just a rough salad of green here and there, no paper-thin wildflowers. It was all view—that was the purpose of the place, I sensed. A world without airplanes, when this peak gave the dizzy biblical thrill: to achieve a high place, to see the world at your feet, to encompass it all with your eye. And like Jesus with his tempting devil, like Francis at the threshold not only of the Renaissance but of the modern mercantile moment, to refuse possession. To forgo ownership and become all attention at this commanding height. To become awe.

A long, low hermitage, looking like a stable, and empty, sat on one quadrant of the summit. It didn't appear to be a ruin, but it was hard to believe anyone lived there. Diana said religious pilgrims sometimes used it a few days at a time. Several American monks, their nylon windbreaker hoods pulled over their heads like cowls, sat here and there, backs straight against the wall, silent, meditating. Some of them had assumed the lotus position. One was simply leaning against the wall of the building, looking out, still as stone. The wind slapped his jacket, jeering.

Out of nowhere a boy on a motorcycle flashed by, the hyena yelp of the engine cutting the air. None of the monks looked up. Where had he come from? Where did any of us come from? From the future this place was trying to hold at a distance. The kid yelled to his buddies, and reared up on the back wheel of the bike, poised there for an instant, and then let the front wheel down in a thump and was off again down the mountain, engine squealing.

The hike down was even worse. It seemed steeper than the way up, and more treacherous, because the path was covered with small white stones, rough as gravel, which made a shifting surface. It was hard to place your foot and expect it to stay put. The stones became little skates.

Louise said they should have indicated this degree of difficulty in the firm's brochure. Ian said a walking stick was the ticket. And Lollie, still in the lead, picked her way sagely, sure as a deer and never slipping.

I skidded down a section of the path, astonished that I kept on my feet. Sometimes I grabbed the frail sticks of underbrush to keep from losing my grip. There was no precipice, but the fear of falling was intense. We weren't taking the road, but a path, just a passage tramped by animals over the centuries. It was so sheer you felt that once you fell you would keep rolling until your broken body landed God knows where.

Sometime about three in the afternoon, things got easier. The awful white stones gave way to earth, and the twisted roots of trees corded over the path. We came to a fountain in a shadowy parklike setting and threw ourselves on the benches around the water which gushed and burbled in the broken light of the place.

Soon after, we hit a paved road. I was exhausted, gritty from falling, my hair tangled from the Subasio wind. I walked stupidly along, passing under a stone arch which was part of a wall I hadn't noticed, lost in the overgrowth.

On the other side of the wall, Lloyd stood lounging. I hardly noticed him and just kept moving. "Don't you realize where you are?" he said. "This is it, girl. You're in Assisi."

We had our last dinner together at what Diana assured us was the best hotel in town. The dining room was formal, almost sepulchral. Soft gray walls, and windows that were great yawning openings, swathed in heavy yellow draperies. The yellow was grave rather than cheerful, as if the color had taken on the dove tones of the walls. Waiters in black and white padded around, bending their heads and speaking in lowered voices.

Lloyd said he hoped dinner would make up for breakfast. Diana ignored the remark. She had stopped bothering to gleam at him in her professionally pleasant way.

Nigel and Jill, the married doctors who seemed always to be off to themselves slightly, although in a friendly enough way, were talking about home. They were eager to get back to their children in Devon.

Cecil said he was glad to be away from the brats, and Alma, whose birthday it was, cried her *"Ce-ci-il."* Diana said she had no intention of having children; children were trouble forever. "I might have a dog," she said. "At least dogs die at fourteen." Louise said toilet training was the big thing. She had strapped her own children to the toilet until they got the idea. "One must learn somehow, musn't one," she said, looking around brightly.

It was all very homey. And when the cake came, we sang "Happy Birthday" to Alma, as if we were a family.

Alma said it was much too good for her, all this lovely attention. She blushed as each of the men rose, in turn, to toast her. And then, as if all this affection were too massive for her to bear alone, she rose to toast Cecil. He was the greatest gift, she said, of her life. "I remember exactly the moment we met," she said, standing up in the solemn room in her very blue dress, which pulled tight around her. The effect was revealing, though not sexy.

"It was at the Wigmore Hall," she said, looking fondly toward Cecil. "I had just come over, and a friend of mine had taken me to a recital. I saw the back of this *head*—he was standing in the aisle, about to take his seat. I didn't even see his face, just the back of the head, and I thought, *That's mine.*"

Cecil's smile was a little brittle, but he said nothing.

Then of course, Alma said, everyone went into the recital. To her astonishment, she was seated in the row behind him, off to the side. What good luck! A sign, an omen.

Later, during the recital, he was about to sneeze, and he reached for the handkerchief in his pocket. He accidentally sprayed all his change on the floor. "It made a terrible din," she said, glancing at Cecil fondly, as if she were recounting the first of an endless succession of charming moments he had occasioned.

Seeing him there, sneezing, in disarray, people frowning in his direction, she felt an overwhelming sensation of sympathy, of wanting to protect him. She fought her way to him at the interval. "I just insisted," she says proudly, displaying her brave moment.

"In fact," says Cecil, pulling on the first after-dinner smoke, "I was interested in another girl at the time—Philippa was her name—and I couldn't be bothered. Who *is* this girl, pushing herself forward, I thought."

Will, shocked in his romantic heart, remonstrates, determined to rewrite Cecil's lines for him. Alma is sitting down, mystified, as if she knows she's been hit but can't for the life of her figure out where the shot came from. "Oh," she says, sinking into her yellow and gold chair, "I didn't know that part of the story."

But everyone is reaching for the last of the wine, the men handing cigarettes around, and in only a second it unhappens, and everyone is chattering, telling plans for tomorrow's departure. Even Alma, I notice, lets it go, doesn't brood, is taking another piece of cake after all.

They left right after breakfast the next morning. I was the only one staying on. "Do your praying at last, h-m-m, Trish?" Cecil said.

Will had never shown me his poems, but he rushed up after everyone was packed into the Land Rover and thrust his copy of Petrarch into my hand.

"I don't read Italian," I said.

"It doesn't matter," he said. "I want you to have it."

I stood on the narrow street in front of our hotel, waving to them with the dog-eared Petrarch, as Will pulled the Land Rover out and lurched off under the San Pietro gate, making his way to Santa Maria degli Angeli, where they would catch the train back to Rome.

I picked up my bag—the first time I'd had to carry it—and headed toward the *monastèro* where I'd booked a room. Back to the nuns, but mourning the loss of my pagans.

The night before, we had walked through the narrow streets to the Metastasio coffee shop—Will, Cecil, Alma, Louise and Lloyd, and I. We sat on the terrace, looking out over the Plain of Spoleto, dotted here and there with lights from houses. The only significant structure was the great sphere of the Santa Maria cathedral near the train station from which, in the morning, they would depart.

No moon. The stars were dancing all over the sky, closer than usual. "Look at the stars," we kept saying to each other. And looked, drinking our cappuccinos reverently, in momentary silence.

"What amazes me," Cecil said at last, "here I am looking at these stars, and then I think—the light I'm seeing may be emanating from a dead star. The star I'm seeing no longer exists."

We pondered this, our heads tilted back, very content with our cappuccinos and death—or this proof of eternal life. *Key*

Into this small, thoughtful silence, Lloyd leans across the table, his face animated by something that can only be called *hurt*. "It isn't fair, is it," he says vehemently. "It isn't bloody fair. What do they care about us?"

It is clear he means the stars and that, for him and for us, too, their light is not without meaning.

The stars are not malignant. Worse: they are careless, without a shred of compassion for us, no matter what cry we send into the dark toward those pricks of light, which every night shed their death upon our mysterious lives. *life is the problem*

MIRACLES

10

Summer mornings I woke alarmed by the pounding of my own heart. I lay in the L-shaped room my father had wallpapered in pink and white. Tidy ranks of rosebuds ran from floorboard to ceiling, punctuated near the door by a wall-mounted lighting fixture with a glass shade in the shape of an oversized tulip. My heartbeat, giant and unnatural, filled the air. I came thudding from sleep into doom, as if I understood the world was not a safe place to enter.

This lasted only a confused instant. Then reality clicked in. We lived across the street from a tennis court, and every morning the high school boy who had been hired to open the place drove an ancient roller over the courts, pounding down the clay like face powder in a silver compact. The heartbeat was just the thud of a secondhand piece of badly chipped equipment, painted a celestial blue, driven by a kid who went to school with my brother.

But the sensation remained: the fatefulness of waking, the dread not of night but of day. Yet even in this dream-dread, I wasn't afraid. Or, at least, I wasn't repelled. I was intrigued: I liked that initial jumble of self and world. It roused me, grabbed me somehow.

The roller cast a blur across the morning that refused to separate us—the world and me—into distinct units of existence. This blur was heaven. I luxuriated in it and had to be called twice, three times to get up. But I wasn't asleep. I was reveling in sensation. The luscious fact of awareness coursed through me. Understanding that the thump was *not* me but somehow had been briefly mine, and was now disguised in a sly camouflage of junky blue machinery—this delighted me, made me float and marvel. The world was so *funny*. This delicious sensation was not daydream but absorption: I soaked up the world. We met each other, essence to essence, oddity to oddity. We fit exactly. Why get up? I was already magnetized to the day.

The booming finally stopped, and the more fragile sounds of morning came forward. I lay there thinking: Which is it—*morning* dove or *mourning* dove? I had asked my father a hundred times, but I never could remember his answer. I could actually feel myself forgetting as he spoke, the answer evaporating between us instantly, the way the name of a stranger introduced at a party gets lost as you look right into the anonymous blue eyes you will never know. This habit of forgetfulness seemed inevitable, a sign that confusion was part of existence, and was meant to be. The doves, whatever else they were, were more blur. Their echoey coos came in the window, another fragment of the delectable, indeterminate world.

I lay there, head turned to the paper roses my florist father had marshaled on the wall. I scanned the field; my eye traced the three doomed ranks that mounted the wall like all the others until they were cut off at the barricade of the light fixture. They emerged briefly again, a small contingent above the petal of the tulip-shade, only to be lost forever with all their pink comrades at the frontier of the ceiling.

I stared at the unreal roses, the doves mourning the morning, and I knew—I felt—why I had been made (*Who made you?* God made me. *Why did God make you?* . . .). I had been made to savor all this beauty. No—this *strangeness*.

"God, you're so *lazy*," my brother with his list of Saturday projects would say, passing my room.

"You're going to sleep your life away, young lady," my mother said.

That's how it was my first week in Assisi: a series of drifting days in a tourist town where I knew no one, not even the language beyond the welcome familiarities of the *menu turistico*.

I had ten days alone, time out of time, before I joined my next group. The next gang, as I thought of them: a group of Franciscan nuns and friars from the United States. I had arranged—or rather, Donnie with her worldwide network had arranged for me—to meet them in Rome, where the Franciscan Study Tour would begin. After a few days there, we would make a pilgrimage—they used the word exuberantly in their correspondence—back to Assisi, the hometown of their order. "Naturally, they want to meet Francis and Clare," Donnie said.

But first I had this floating time, solo. Assisi presented itself as part monastery, part carnival. Many of the town buildings were made of the same stone, a blush color with a faint gray cast, making the stones seem oddly tender. I felt securely shouldered in between the walls of the narrow pedestrian-only streets, as if in a cloister corridor. The slice of the Plain of Spoleto I could see between buildings might have been the slender view from a monastery cell window set at a transcendent height. The town was so steeply built on its hilltop that sometimes, pausing on a stony path, I had the sensation of being pitched over a sharp drop.

That was the monastery part. But the central areas, especially the twisting streets leading to the Basilica of St. Francis, were chockablock with souvenir concessions built into the ancient walls, places as T-shirt-ridden and geegaw-bedecked as the midway at the Minnesota State Fair.

I had been warned. A friend who had lived in Italy said before I left home, "We only made a day trip to Assisi," and added, "You may be disappointed; it's awfully . . . touristy."

But when I looked up from a plaster beer mug made in the shape of a rotund friar to see, walking by, a sandaled friar in the shape of the beer mug, I was not perturbed. I bought the mug.

It was another of perception's watery ripples, another of life's scribbles that refused to stay within the lines. Besides, my understanding of St. Francis, the playboy son of a big-deal cloth merchant, required the keen scent of retail sales somewhere on the scene.

I was staying at the Poor Clare monastery of Santa Chiara (i.e., St. Clare) on the Borgo San Pietro. The monastery had a strict cloister as well as common rooms—a pleasant, shadowy lounge and library with easy chairs and a piano, a breakfast room with several small tables—and a chapel open to visitors.

"You can't beat the price," Donnie had told me when she suggested the place. Hospitality, she explained, is one of the oldest missions of the monastic life. The ancient monastic idea was to provide lodging for "pilgrims and strangers," as St. Francis called himself and his followers. There was a lot of wandering about during the Middle Ages, much of it by pilgrims and itinerant monks attached to no specific monastery. Such wandering monks, called *girovaghi*, were a social embarrassment, trading on the commitment to hospitality that governed the grand monastic houses. "Concerning their miserable way of life," the great monastic rule maker St. Benedict wrote, "it is better to be silent than to speak."

This medieval tradition of hospitality has carried over easily to the contemporary mass tourist trade; it is not hard, especially in Italy, to find lodgings in active monasteries where the communities see the enterprise as part of their mission and as an appropriate way to support themselves. The Frommer guidebooks are enthusiastic about these monastery-inns because they're cheap and they're clean, and often they're beautifully situated. Which exactly describes Santa Chiara.

The Santa Chiara community had come from Normandy originally, and the language of the house was French. I took out my high school French as if I were unwrapping from long storage my hideous senior prom dress, and I did what I could with it as pretty Soeur Marie Ange (a nun straight out of my bridal night dream) led me to my room. I jabbered in the present tense, the only one under my control, about a limited number of topics dictated by my vocabulary, which tilted heavily toward food items and the colors of things: *Ah, les grandes roses de votre jardin, ma soeur! Oui, j'aime le café au lait pour le petit déjeuner demain matin* . . .

Soeur Marie Ange said, with great round eyes that were all kindness and no truth, that my French was *excellente, superbe*. Especially for an American.

The Sisters smiled and floated in their beige habits and black veils along the gleaming corridors and in the garden—where the roses really were huge, great pastel cabbage heads above dry branches. The roses were nourished on threads of water strung out for them by an old bent nun wearing a battered straw hat over her black veil. The camel-colored earth was so parched the water sat atop it for a few moments as if it were not liquid. Then, finally absorbed, it left a shadow at the base of the plant until the color of the desert reasserted itself. Yet the roses thrived, the petals were moist, the air fragrant.

The bedrooms of the place, each named for a saint or some part of the liturgical year, were located in a wing of the main monastery and in two separate buildings which provided, on one side, an intimate view of the walled garden. The other side gave onto a kitchen garden strung with laundry lines, and beyond that to a trellised grape arbor. Finally, the Plain of Spoleto spread out in a misty stream, the dome of Santa Maria degli Angeli, where Francis had gone to die, bulging in the distance.

This was the view from L'Annonciation, my room. Next door, in La Joie, a man I never saw coughed a racking smoker's cough on the first night and then was gone—or dead. I never heard him again. I seemed to have the whole suite of little rooms to myself the entire week. But that first afternoon and evening the cough in Joy didn't bother me anyway. I was too content in the Annunciation to notice.

I'd been here before. If life is not like a novel but something more strictly musical—a theme with variations—I'd first heard this central motif long ago. At home in St. Paul, of course. At one time, the little mustard-colored room where I was sent after lunch to practice the piano at the convent had been a dormitory room. Years before, farmers and bankers as far away as the Dakotas had sent their daughters to the nuns in St. Paul to be finished, as the rather sinister phrase of the day put it.

But by 1964 the boarders were long gone. We were all day pupils, studying trig, hoping to score high on the SATs. Most of the old dorm rooms, opening onto a long, dim corridor, had been turned into practice rooms. Another, used for storage, was filled with Singer treadle sewing machines from some ghostly home ec class of yore. But one room, always locked, at the darkest end of the corridor, remained a mystery.

This room was next to a door on which a yellowed cardboard sign that looked a century old announced in block letters: ENCLOSURE. This was the ultimate STOP sign of the convent. No girl was allowed past this door or past any Enclosure sign posted throughout the building. Such markers indicated the border, strictly observed, between school and cloister. The whole place, even the big, walled courtyard, was divided in half this way. Them and Us. "I'll fetch it, dear," a nun would say affably when one of us lobbed a tennis ball out of range into the cloister garden behind the tall hedge called the Maze. It was unthinkable that one of *us* might trespass Over There.

The building was romantic, made of red brick and laid out in an L-shape, with a great bell tower from which the hours tolled. There was an arched walk, a reflecting pool, statues, a grotto— the works. Though it was only a few blocks from my own house, the convent seemed—and was—foreign. The design of the building had been taken from that of an old French monastery. The fact that the nuns casually referred to their bedrooms as *cells* only heightened the exotic allure of the place. So complete was the injunction against entering the cloister that no one flirted with the idea of a raid. It was impossible to imagine putting a hand on the doorknob of an Enclosure door.

Yet the cloister calm reached us. I loved the cramped, yellowed room on the fourth floor where I did precious little prac-

ticing. After a few swipes at "The Jolly Farmer" and "Für Elise,"
I threw myself on the flowered daybed behind the black grand
piano (said to belong to the archbishop, who stopped by at times
and spent a solitary hour playing "Begin the Beguine" and
"Sweet Georgia Brown"). The long window rattled in its sash,
and I stared down upon the courtyard. The room was up so high
that no ENCLOSURE sign could deny a view of the cloister garden
below. I could catch a glimpse of the greenhouse attached to
the south wall of the monastery where Sister Mary Louis encouraged gift plants the nuns received to keep blooming. But
otherwise, the view proved to be disappointingly ordinary.

I lounged on the daybed in my blue serge uniform and brown
oxfords, and considered my future. I had many airy castles in
mid-construction. I would travel, I would see the world. The
scriptwriter scrolled up, and I eased into my third-person life:
*It was some kind of oversight, a mistake, that she had been born
in St. Paul, Minn., in the first place, a girl really destined* Imagination
for . . .

One afternoon, emerging from the practice room, I saw that
the door to the always-locked room at the end of the corridor
by the ENCLOSURE sign was open. A shaft of light fell across the
dark hallway. There was a window in the room, south-facing,
and the sun was flooding in.

Strange, the rooms that strike one as perfect. They needn't
be beautiful, but they must somehow *register*, touch a core of
harmony. A room, after all, is an interior: it speaks to the inner
self.

The floor of the room was golden maple, highly polished.
Nun's work. There was a small blue rag rug, a plain table meant
to be a desk, a chair. A tiny mirror above a sink in the corner.
No crucifix; instead, a print of a ship at sea. Behind it, someone
had stuck a dried frond from Palm Sunday that curled around
the wooden frame. But it was the bed, I think, that did it. A
narrow white bed with a candlewick spread. A great wafer of
sunlight fell upon it from the open window. I wanted to go in
there, to lie down and sleep for maybe a hundred years. The

entire cube (it was tiny, another former dorm room) was engulfed in light. It seemed not part of the school, not part of the cloister, but some middle ground of utter serenity.

Sister Marie Therese, the biology teacher, was placing a vase of lilacs on the table. She had a bundle of bedding under her other arm. She gave the white bedspread a final flick as she came to the door.

What was the room for, I asked her.

"This room, dear? This is for visitors."

"Visitors?" Who, I wondered, came here overnight.

Sister took a final look around the little chamber; it seemed to pass inspection. She stepped outside, near me. "Strangers, dear," she said, closing the door, which left us suddenly in the dark again. "We must always have a room for strangers." Then she opened the ENCLOSURE door and went on her way into the cloister, out of my part of the world, the bundle of laundry balanced on her hip like a baby.

This was the room I entered now as I took the key to the Annunciation from pretty Soeur Marie Ange. "Bye-bye," she said, turning on a gorgeous smile with her single English word. She rustled away, leaving me to the cleanliness-is-next-to-godliness polished floor I knew so well, the little table with a bunch of blue flowers, the French doors open to the balcony.

I lay down, as if on command, on the white bedspread. The sunshine showered down, flooding every surface of the tiny room, including me. I fell asleep in the rich Italian sun. Maybe it was a small version of the hundred-years sleep I wished for that day in high school when I saw, briefly, the flood of light coming from the locked room for strangers.

Now I was the stranger, and I sank into strangeness—into the odd seclusion light affords, into the anonymity at the core of travel, the solitude that must be heaven.

11

At breakfast the next morning I sat with an elderly woman whose white hair was swept into an elegant twist. She was a retired professor of French literature from Nice. Unlike Soeur Marie Ange, her eyes were not round and forgiving; she said nothing about my French.

She could tell, she said, that I was well trained.

Trained? I felt like a dog.

"*Chez les soeurs*," she said. "By the good Sisters."

I smiled—sweetly. The convent school insignia flashed again, the overripe *politesse* of the eternal ingenue: it was the desire to be approved of, preening when she complimented me for being innocuous. I beamed at her, as I had beamed at Cecil, at Lloyd and Louise. And then, hunched up at night in bed, chummy with my notebook, I would wipe the smile off my face and get real.

The truth was, she depressed me, this worldly woman. I was exposed in the light of her arch smile, the effort of my infantile French betraying me. Or maybe it was the toil of social effort. It felt like the weight of a lifetime's exertion, as if I had slept all my life not on the candlewick bedspread of my dreams but on a pillow embroidered with the words *Keep trying* pressed into my cheek.

Mme X had long ago ceased striving; many years of calm judgment lay behind her, years of looking neutrally across tables at strangers, seeing them for what they were, not for how or whether they might like her. She, too, practiced her *politesse*, in birdlike chirps to the nuns who served us, but it was a courtesy so regally impersonal that it allowed her soul a privacy, even a disdain, I could hardly imagine. She gazed across at me where the buttery crumbs from the croissant blotted into the paper tablecloth. Her own place was as smooth as the controlled twist of her white hair.

Somewhere in the middle of our *café crème* she adroitly shifted us into English, where she was visibly relieved to leave me, having finished a second cup and declined a third, and now entirely absorbed in her next project: off to see the Giottos. "I do think it's best to see art alone, don't you?" she said, glittering slightly. Another solitude freak. It was her only slip: she had no need to worry I would attach myself.

I wandered around alone, visiting some of the major Franciscan sights I had mapped out with Donnie's help. Before long, I abandoned even this loose discipline. The second morning, I left the monastery to buy a pair of shoes and felt, yes, that's enough for today, and returned like a lap dog to my perch on my balcony at Santa Chiara. The next day, I tried, without success, to use my phrase book to get enzyme tablets to clean my contact lenses. That, too, seemed enough of a day's outing.

On the third day, I walked up to the *centro* and drank coffee at the outdoor café by the Temple of Minerva, a blackened pagan site in the middle of town—a building that proved, however, to have been turned into a Catholic church centuries ago. I lit a candle for world peace in the dark interior and wandered out, squinting, into the sunlight, and rushed back to the monastery as if I were expected at home.

I was spending most of my time sitting on the little balcony of the Annunciation, gazing down at the bent nun in her heavy habit, her outer skirt hitched up, slightly showing her woolly stockings. I couldn't make out her face under the broad straw hat, and she never looked up at me. Birds dipped and paused, twittering and scolding. From time to time, I heard the nuns' voices coming from the choir, chanting a wavering line of a Psalm in French. I had no desire to go anywhere.

Idly, that third day, I took out of my bag the portable water-color set my husband had insisted I take along. He often sketches when he's on a trip, and I marvel: "You got it! You got it!" astonished at his facility. I could not make him understand that I wouldn't use the paints—wouldn't, *couldn't* draw. Never had, never would. "When we did murals in grade school," I said, "I was the one the art teacher assigned to do the lettering underneath. I can't draw. It's a known fact."

This made no sense to him. "Why do you think people take cameras on trips? Pictures get it better than words." But he knew he'd just skated onto thin ice there. "Look," he said, "it's no big deal. Just little sketches of where you go. I'd like to see what you come up with."

"I won't come up with anything."

He had even bought a postcard-size tablet of watercolor paper. "You can send me your own postcards."

"I can't draw, I've never been able to draw."

He tucked the little metal hinged box in between my socks. "You'll be glad to have it," he said, and slid the tablet flat on the bottom. Then he gave me the airplane brooch and, to cheer me up, the magazine article about the statistical unlikelihood of any given person perishing in an airplane crash.

I filled the tooth glass with water now, settled back in my chair, and opened the black box. Maybe I could do abstract art. Inside, a small pencil, its pin of lead in a wooden shaft of black enamel, the point dart-sharp, and a white eraser; also a minuscule brush like trimmed whiskers bound in a blue wooden wand. And, marshaled in their immaculate ranks, the bright candies of paint. Just waiting.

I picked up the pencil, looked at the nun's straw hat below

me and the huddle of her black, crouched shape, and took the leap, not even looking at the page. I let the pencil buck where it would. When I looked down—there was a hat. Or an ellipse so reminiscent of a broken straw hat that it made my heart soar. I was off to the races.

Straight lines, I found, were easier than curved: I abandoned people, even conveniently lumpy ones like crouched nuns in full habit facing away from me. Flowers, though powerfully seductive, were dangerous. Buildings were best, affording many satisfying moments of illusory power: I got it! I did bell towers, parts of monasteries, walls with fountains, even managed, with much use of the eraser, a bas-relief lion dribbling into his font.

My Assisi listed strangely, and certain objects tended to loom, others to recede in unaccountable panic or reserve. At first especially, I laid the color on as if I were covering the side of a barn. Assisi, according to me, was heavy, impenetrable, a Dark Age of somber brocade.

Eventually I lightened up. The drawings I sent off to my husband looked as if, in this place where I found myself alone without him, all buildings tilted and dipped, softened to mush by the eternal rain they endured (I hadn't mastered the dripping and running of my watery palette). Still, I sent him a postcard each day, barely able to part with it, so smitten was I, so attached to those melting, merging, unstable structures I could never explain: the world, as seen by me.

All this drawing and sloshing of watercolors was absorbing: hours went in an instant, days galloped. But the effect of this riveted attention was oddly dislocating. I felt vague as a watercolor myself, vacant, blank—but happily so, blank as paper is blank: ready to receive.

Even my encounters with other tourists had an insubstantial quality, as if we were passing under water. Sometimes I joined people for a meal, occasionally I fell into conversation at a café, but it all felt slightly out of focus, not quite real. It seemed I kept meeting people and yet not meeting them, as if we approached the cliff of encounter and then they sheared away, lost. Mme X, for instance, who kept hailing me in the breakfast room each morning with her phony friendliness, which I couldn't help but admire: *"Bonjour, bonjour, ma chère!"* she exclaimed, backing away as she greeted me.

Even the most chance encounters had a way of deflecting me from people, sending me back where it seemed I belonged. Early one morning I walked to the edge of town to the chapel of San Damiano. The church with its small monastery is one of the most beloved of the Franciscan sites in Assisi. Here Francis received his second, and greatest, vision; the icon spoke to him directly: "Francis, rebuild my church." And looking around, he saw the little stone structure was indeed falling apart. Being a poet and therefore irredeemably literal, he set about trying to fix the building. It took another, revised, vision to set him straight: he was to reform the Church, the icon explained, not restore the church.

San Damiano eventually became the monastery of St. Clare and her early followers. Her tiny garden remains, and the room—reminiscent of a hayloft—where she died. The source of Donnie's way of life, transported to a Minneapolis suburb. Here, too, in 1937, the French mystic and philosopher Simone Weil had come as a tourist; kneeling in the same chapel before the same image that had spoken to Francis, she received her own conversion vision, which changed her life forever.

I had walked the mile or so to San Damiano just past sunrise in order to beat the tour groups. San Damiano is not a place for groups, maybe not even for a companion. As I approached the small piazza in front of the chapel in the early light, a stern Francis look-alike hustled out of the chapel, on his way up the pedestrian walk that keeps the tour buses at bay out of sight. He bore a striking resemblance to the Cimabue portrait of Francis: the wasted face, framed by dark hair; the sallow cheeks of a Byzantine icon with its family resemblance to Christ. He glanced at me, frowned, and walked away purposefully, down the road.

I went on to sit by a pool of still water behind the church. A stream ran into a small stone basin above the pool. It tipped the water over a sheet of emerald moss at one side where it drenched its way into a debris of poppy blossoms which floated on the pool's surface, their petals drained of red, a splash of black at each pale center. Their skirts flared in a circle like transparent water lilies. Cypress hemmed the place in, and a clump of silvered olive trees blocked out the hillside's drop.

I was thinking, with low-grade envy, of crazed Francis and of Simone Weil behind her owlish glasses, both children of the middle class, grabbed by visions, miracles of the mind. I felt kinship with them, I was *here* because of them and the peculiar quirk of existence that gives the word *sacred* meaning, even to those who prefer to elude the whole notion of belief. But I was also—or really—thinking of breakfast: would I make it back to Santa Chiara before Mme X and the others had wiped out the morning's croissants? Engulfed in pettiness as usual. And somehow, amid the lush sound of the dripping emerald pool, the birds jetting around the leafy place, the aura of the real-life Cimabue's frown still hovering in my heart, I knew my destiny was with the croissants. *God is in the details*—one of Donnie's key themes. But *only* in the details? Where are the whirlwind, the stigmata, the burning bush, the murmuring icon? The old greedy transcendent hunger gnawed in my morning stomach, though my soul belonged to the sweet rolls.

Just then, along the narrow path running under the high stone wall, came a friar holding up the skirt of his brown robe, tonsured head down, speeding along like the rabbit in *Alice*. He caught sight of me and stopped dead in his tracks for an instant. Then he rushed toward me. He was a small man, I suppose about sixty, though he had one of those eternal faces outside the reckoning of age. He looked thrilled, his smooth face glowing, round and solid as a figurehead on a cane, much rubbed. He held out his hands, as if we had not met in a long time, far too long a time. He spoke in Italian, saying something about the morning, something about music, maybe in reference to the birds. I couldn't understand him. He saw that, and switched to French.

He stopped only an instant; later I thought maybe he hadn't paused at all, though he held my hands and spoke straight into my eyes—whatever he was saying—smiling and, yes, loving me. That total Franciscan charm, the inability to believe we were strangers: being human, we must be kin. He was the flip side of the earnest young friar, the Byzantine icon who had frowned and rushed away, off to his cave and his Search. This was the old man—this was Donnie's ageless face framed by the pixie haircut—telling me things I couldn't understand. Simple things, but not in my language.

Then he was off, pointing to a yellow-breasted finch that dipped its marionette head pertly into the pool and immediately, like the friar, flitted off its own way.

Soeur Marie Ange was waiting for me when I got back to the monastery. She had *une petite faveur* to ask of me, she said, just a little request. There was an American novice in the community, a young woman from Detroit, and the Sisters worried that she often felt lonely because she had no one to talk to in English. She was studying French, of course, but French was *une langue très difficile*—even, pretty Marie Ange said, blushing with her charming falseness, for someone whose French was *superbe*. Would I be willing to visit with the novice for just a little while that afternoon? Just for the home feeling, *un moment de chez elle?*

I had heard of Soeur Agnès. Donnie knew her the way she seemed to know everyone in the Poor Clare network. She was about forty, a physician who had entered the Poor Clare monastery in Detroit but had left the community before her final vows. Then to everyone's surprise—including her own, apparently (she had come to Assisi as a tourist, with no intention of staying)—she had entered the Santa Chiara monastery here the year before, to start all over again being a Poor Clare. Contemplative monasteries tend to be highly autonomous, without the centralizing (and controlling) "motherhouses" that characterize some of the "active" orders with their far-flung communities. Contemplative communities do band loosely together in "federations," which meet occasionally and communicate by mail —there is quite a lot of to-ing and fro-ing among individual monasteries. But each monastery (or "foundation," as the establishment of each house is called) is left to determine its own habits, really its own *style*, within the larger "charism" or spirit of the order.

As for the word *charism*: Donnie had spent a lot of effort trying to get that straight. It has nothing to do with being "charismatic," but is simply the term used to suggest the *esprit* of a given order. While each order has its "Rule," one usually patterned on St. Benedict's famous manifesto for monastic life, each order's charism is its heart, its way of interpreting its Rule. Even the Rule tends to be a document less like a list of rigid commands than like the United States Constitution: it is a formal document to which its citizens adhere but which, by common assent, requires constant reinterpretation in order to survive over time as an organizing and governing principle. The Rule, Donnie would say, is the life. As such, it isn't a law but a way. As the Tibetans say, the Tao.

Members of the various orders—active or contemplative— refer often to their charism, because that is where they ground themselves. They may speak of the "earthy" charism of the Franciscans being different from (even inimical to), say, the "intellectual" charism of the Dominicans, even the "severe" charism of the Carmelites (but that wouldn't be a Carmelite speaking; perhaps a Franciscan would say that).

To complicate things still further, a Poor Clare in Minneapolis (who is part of the supposedly non-intellectual, "earthy" Franciscan charism) might actually have more in common with a desert hermitage Carmelite, whose charism represents a sort of Rolls-Royce of Western contemplative life, than she would with an "active" Franciscan who teaches fourth grade in Fargo. Yet to be "Franciscan" is to claim and share with other Franciscans a certain charism (literally, *way of love*), while to be a "contemplative" is to claim an identity distinct from "active." A charism is rather like a tribal identity. The identity (contemplative) without the charism (Franciscan, say) would be a bottle without wine.

The charisms of each order spring from the personality of the founder or foundress—sometimes a personality astonishingly vivid centuries after death. In no order is this as true as with the Franciscans, whose founder is the most beloved and vivacious figure in Christian hagiography (there was even a troublesome short-lived heresy that sprang up after Francis's death which claimed his life as the Second Coming). There is certainly no saint of the Christian calendar who has displayed his capacity to stay *alive*. He was the medieval chivalric knight who became the "day star" of the Renaissance, and his charism easily transcended the splits and seizures of the Reformation.

More striking, he has managed to sail into the secular age without a nick on his garden statue. He doesn't seem to *annoy* atheists or agnostics as, finally, most saints do. In the sixties he was, perhaps facetiously, "the hippie saint," tripping barefoot in the woods, bearded, and with much appeal as a troublemaker who drove his merchant father crazy. More recently, and probably more significantly, he has been fixed upon as the patron of the environment, of ecology and all the save-the-Earth movements of the day.

Unlike many attempts of the Church to be "relevant," the choice of Francis as patron of the planet's vulnerability has none of the Holy See's usual flatfooted way with its own poetry (Saint Clare, for example, was proclaimed patroness of television in 1957 because of a vision she saw projected on her cell wall). In any case, the Church did not proclaim Francis the environment saint: people simply recognized him to be the man for the job.

As with everything attached to him, there is something spontaneous about this new identity for Francis. Something radical, a grass-roots choice free of the machinations of Rome's CEO. Francis's first conversion act, after all, had been to rip his city clothes off his body and run into the woods, away from the greedy and brilliant urban centuries he was right to sense were coming to Western civilization.

Franciscan contemplative charism, rooted in a personality still palpably radical, fits the autonomy of individual monasteries, and it is not surprising to hear of a woman leaving one Poor Clare monastery and later entering another. Especially after Vatican II, with its call for reform, monasteries have defined themselves with a rainbow of difference, even while claiming the same root charism. Donnie's monastery, for instance, was a foundation established from another Poor Clare monastery. This founding monastery still exists in the northern Minnesota woods. The women there live a life very different, at least stylistically, from Donnie's. They retain a strict cloister (grates, curtains, the old-style habits, barefoot in the manner of the first Franciscans, a truly "removed" life). They are virtually unknown to the world. It would not have been possible for me to go there, as I did to Donnie's monastery, and "taste" the contemplative life. They shut the door for life—some would say on life—and get to work praying. Their job? The *opus Dei*, the work of God. Put simply, it is to pray without ceasing. That is Donnie's work, too. But her community has defined the shape, the look, and feel of the essential identity differently.

The change has been slow. The monastery Donnie entered in the early fifties offered a very different way of life from the one she lives now. The changes, achieved at a snail's pace through a process of "discernment," are made through democratic community vote. In the almost three decades since Vatican II, the veils have gone, also the sweeping habits, and, more significantly, the grates separating the nuns from "the world." Donnie, sounding for a moment like Rima out of *Green Mansions*, looks wistful when she talks about the barefoot days of her first twelve years as a nun. "It was so free. The floor felt cool and fresh every step you took along the corridors."

Soeur Marie Ange, barefoot in sandals under her beige habit, led me now down a dark corridor of the monastery and pointed to a door with a small sign on it: PARLOIR DE SAINT

FRANÇOIS. She motioned me inside and shut the door behind me. I found myself in a small, light room. A straight-back chair was placed before a counter framed by a squared arch which formed one end of the space. I sensed the chair was mine.

Behind the counter another chair faced this one; behind that, a small window, placed high, framing a Piero della Francesca landscape, a smooth pale green hill with a few well-drawn trees, the whole small scene wrapped in a gauze of light. On the other side of the counter, to the left, was a door. The effect was of a miniature theater, perhaps a puppet theater, with my lone chair representing the audience. It was placed unnaturally close to the action. The actor, still offstage, was clearly meant to enter from stage left. I sat there for a while. It was like waiting for the dentist to come in after the nurse has put you in the chair.

There was a faint sound of drapery moving somewhere, but it was a surprise when the door behind the counter opened. I jumped up. She came toward me, a solid but not fat figure in the same graceful folds as the wandlike Marie Ange, except she wore a white, not black, veil. She leaned across the counter and greeted me with the French air-kissing embrace on both cheeks. It seemed an odd thing between two Americans meeting alone, but I was glad she took charge.

"Mother," she said, referring to her Superior, "thinks I'm homesick. She's always asking Americans to visit me. I can't convince her it's unnecessary." It was clear I was no treat. She said each sentence with a strange upturn at the end and a questioning little "hmm?" that sounded affected but was actually unconscious, a tic of shyness, I decided. It was as if English, not French, were foreign to her. She carried a French grammar, and looked frankly at her watch as she settled into her chair. She radiated distance. It occurred to me I might be a minor penance, an occasion for holy patience. She responded to my questions, but a conversation did not at first develop. Why had she left the American monastery?

Because, she said briskly, she was looking for greater commitment to poverty. She had worked with the poor before she entered the Detroit monastery and she was impatient with bourgeois religion. As for entering the monastery here—that was a surprise, something she'd never planned.

Did she plan to spend the rest of her life here?

As far as she knew.

I realized, when she had taken up her position behind the counter, that the open space had once been covered by a grille. The places for the fastenings were visible in the frame that gave the space its proscenium arch. The monastery was molting from strict cloister to something more relaxed. But apparently they were not yet ready, as Donnie's monastery had done before I ever arrived, to do away with the entire apparatus. They kept their distance, the stamp of the cloister. Soeur Agnès seemed content with that. She leaned back in her chair, away from the counter that connected us. I found myself leaning forward.

Yet I was aware of some resistance in myself, too. Even nervousness, verging on panic. It didn't make sense. I ignored it, trying to be *interested*—which I was. An American doctor entering a monastery in Assisi: interesting. But the panic was there, and it lent my questions a slightly clipped, almost hysterical insistence. Still, she kept answering.

It turned out she was a convert, having come from a Protestant family that didn't bother much about religion. At twelve she had somehow been drawn to Catholic Sunday school, probably, she thought, because her friends went. Her parents didn't mind. They didn't even mind when she wanted to be baptized. Then, when she made her First Communion, everything was decided for her.

"I thought, Hey, this is *great*," she said, for the first time sounding American. She had a nice smile. She had appeared to be frowning slightly the rest of the time, but it was probably just her heavy eyebrows; they made a severe line across her forehead. At that First Communion she had simply had some kind of experience, a union with God. "All I knew was I wanted to feel that way all the time." The love she wanted was God's. She understood she was a contemplative.

She kept the information to herself. She seemed to know it was not a young person's career, had gone to college, taught for a while, gone back to medical school, worked at a walk-in clinic. And entered when the time was right. Leaving the Detroit monastery hadn't changed her sense of herself. She just took her vocation on the road. And here she was. Of course, for a Franciscan, Assisi was a nice touch. But Assisi wasn't the real point, she insisted. She simply saw that here she could do her work.

Which was?

She looked surprised that she had to say it: "To pray, to find God, hmm?"

She believed in the idea of cloister, she said. It was obviously something she had worked out. She had a certain impatience *Point* with all the New Age-ish searching of American communities, the guitars, the trendy liturgies, the psychologizing of prayer, ✗ the endless community meetings about habits and veils. Nor could she stomach the pretense of a self-conscious old-style orthodoxy, parading around like medieval dames, living a sham feudal life like a person hired at a Renaissance fair. She had the look of someone who wanted to cut to the chase, who wanted to do business. A cloister, to her, made good occupational sense, and she wanted to be inside one, working. Praying. She looked at her watch again.

I asked her if there was anything I could do for her. I expected her to say no: her don't-tread-on-me personality was convincing. But she drew an envelope out of the depths of her habit. "If you'd mail this in the States, hmm?" she said. "The Italian mails are so slow." It was for her father.

Anything else? I asked. The strange panicky sensation was still there, but I also wanted to *give* her something. I had the mad instinct to cram a twenty in her hand.

She would be very grateful, she said, if I sent her a calligraphy pen. She was taking up the art, and it was useful to the community because she could write all sorts of cards for feast days and as little gifts among the Sisters. She had only a dip pen; it was hard to use. I promised to send her one with an ink barrel.

103

We both stood up, facing each other across the counter. The panic flipped into vertigo. This was the sensation: I was looking straight into a mirror. I knew I was looking at myself, but I didn't recognize the face. My hands prickled with sweat. *This is nuts*, I was saying firmly to myself, *get out of here.*

But I found myself saying, as we each went to our respective doors, "By the way, what was your name before you entered?"

She smiled. Right through me. "It was Patricia," she said.

That evening I went to dinner with a middle-aged French Canadian couple who were staying in the main building of Santa Chiara. I had met them in the breakfast room, and it had been their idea that we meet later in the day to choose a restaurant for the evening. "Where do you suggest?" the wife asked, as if she were a woman who relished her food. But she discarded each place I mentioned. "Oh no, I'm quite sure I heard the Sisters warn against that one—who knows what goes on in the kitchen?"

The husband seemed not to care where we went, but the wife became almost hysterical as she pored over her red Michelin guide. "How," she asked with real anguish, "can you tell what's *clean* from the little symbols? There is no symbol for hygiene."

In desperation, she was driven to choose a place located on a second floor because at least it was off the street. But once up the narrow stairway and seated in the tiny room, she was visited by terrible doubts. She was unable to bring herself to take anything but bottled water and little pellets of bread she tore from the loaf the waiter brought to the table in a basket. "You can always trust the bread," she said conspiratorially.

The husband and I ordered our way heedlessly through the menu. With each course, her face took on a look of horror, unable to comprehend the trust we placed in the tomato salad and the tortellini. Her eyes widened in dismay when the vitello tonnato arrived. Toxins abounded. "Claude, Claude, Claude," she murmured miserably to her husband as each dish arrived at the table, though she never cried out my name and seemed willing to see me bite the dust.

Claude took it all in stride—the parade of possibly poisoned food, his wife's dolor, and the very nice bottle of Orvieto he ordered for the two of us. As the meal went on its strange way, it seemed he and I were dining alone, holding down the physical fort, while the wife deserted to pure spirit, a dark angel attending the feast.

The oddity of our arrangement had reached such a level of normality that I wasn't surprised when, apropos of nothing, she leaned across the table and said, *sotto voce*, "I was unable to have children."

"Oh," I said affably enough, my mouth full.

"And now I have had to quit my job at the hospital," she said, warming to intimacy as if I had proved myself a good listener. "I had to quit. I had to work with people who would *not* take things seriously. They have time for coffee breaks—oh, plenty of coffee. But sort out the supply room?" A snort of derision. "No time for *that*. It was all on my shoulders. Everything. And so . . ."

We walked back to Santa Chiara in the dark, the wife long gone into fret, the husband just gone, a man who had checked out long ago. They did not seem unhappy together, companionably traveling their separate ways. The next morning they left before breakfast, without giving me their Quebec address, which the wife had been intent upon doing.

They dropped into my notebook without a splash, and I was solo again on my balcony, attending the apparition of another watercolor, but now with that added layer of solitude that comes from realizing I had been alone even as we sat together across the dinner table toasting each other, the husband and I with white wine of the region, the wife with the abstract champagne of her carbonated water, which she assured us again and again was one thing you could trust in this foreign place.

like the stars

12

Two weeks of brief encounters seemed to erase themselves, leaving real time amorphous, mistily vague as the Plain of Spoleto below the balcony of the Annunciation, where I spent most of my days alone, staring out, giving myself over to my drawings, staring some more.

Sometimes I left the balcony and sat in the cool interior of the room, flipping from *The Cloud of Unknowing* to the *Revelations* of Julian of Norwich. "All will be well, and all will be well, and all manner of thing will be well," Julian the anchorite had written in her famous reassurance in Chaucer's day. Probably the coziest mystical revelation ever imparted. ". . . And all manner of thing will be well." *Maybe*, I called back across the centuries. *Maybe.* I had taken to talking to myself in a mumbling, monosyllabic way.

Sometimes I went into the garden and walked along the gravel paths, crushing thyme underfoot; its sharp pine-forest scent rushed up. Then I went back to the balcony and stared out, waiting for Vespers at five o'clock, when bells started up all over town, from church to convent to monastery in a wild cuckoo-clock-shop effect. I sat even past that, until the light faded. At

Not much by stillness

dusk the horizon turned briefly vivid in a magenta flare, before night swallowed the color and the stars came on and I could call it a day.

Each day expanded with its own emptiness; the present got lighter and lighter. It puffed into the air like the dusty earth the monastery roses grew from, making the view to Santa Maria degli Angeli swim in the famous mistiness that gives Umbria its reputation as "the mystical province." *aura*

The funny thing was, the longer I stared from the balcony, the less the landscape seemed to touch me. I was elsewhere. I was long gone. Not Mme X, not the nuns sweeping by in their graceful drapery, not the friar with his polished head who had grasped my hands, not the dizzy occult moment in the *parloir* with Soeur Agnès, not even my attempts to sort out the impulses of Francis or the modern, edgy conversion of Simone Weil (I had brought some of her essays along, too)—none of these encounters seemed capable of anchoring me in the present. Even the watercolors, created out of close attention to the world around me, had this dislocating effect: they were minor miracles, not mine. *They were here, but I was* . . .

For the most part, I was in St. Paul again. Or I was in my childhood, or my girlhood, or whatever condition pulls a person toward the tiny pinhole of consciousness through which personality first asserts its light. I found myself entirely absorbed by stray bits of memory, shards long discarded. *memory*

Nobody was expecting me anywhere, nobody needed me. Even English was an island I lived on alone here. I hadn't been so free and unfettered in years. I could understand why Soeur Agnès, against the solicitude of her Superior, was not lonely marooned in her French-Italian world. There was so much to *see*. I would have called my state of mind pure laziness—like those summer mornings when the heartbeat of the tennis court roller pounded into my brain and the doves cooed their blurry requiem. But this difference: now the heavy traffic of memory was running through my head. I was busy on my balcony.

Memory had always seemed a series of stories, vignettes with beginnings, middles, and ends which gave them the sturdiness of a book. But these things that captivated me as I sat on the balcony making my blurry drawings, letting the days drift by without making a mark—these things were not stories. They were brief testimonies of perception, bits of consciousness. Although they arose from my life, they were hardly personal. If memories *are* stories, then these mental fragments were from an earlier mind, lyric rather than narrative. They were the unformed water, not the sea with its confining shore. The images washing over me were part of the blissful anonymity of that first sleep on the candlewick bedspread in the Annunciation. They lent me the neutrality of Mme X and her perfect head. By the end of the first week I realized that, for once, I wished to be nobody else. Yet I felt a comfortable distance from my own life as its odds and ends sifted over the weightless days.

The aloof part of my mind (of anyone's, I realized from this detached point of view I seemed to inhabit on the balcony of the Annunciation) had always been there. I was free—always had been free—of the slavish convent-school girl I had been railing at all these years. Mme X did not have me pegged. There was no convent-school girl, there was no eternal ingenue. I would wear my hair in a chignon one day, I would retire from whatever it was that enslaved me, just as Mme X had retired from her teaching job in Nice. It was so easy. There was no daughter straining to break free, no mother, no father, no stockade of love and loyalty. No Catholic girlhood to ransack for jokes or outrage.

There was only this mind—the simple room which turned out to be a camera, admitting light; it had been taking its quirky snapshots all along. Everything from the past seemed valuable, yet almost weightless, without the usual attachments of pride or grief, regret or resentment. Just these slides soundlessly presenting themselves in no order, but creating out of their ceaseless flow a fascination like a plot line in a novel. Only there was no plot. The experience was this: An old shoebox full of snapshots had been dumped on the polished floor of what a nun would call her cell. I had only to regard them. The sense was already there, waiting to express itself.

One after another they came: My brother, calling from his room, "How do you spell *could*?" And my answer, just hanging there, "You're so *dumb*!" The accuracy of the cliché struck home: contempt dripped from my voice as I reheard myself. It was another of those pinholes of light through which I passed. But this awareness was not attended by shame (which would have struck me as false, a pose) but by a sort of vital *interest*: ah, so *contemplate* *that* is there, too.

Then the perfect O of my aunt's mouth scrolled up, the moment when, age ten, I stood next to my father as he told her their father was dead. It was the first moment I realized adults did not live for children. Her familiar mouth was suddenly a zero, falling away from its usual attentive auntishness.

Now, sitting on the balcony of the Annunciation, I saw the moment for what it was: not simply my first encounter with death (my Irish grandmother, whom I adored, had died earlier), but my first experience of detachment. In that instant of seeing *alone* my aunt absolutely in her own life and knowing I wasn't part of *detached* it, I got a sharp whiff of liberation. I understood in some subtle way that my family's love, all their protection, the rules and restrictions of Catholic life that kept everything going, but especially the anxious smiles that always seemed to greet my presence—these things were decorative veils over the real.

What was real was the zero, and what was essential was to be there to see it. True, the zero was death. It was New Year's Eve and my grandfather had been getting ready to go to a dance at his lodge hall when the heart attack hit him; perhaps part of the force of the memory was imparted by the cold of the hospital vestibule where we waited. But as I stood between my father and his sister, and my aunt's face refused me, I was admitted to the domain I had been denied by that European eiderdown of family love that was always pulled up to my neck.

I took the moment, instinctively, as a privilege. I understood, though I couldn't have said so, that I would never feel closer to

Paradox ?

One when Separate

my aunt than at that instant when she forgot I existed and just let me *see* her. I had not known people could stand in such stern solidarity with each other, that we were One when we were separate.

I liked standing right next to my father, near my aunt, and I liked very much that I was forgotten, that something huge had happened, and I knew what it was, saw it, took it in. I remembered the opening line we said at the noon Angelus prayer in school: "My soul doth magnify the Lord." And I was dilated, enlarged, standing there, fixated by my aunt's open mouth, which was the family abyss where, for once, I was allowed to stand unguarded.

admitted to the real.

Then it was full summer. My memory made a jump cut to the black tub in the palm house at my father's greenhouse, where the sluggish goldfish, sold for aquatic gardens, hardly moved in their dark pools. They eluded my hand, though they were torpid, phlegmatic things. Joe Vero, an old Austrian grower, was passing by with a flat of petunias. "They eat them in China," he said, looking at the fish and at me without stopping, sending a clairvoyant fright of exotic desires down my spine.

With an uncanny sense of timing, my mind had chosen this misty Italian place, these empty days, to mount its traveling exhibition. I sensed this wasn't nostalgia. "You're so *lazy*," my brother had said. But these days felt like life's real labor. The question remained, however: If this wasn't simply reminiscence, what was it? It wasn't prayer—I was still far from prayer—but these days were some kind of genuflection, a necessary acquiescence.

Between reminiscence + prayer

I was on my knees—not as I had been on the plane, in the foxhole fear of extinction, but with the other kind of urgency, born of wonder. Like a tune that takes up residence and refuses to leave, an interior chorus murmured, *Charity begins at home*, and kept playing this line across the snapshots my mind cast on its screen. It was a subliminal sound track running softly under the moving slides, telling me—what? That I loved my life? But something else, too, something I could not grasp. It was beyond my life, although the materials of this strange but simple experience came only from its scraps.

In this spirit, my life—or the refuse of my life—passed before my eyes in all its smallness. I gazed fascinated at everything that came my way: the indescribable loveliness of the St. Paul lilacs every year that second week in May, their dark pellets opening, flooding the back alleys with fragrance before turning finally to rust. And the hard face of the nun who said, when I told her I was going to the university and not to the Catholic women's college, "Patricia, you have turned against your friends. You will lose your religion." And there was my ecstatic face lurking all these years under the head I had been canny enough to bow submissively before her.

My father's sensible hand appeared, the knuckle cracked, turning the dead ignition of his Ford on a 20-below-zero day: the patience of his face and its haunt of greenhouse work, decades before I ever thought of his death.

Click, click, the carousel of slides: the powerful Minnesota seasons marking each year in four bold strokes, revealed now as analogues of the spirit, its savage contradictions. The feints and lunges of family love: my mother's hard face and then her tender one; the teapot that played "Tea for Two" when you picked it up to pour; my brother Peter talking sensibly to his dog, which understood him, and my mother saying, "Don't tease him, he needs to talk to someone." And Mr. Bertram next door saying to my mother, "Well, it's this way, Mrs. Hampl. I am afflicted with perfect pitch, so of course, in the summer with the windows open, your daughter's practicing is painful to me. I might add, my wife has encouraged me to be frank."

Occasionally a skit. Peter goading Mother the year Kennedy ran for President: "Admit it, Ma, you're voting for him because he's a Catholic." Her outrage: "How can you even *suggest* such a thing? You know I believe in the *complete* separation of church and state. Your father and I always vote yes on bond issues even though we will always provide you with a Catholic education."

111

He couldn't resist, though: "You wouldn't vote for George Washington if an Irish Catholic was on the ticket."

"Well," she said, taking the bait, "I seem to be the only one in this house who thinks it wouldn't be so awful to have someone of The One True Faith in the White House."

And then, three years later, like an epilogue giving her the last word on the subject, her face, streaming with tears in front of the Magnavox that whole weekend in November. She reached out and touched the screen when the caisson rolled by with the coffin.

More than once—several times—during the week that I sat on the balcony of the monastery room and let my life present itself in all its lost details, the beautiful little girl appeared, as if her presence were the most insistent of all, her departure the most unwilling. I must be four. I don't go to school yet. I can't read. People are always telling me to go outside and play. I can walk to the end of the block. That far. I must not cross Oxford Street. But there she is, standing across Oxford. I have seen her many times. And now again. Her hands are clasped behind her back, and she is swinging back and forth in a self-contained motion. She is answering the question I have finally emboldened myself to ask her. "Grace," she calls across the great neighborhood divide. "My name is Grace."

"I'm Patricia," I holler back. The next thing seems inevitable, easy: "Will you be my friend, Grace?" My brother has friends, but there are no girls on our block. She is the nearest one, as far as I know. Her hair glows in the sun. I don't understand I am not looking in a mirror of desire, wish meeting wish. Isn't what's in my heart in every heart? Doesn't Grace need Patricia?

She shakes her head, her hands still behind her back, still rocking to her own rhythm. "No," she says. "No, no, no." It doesn't occur to me that, after all, she lives by remote control, too, and cannot cross the street. I only see her now as she turns from me, her honey hair swinging back and forth as she runs away, calling out *No no no* forever, escaping down the block where I don't dare to follow.

The only slides that seem already sorted, as if they had been stashed for retrieval at a safer time, come in a rush one after another: Bonnie Binder, too popular to like *me*, inexplicably inviting me to her house overnight in fourth grade. Lights out, and her bossy voice, softened with desire and fright: "I'll show you mine if you'll show me yours. You go first . . ."

Father Flannery in the confessional: "And are these thoughts and actions something you do alone, my child, or with others?"

With others! What is he *thinking* of! (I repress Bonnie Binder, I drown her like a kitten in a sack.) "Oh, alone, Father, alone," I say, grasping for what must be the lesser sin.

"I suggest when these thoughts come that you listen to music on your hi-fi," he says.

"We don't have a hi-fi, Father."

"Well, do you have a radio?"

Yes, we have a radio, we also have a television. There is a way out of this thing if I will just flip the right switch and get some public noise going in the too private air.

A few years later, the first sensation of *lips*, my eyes springing open into Tommy Ryan's close-up face; I was so startled: *Hey, they're soft. Like ours.*

Then Benson Masters, with his thrillingly non-Catholic name that sounded like a law firm, saying impatiently, "How should I know? They call it French because the French *invented* it, that's why. What difference does it make?"

But even that damp convent school don't-touch-me patter had lost its capacity to humiliate me. The slides clicked along, throwing their curio shots against my memory: the flustered first dates, the hideous rust-colored sateen dress, bought on sale at Scheunamen's, gleaming grotesquely like a mother-of-the-bride getup amid everyone else's pink and powder blue at the St. Thomas spring dance. And Benson Masters, that flashy Protestant, lost finally, his disgusted voice in the back of his dad's Olds: *You Catholic girls—every one of you's a prick tease.* The early memories of the everything-but girl, roses in my hair for the senior dance, and my date saying, "Yes, I've decided to join the Christian Brothers after graduation." My antique innocence, bred in an age—or maybe just a neighborhood—which had crumbled to dust although it was supposed to be just yesterday, seemed far away, not me, not anything, as it revealed itself in picture after picture. It evaporated, joined the mist of Spoleto far off there somewhere. I caught myself smiling slightly as I came out of these reveries.

I had the feeling I was standing again at the old Union Station in St. Paul, a sharp winter brace in the air, putting difficult relatives on the train, waving them off on the rails of oblivion, sending memory after memory far away, where they belonged, where they would be just fine without me.

Dealing with unfinished Business?

Process Reminiscences — For its own sake? or for the psychology?

13

"We're Chaucer," Sister Francine said. "Pure Chaucer." She sounded happy. Sister Francine had won her place in the two-week Franciscan Study Tour in a lottery at her Philadelphia convent. She was marveling now at the "human variety" in the tour group as a few of us sat at the Caffè Minerva in Assisi, ordering coffee. "I think you should say we're straight out of *The Canterbury Tales.*" She pointed to my notebook.

"Does that mean I should be telling a dirty joke?" Brother Philip asked. He turned to his sidekick, Brother Sylvan, who snorted on cue and raised his glass. They had decided against coffee and had ordered a local aperitif made from truffles.

Philip was portly and bald; his red face gleamed under a pork-pie hat. Sylvan, a reedy ectomorph with a pencil mustache, cocked his hat at a dapper angle, which gave him a David Niven dash. The two of them had the look and timing, and the Brooklyn accents, of an old vaudeville team. They wore double-knit trousers and pastel no-iron shirts open at the collar. "I'm sure," Sylvan said deadpan, "Sister would like to hear the one about the Holy Father and the postulant from Mount Pisgah, wouldn't you now, Sister?"

Sister Francine rolled her eyes. But she was playing to them, not me. Clearly she wasn't offended. She had the family routine down as pat as they did: proper older sister scandalized by rascal kid brothers.

In fact, none of them was a kid; they were retired, and had met for the first time a week before in Rome at the beginning of the study tour. The family dynamic had clicked in place soon after the thirty Franciscans from all over the United States (with one from Ireland) had gathered the first evening in the hotel lobby of the Casa tra Noi, not far from the Vatican. They spoke of their "communities," swapped information on the year they had "entered" and the date of their "profession," the way strangers meeting on another sort of tour might speak of wedding anniversaries and the birthdates of children.

Most of them had entered their orders well before the changes following Vatican II in 1963, and had weathered the departures of the late sixties and seventies. They regaled each other with "before" stories. Philip and Sylvan's tales tended toward high jinks and rascal behavior of the boarding school sort: sneaking out of the novitiate to go to the movies, saving the nickel they were given for the streetcar and walking to their school work so the nickel could go for a beer.

For the women, these "before" stories tended to depend for their hilarity on the "outlandish getups" (Sister Francine's term) they once had worn. Most of the nuns in the group dressed in street clothes now, the younger ones sporting sweats and running shoes for casual wear, the older ones the wash-and-wear acetate blouses of the frugal traveler. Some of them did wear an abbreviated habit or a short veil for formal occasions, but, "You'll never catch me in one," Sister Francine said. She tended toward natural fibers and was wearing a white cotton blouse with a touch of lace around the collar. "They bring back those monstrous clothes and I'm out." She spoke with the happy bravado of a long-married wife who adores her husband and says cheerfully, "I'm divorcing that man if he ever brings that outboard motor in this house again."

Sister Francine had taught high school English for forty-two years in Philadelphia and New York, and was perhaps disposed to see life in terms of the language arts curriculum. She lamented the absence of *Great Expectations* from the current course offerings and indicated that things did not augur well for a society which had ceased to place Dickens firmly before its children.

"What do they teach them now?" she asked, with a dismissive flip of her hand.

We were sitting at a wobbly table facing the blackened Roman temple in Assisi's Piazza del Comune. There had been a moment's hesitation about taking our espresso *al fresco*—the same drinks were cheaper inside the dark café than outside on the piazza. But we'd gone for the total experience. The vow of poverty seemed to bestow on the Franciscans a regal disregard for small change. They egged each other on to little treats in Assisi. "Go ahead, Sister," one of the friars would say to a timid nun hesitating over the purchase of an I ♡ Assisi T-shirt. "You're only in Assisi once," they kept reminding each other.

This wasn't a vacation for them. It was a reunion—and not simply with each other. They spoke of Francis and Clare as of people who had just left the room for a moment. On the bus from Greccio to Assisi, Sister Francine had been discussing a woman's hair with another Sister. It was blond, of course, she said. But she couldn't remember if it was curly.

Oh yes, beautiful natural curls, the other Sister said.

It took me a moment to realize they were talking about St. Clare, dead since 1253. "I sometimes wonder what she saw in Francis," Francine said. And they were off again, discussing the unlikely passion for spiritual perfection that crazy, converted Francis from the merchant class had fired in beautiful, patrician Clare. They mused over it in the timeless manner of bystanders contemplating any improbable romance.

The Franciscans didn't treat Assisi like Mecca—and it wasn't Rome. It was *home*, and its power was intimate rather than ecclesiastic. It imposed the holy commandment of celebration. And they were happy to oblige, wandering the little tourist town with their maps, taking family pride in the Giottos, diving into the dark of the souvenir shops for mementoes for their communities back in the States. "It used to be," Francine said, "that people asked for holy medals, blessed by the Pope. But now they all want you to bring back a bottle of grappa." She didn't seem troubled.

Perhaps these celibates, related by vows, not blood, had settled into the most profound kind of family after all: one entirely poetic. The mystery of family, which bedevils every generation, remained for them a series of eternal tableaux handed down over the centuries from the dawn of the Renaissance when Brother Francis, accused by his clothier father of selling his retail goods to give away the money to the poor, stood before Guido, the bishop of Assisi, for judgment. It was a shrewd move on Francis's part to agree to this showdown on the bishop's property, for it shifted the law from the state to the Church—which, after all, was the family Francis sought to serve with his father's goods and which was predisposed to see things his way.

"From now on," Francis shouted to the crowd gathered in the bishop's courtyard, "I can say with complete freedom, 'Our Father who art in heaven.' No more is Pietro Bernardone my father, but only the Lord God in heaven is my Father." He threw down the little bag of money, and ripped off his clothes ("not even retaining his trousers," Thomas of Celano, his earliest biographer, notes).

The garments represented not only social decency but the very stuff of his father's business. Francis stood naked before his enraged father and the astonished townspeople. Then he ran—howling like an animal, some reports say—into the woods to join the lepers.

"Did he ever make it up with Pietro?" one of the Sisters had asked Francine on the bus.

"I don't believe so, Sister," she said. They fell silent for a moment.

It was a strange sensation to listen to this sort of conversation. Like eavesdropping on the gossip of the ages. Nor did it sound like the babble of cultists. The references were casual. The immediacy of these historic figures was family lore, not pious fiction. *Did he ever make it up with Pietro?* the Sister had asked in a simple way—the way you ask about a brother or nephew.

They weren't "living in history" with its throwaway pageant of changing characters. Rather, in this Franciscan world there was only the eternity of primal relationships. Although they enjoyed trading stories about Francis and Clare, it wasn't the stories that packed the punch of immediacy; it was the characters—wild Francis, regal Clare—whose temperaments radiated real life from the charter bus on the autostrada from Greccio, and now here at the Caffè Minerva, in between tourist stops.

Every story seemed to resolve itself into a tableau of character, an image that refused to fade with the centuries. These tableaux—Francis tearing his father's garments off his body in the bishop's courtyard (we had gone there that morning), Clare escaping from her father's palace in the dead of Palm Sunday night to pledge her life to Francis's poverty (we had stopped for *gelato* at a café across from the Church of San Rufino, where she had gone to Mass that Palm Sunday morning)—these vignettes were scrutinized not for story but for a reading of character. And character itself, whether in hothead Francis or the serene lady Clare, led back to the eternity of family, the broken heart of each generation.

The actions of these figures ceased to be primarily historic. They became poetic in the essential sense: they were real *and* they were symbolic. This made them irresistible. Not simply enormously appealing, as Zeffirelli had rendered them in his movie *Brother Sun, Sister Moon* (which all the Franciscans had seen at least once). Francis and Clare were irresistible to the soul seeking correspondences and guides to the mysterious web of human relationships that attaches people to each other through the ages, even as they struggle to break loose from this connection into the glory of individual consciousness.

Religion is literary. If Jesus was the greatest of all storytellers, and St. John is the William Blake, the visionary of the Gospels,

119

then Francis is Keats, the lyric genius of consciousness regarding the created world. He is the patron saint of perception, a proto-Romantic. It's no mistake that anthologies of Italian poetry begin with his "Canticle of the Creatures," a litany of the created world which is united in praise to the Creator.

In pondering Francis, the Franciscans on the tour were not on a historic quest. Rather, they touched the two gushing sources of contemporary psychology: the family and the self. In Francis they encountered the self held in the communal embrace of family and Church, *and* the individual mind desperately seeking free flight away from that very clutch, seeking the Godhead, where all divisions are lost, where self, family, you, me cease to exist, and everything becomes It.

His father wasn't the saint's only trouble. Francis's vision of Christian poverty was so radical (or so nuts, as one of the friars on the tour said cheerfully) that the Brothers of his own order took control of the community before he died; he was relegated to the sidelines of the very family he had founded.

Francis was drawn to create the family, the community, but his temperament was mystic, anarchic—individual. It sustained visions, not a social structure. His was no patriarchy. He was Brother Francis—all his life he declined to be ordained a priest. He refused to call Pietro "Father," but no one could call him "Father" either. To father a family—or found a community—is an act of the communal imagination. In the end, the cross Francis was spread on was made of the green-cut plank of the self laid across the ancient wood of the tribe. And there, looking very contemporary, he writhed.

To ponder at all this distinction between communal and individual is very modern—and very Western. And to put fundamental trust in individual perception is, more than the "isms" the twentieth century acknowledges as its secular religions, a sign of the real faith of our own age in the West.

The Franciscans read Francis and Clare not for stories but for signals. They read them as moderns who had performed a miracle: from the bloody family battlefield to have plucked the

unbruised rose of individual consciousness, and to have found
in this flower not isolation and self-absorption but full union with
God and the world. This union was mystical and eternal in a
way that the family, based on the body, could never be, in spite
of its age-old claims. It was a reclamation of the radical Christian
idea: A *People* could be forged by the miracle of the imagination,
what Keats much later called "the holiness of the heart's affec-
tions." The most basic act—eat this, drink this—became the
way to union, a tribe for all seeking the All.

Nor was the Franciscan vision pietistic or lost in interior moments untranslatable to the world. Francis ran first to find the
lepers. He didn't run howling into the woods to *help* them. He
simply went to join them, to *be* with them. He wasn't a do-
gooder, not a missionary in the convert-the-heathen sort of way.
He was a joyous mystic who *needed* to suffer the great pain of
his age, because not to suffer, especially to miss out on the
suffering of the world, was not to live. If he was the first modern
man, discovering the self, he recognized the self as an instru-
ment, not a thing unto itself. Individual consciousness, that astonishingly tiny pinhole of light, was his lens for viewing the
world.

This suffering-with/being-with creates a ground of equality
missing from other missionary motives with their inevitable one-
up/one-down benevolence. Perhaps this is why Francis has been
an attractive model for the liberation theology in the Third
World. Francis performed a miracle when he stripped naked
before his father and his townspeople. For discovery is a kind
of miracle, and his miracle was to discover that out of individual
perception, not out of blood ties, came solidarity. Individual
consciousness was not, in this view, made for the "pursuit of
happiness," but radiated forever as proof of the fundamental
Christian belief, already betrayed in his own day: the faith that
we are all One Body. Forever and ever. Amen.

His miracle retained its capacity to endure, which meant that
two thirteenth-century saints were not dead but uncannily alive
not only in Assisi but in the lives of the American Franciscans

who had finally made this trip home to find them. So it did not seem strange when Sister Francine turned to the Brothers and said, "Look, the young Francis." She was pointing to a young Assisan in tight jeans and a leather jacket, who was lounging by the *gelato* bar across the piazza, lighting a cigarette. He had just said something that made his buddies laugh, and was grinning now at his success.

Brother Philip turned back from looking at him and nodded: "Just like him." He said it without a trace of humor or irony, just acknowledging Francine's observation of the pre-conversion Francis, the charmer, the poet, the leader of the town's fashionable youth (a Francis for whom the Franciscans reserved a special affection, rather like a child beloved partly because he is a terror).

Philip and Sylvan had been firm champions of the higher-priced-drinks-on-the-piazza. That had been fine with Sister Francine. She drank down the little glass of *acqua minerale* that came with her espresso and went back to the Wrong Turn that the English curriculum had taken. "First it was Bob Dylan," she said. "We did units on 'The Poetry of Rock,' that sort of thing."

She had been chair of her department at the time, in the late sixties, just after Vatican II. "Everybody wanted to be Relevant," she said. "But now Bob Dylan's somebody's grandfather, and the kids don't want the poetry of rock. They want rap, and so the English curriculum is off chasing *that*. Meanwhile, where's Dickens? Wasn't *Great Expectations* relevant all along?"

She paused and took me in for a moment. "You have read *Great Expectations*, haven't you?"

"Pip?" I said. "Miss Havisham?"

"A wonderful novel," she said, reaching for her espresso. "A wonderful *teaching* novel." She brought the little cup to her face and smiled as she took in the aroma.

Philip and Sylvan had been born and raised ("baptized and confirmed," as they said) in the Brooklyn diocese where they had spent most of their working lives teaching in Catholic boys' schools. Their places on the tour had been given to them as retirement gifts from their provincial. Ruby-faced Philip had taught shop; the lightweight Sylvan, surprisingly enough, had been the principal, known for his iron rule. "Oh," Philip said, "you should have seen them tremble when he took the stage for Friday assembly. Terrifying—kept the boys in line just lifting an eyebrow." Sylvan smiled his feckless David Niven smile, then let his mouth go thin, the barest hint of something like contempt playing around its edges, his eyebrow just slightly elevated, the ice cracking from his eyes. "Like that?" he said, breaking the pose, grinning at Brother Philip.

"Like that, like that!" his pal cried. "I'll drink to that, Brother." And he raised his glass to Sylvan, who made a slight bow, acknowledging his skill like a modest character actor.

And why not see them Sister Francine's way: the bon vivant brothers living it up on the way to the shrine, and Sister Francine herself, delicately wringing a sliver of lemon zest over her espresso so the oil beaded from the pores of the rind before she let it fall into the cup.

She lifted her demitasse with her little finger crooked, a dainty Prioresse scanning the piazza contentedly, ready to recognize Francis, in case he should materialize again, as he so often did.

Relations

14

My roommate on the study tour, Elsie Pickett, was determined that I should not suffer from her need for a cigarette. She waited until we were both in our narrow beds, lights-out in the little room we shared at the Casa Papa Giovanni in Assisi. Then, giving me a decent amount of time to fall asleep, she crept out of her bed and made her way to the bathroom. Sometimes she stubbed her toe in the dark and let out a suppressed yelp while she hopped forward on one foot. She sat in the bathroom, smoking, most of the night.

Toward morning she went back to her bed. When I got up, I found her twined in her bedclothes like a corpse in a winding sheet, her gaunt face flattened and exhausted. The pent-up murk of her cigarettes enveloped me like bad weather when I opened the bathroom door. Long before she confided in me, I sensed Elsie was not happy on the tour.

And not for the obvious reason which she had mentioned casually the first night at the hotel in Rome when she and I found we had been assigned as roommates. "The bride and the divorcée," she had said sardonically, with a laugh I liked. "You're before and I'm after."

She had been divorced less than a year, and was a charismatic

Catholic. It wasn't clear which had come first, the divorce or the charismatic conversion, or if they had anything to do with each other. She came from "an itty-bitty town in Kentucky you never ever heard of," and worked as an attendant in a laundromat. She had decided to join the tour at the last minute, thanks to a collection her prayer group had taken up. That took care of the airplane ticket. She was charging everything else on her Visa account. "Pilgrimage by plastic," she said, snapping her card down on the counter of a souvenir shop where she had bought twelve St. Francis trivets for the members of the prayer group.

Everyone in the prayer group had recognized it would be best for her to get out of town that summer: the ex-husband was marrying the daughter of their former next-door neighbors, a young woman Elsie described as "an intsy thing with a waist no bigger than your arm and young enough to be his daughter." She paused and said, "Or my daughter, I guess." But she didn't have children. "That's a sadness," she said.

This new marriage was nothing more or less than she would have expected of him, but it hurt. Again she said, "It's a sadness." There was a steely integrity in her habit of using the noun, instead of an adjective, to describe her suffering. She gave the emotion a life apart from herself, recognizing the impersonality of pain, not questioning its right to exist: *It's a sadness.* But the effect was that her melancholy, thus formalized, invaded the atmosphere like her aura of cigarette smoke, leaving Elsie herself, sporting a game smile, the plucky harbinger of the grief that is ever in our midst, and not simply a loser with a sad-sack history. She had a cheerful, accepting temperament, a birdlike face that was winsome though it was gaunt.

We had spent the first week of the tour in Rome, then came up the Rieti valley past fields of huge-faced sunflowers, and had arrived in Assisi for the final week. A chartered bus hauled the thirty of us around, from catacombs to Vatican in Rome, then north to Gubbio, where Francis had gentled a wolf, and on to Greccio, where Francis had made the first Christmas manger scene.

125

At every stop, we were given long—and I thought superb—lectures by Paul, our guide. I scribbled furiously in my notebook in shadowy basilicas and next to altars harboring the bone fragments of martyrs, making Paul's meticulous notes my own: *Francis: b. 1181 (82?) d. 1226 (Oct 3) . . . vision at San Damiano 1205, strips naked and disowns father 1206 (April 10), Clare joins his band 1212 (Palm Sunday), composes "Canticle of Creatures" 1224, canonized 1230 (on Clare's 34th birthday) . . .*

Paul was an American friar whose regular job in the States was to run a retreat center in the South Bronx. The mission of the place was to give the poor somewhere to go for a little peace and quiet. During the summers, Paul was assigned to the study tour. He took the job seriously and had boned up on the history of the period, on the scholarship surrounding everything from Bernini's monumental sculptures to the details of Francis's biography. He crammed the day with information, which suited the places in Rome, jammed as they were with the fevered art of centuries. Then he packed us back into the bus, got us singing folk songs, calling us to order with the address Francis used: *Buona gente*, good people. Paul avoided being a scout leader because he wasn't jolly and wasn't interested in being beloved. His eye was on the job, and he kept the day going at a brisk allegro clip without trying to make friends with anyone.

The nuns (who made up the majority of the group) and the several friars and Brothers were all Franciscans from one order or another. Like Paul, they were used to the peculiar mixture of intimacy and distance inherent in community life. They were family, but they did not insist on being "close." Paul's cool, if affable, professionalism didn't offend them. There had been a little mumbling that you couldn't get to *know* Paul, but in general his neutrality seemed to work, leaving people free to make friends among themselves and to view him as a resource rather than a buddy.

But among the lay members of the tour—just four of us—this distinction seemed harder to bear. I had felt it myself. I had tried to engage Paul in conversation on the literary Francis and been adroitly rebuffed. "I think you'll find what you're looking for in Bodo," he said, handing me a volume by a friar who specializes in popularizing Francis. And Paul kept moving, working his way through the post-*cena* group still lingering by the Casa Papa Giovanni dining room.

"That's how they all are," the bitter voice of Justine said behind me as we watched him pass without missing a beat from the dining room to the dark corridor on his way to his room and his privacy. "That's why I stay away from priests. They always give you the brush-off." *✗✗✗ Personal Relations*

Maybe Paul needed a rest before the afternoon tour, I said. She shook her head. "I know them," she said darkly.

Justine had been a Poor Clare for five years just after college, and had left—or been asked to leave—for reasons she liked to keep tantalizingly unclear without ever letting this central wound of her history fade from view. "I was too sensitive," she said. "I'm sure they're very different now." But questioned about her life in the convent, she shrank from disclosure. "I can't talk about it," she said. Then, as if gazing at a light far off, she said dreamily, "I still think of myself as a contemplative. But you can't be sensitive in a community. I see that here." She was referring to the tour. "It's the convent all over again, the groups, the cliques, the priests playing favorites." *??? key*

Who were the favorites, what clique was she left out of? *Just felt left out*

No, she couldn't do that. She didn't want to name names. "It's because I'm sensitive," she said, radiating her obscure anguish. "I feel things." She seemed preoccupied by a collection of slights and injuries she had been tending since her departure from the convent sometime in the sixties, hurts and subtle humiliations which, she told me, she offered up but which nonetheless were a constant cross. She had the looks of a once-pretty girl, over fifty now, but retaining the good bones of someone much younger.

She lived in Philadelphia, her hometown, but made a point of mentioning every now and again that she had no family. "I'm alone in the world," she said, and smiled a brave, dotty smile.

"I'm one of the little ones." There was an eerie abstraction to her. She worked in an office, filing things. What things? "Papers," she said. "In alphabetical order."

"I go to my job," she said when I asked her about her life, "and I live alone." She delivered even this minimal bio note drenched in the mordant unction of her invisible travail.

"That woman gives me the creeps," Elsie said after Justine had sat with us at lunch one day. "She slithered right out of the catacombs, that one." Nor did Ray, the other lay person on the tour, inspire much confidence. There was some speculation that Ray had no business being on the tour, and had somehow falsified his medical records to be allowed to go.

It was true that he hadn't been able to manage the walk into the catacombs, or the hike up to the caves in Greccio, and in general had to be attended to wherever the bus let us off. He was a huge lard of a man, suffering from diabetes, his legs painfully puffed up, his Bible often open across his great middle as he sat snoring, taking up two seats on the bus. He lived in Dayton and belonged to the Third Order Franciscans, a group for lay persons; he wore an ornate cross, big as a bicycle wrench, roped from his neck.

He had joined the Third Order because, he said, the OFMs (the order of friars) had rejected him. "You want to know why?" he asked.

Sister Francine, ever encouraging of open class discussion, said, "Yes, Ray, why was that?"

Because, he said, his mother hadn't been married in the Church. That was why his vocation had been thwarted. On a technicality.

Francine regarded the heap that was Ray and apparently decided on charity. "It was a different Church in those days, wasn't it?" she said.

It hadn't been all bad, Ray said. Unlike Justine, he bore no grudges. He had taken care of his mother until she died. Who else was there to do that? Everybody else was married, busy, moved away. And he had joined the Third Order. "You don't hear much about the Third Order these days," he said. "But it's been very active."

Really? I asked. When was that?

"In the Middle Ages," he said, as of a time no more distant than his boyhood. His group was doing a lot in Dayton, he said. They had been putting together household items for poor people, no junk, just good things like vacuum cleaners that really worked, toaster ovens; they even had some microwaves. They worked out a deal where they left things at the parish garage and the people could go in and take what they needed, nobody watching them or making them feel bad about being poor.

"But we've had to change that," he said, "because a bunch of suburban housewives heard about it, and they started coming and getting the stuff in station wagons, and were running garage sales with it."

"That's pitiful," Sister Francine said.

"I guess they were making money for their kids' college educations," Ray said, trying to see both sides.

"That Ray is a moron," Elsie said. "I'm just praying he doesn't *explode* while we're on the tour. That'd throw Paul for a loop." She had a certain feeling for Paul's position and didn't seem to want anything personal from him. In fact, she wanted less from him than he was giving.

Paul was fluent in Italian, and over the years had become a familiar figure in Assisi, sometimes garbed in the classic Franciscan brown habit with the rope cincture with its three bold knots for poverty, chastity, obedience. At other times he led his band of gawking Americans around the town in shorts and a polo shirt. He looked then like an aging member of the Kingston Trio, amiable and handsome in a very American way. The shopkeepers along the narrow street up from the Piazza del Comune leaned against their doorframes as we trooped along toward the Casa Papa Giovanni (named for Pope John XXIII) the first day in Assisi, and called out to Paul as to a neighbor they hadn't seen for a while. "They like us," he told everyone on the bus before we were let off outside the gates of the town (no tour buses were allowed inside the city). "They like the American religious; you'll be popular."

This popularity stemmed mainly, it seemed, from the easy American smile. "You smile, nice smile," a woman explained to Sister Francine when she sold her a tile with Francis's standard greeting painted on it, *Pace e Bene*, Peace and Goodness. Italian nuns, the woman said, never smiled. "All the time sad faces, black clothes," she said. "American nuns, bright colors, big smiles. Joking all the time. Normal, all normal people."

This, in fact, was what sent Elsie Pickett for her brooding insomniac smokes. The nuns and the friars were all too normal. "Too secular for my blood," she said. "And you can quote me." We were sitting in our tiny room, both of us in nightgowns, and Elsie had been saying she knew she smoked too much. "I'm smoking more now than at home," she said, "and I can tell you why."

The tour was a big disappointment. "I'm nervous as a cat," she said. "And I've been filled with the joy of the Lord for months at home." She had expected the trip to be a spiritual bonanza. "I thought there'd be special gifts of the Spirit every single day," she said. "But they're all of them talking about that *gelato* ice cream and trying to decide whether it's red wine or white wine they want with their meals."

She frowned, but at herself, not at the nuns and friars, it seemed. "Now that's judging. I don't mean to be judging. They're nice people. But I got nice at home. I got a lot *more* at home. How is the Spirit coming on us with all this running around, jumping on and off that bus, Paul giving us lessons all day long about this artist and that painter, and I don't know what all. Did we sign up for a history lesson?"

Paul was confusing everything as far as she was concerned, when he read to us from a study suggesting Francis's mother, Pica, might well have been Jewish, noting the trade routes Pietro, the father, had traversed, and piecing together little-known intermarriage patterns of the era. Then he hauled in another piece of scholarship citing evidence that Francis was a devotee of Sufi dancing. "He's got him a Jew and a Muslim, and there's hardly any room for him to be a Catholic, which is the one thing he was, if I know my right from my left," Elsie said. "This ecumenical bit can go too far."

She had never spent much time around priests or nuns, she said. There was no parish in her town. She'd always felt sorry about that. Now she wasn't so sure it was a bad thing. A priest drove over on Sunday to say Mass for the assembled Catholics in a former gas station which had been abandoned when the freeway came through another town, leaving Elsie's town stranded on a has-been road. The gas station had become a sort of community center; it was used by the local AA meeting, Weight Watchers, the Catholics on Sunday morning, the Red Cross chapter, and Elsie's prayer group, which was her real parish, more than the priest coming over on Sundays for Mass. The group met twice a week for prayers and witnessing. The Spirit, she said, was always with them.

She said this in the same no-nonsense way she spoke of the faithless husband and of the various sadnesses that attended her: a fact stated, not an indulgence of sentiment. But her disappointment was serious: she wanted to fly home. She had stopped at a travel agency in Assisi to see what could be done about changing her ticket.

Not much, it turned out, unless she was willing to pay extra. "They want an arm and a leg," she said. And though the travel agent spoke perfectly normal English to her, who knew what the woman was cooking up on the telephone jabbering Italian lickety-split with whomever it was she called in an alleged attempt to get information for Elsie. This was not a sadness. "It's a worry," she said. "Maybe I'm just homesick," she added.

This struck her as strange, given the fact that her home had been taken away from her and she was firmly convinced her only habitation now was "in the Lord." That was the whole point of the trip, wasn't it? To walk in the footsteps of Francis, who had refused every sort of human comfort, who had stripped himself naked as the birds he preached to, and who slept in the dripping caves we had visited on the way up the Rieti valley. Francis who, Elsie saw, was supremely happy precisely because he was willing to suffer. "You don't get the gifts of the Spirit," she said, "making a fuss about that Orvieto wine they're all so crazy about."

Francis would have been a charismatic, she said, though nobody else on the tour seemed interested in being wrapped in the Spirit. Francis had often prayed with sighs and groans— Paul had even mentioned this. But was there any sighing or groaning in any of the liturgies we attended? Pretty thin gruel, she felt. "Not much for the Spirit to latch on to in one of Paul's Masses."

But a statement like that brought her over the edge of what she meant. "I'm being critical now," she said, frowning. "And I'm not critical." She just wouldn't have come if she'd known it was a *trip*. She had had in mind a sort of traveling retreat on the very ground where the Spirit had seen fit to consume an ordinary man with the fire of mystery, a guy anybody could identify with who had been marked by God indelibly.

It was the inarticulate sighs and groans—and especially the stigmata wound—not the poetry and *chansons*, and not the saint eloquent of contemporary psychological process, that drew her from the laundromat in Kentucky to the caves of Umbria, where Francis had shivered and roared. She wanted to do what he had done: make contact. The tour wasn't helping a bit. "I'm dry," she said. "Awful dry." The Spirit was clearly elsewhere, in the abandoned gas station at home.

"I don't need all this," she said, gesturing with her hand to indicate Assisi, the Rieti valley, and stretching even to include Rome invisible but glowing beyond us with its priceless horde of paintings and statues and churches.

"Lord above, did I *hate* that Rome." It was great for the art, she said, trying to give the place its due. But she hadn't come for the art, and say what he would with all that lecturing on the spirituality of icons, Paul wasn't going to talk her into anything. "He means well," she said, turning out the light. "But it isn't the Spirit. That's the sadness."

15

The town, Paul said, existed even in ancient times, when it was called Ascesi, which means *to ascend*. The word *ascetic* comes from the same root.

"Isn't that something?" Thaddeus said. "How all this stuff fits together?" Thaddeus, a friar from New York, was chaplain at a church in midtown which had lost its stable family membership and had turned itself into a food shelf and way station for the homeless. "We're on the frontlines," he said. "You come to New York, you better come to Thirty-fourth Street or you miss the whole point."

We were leaving the conference room in the Casa Papa Giovanni, which served as our classroom, where Paul gave his lectures standing under a big poster of Pope John Paul II embracing the Dalai Lama, a picture taken when both leaders had come to Assisi a few years before for an international environmental conference. The Pope looked like a severe, if benevolent, father in a costume made of stiff brocade; the Dalai Lama, in his diaphanous saffron, an exposed arm naked to the shoulder, appeared to have thrown himself in a real hug at the Holy Father, embracing him like a joyous child.

Thaddeus said he had to hand it to Paul, how he laid everything out in the mornings before taking us out for the day's tour of sights. "Not that I can follow it all," he said, shrugging his aging athlete shoulders. "Francis wasn't much with the books either, and he's my main man."

Thaddeus had the sag and heft of a career military man, his big, shambling body topped by a baseball cap. In the mornings, he passed by Sister Francine and her circle of older nuns who sat stirring their milky coffee companionably, like a group of widows on a charter tour, and he called out to them cheerfully, "Hi, troops."

Yet he didn't charm them. Sister Francine allowed herself a small frown when he showed up at the basilica of St. Francis for Paul's lecture on the Giottos wearing the baseball cap backward, polishing off a *gelato* cone. "Want a lick?" he asked chummily. He seemed unable or unwilling to read her pursed lips. "Anybody seen today's *Herald Tribune*?" he called around as we entered the church. "I'm trying to find out how the Mets did yesterday."

Absence from New York was a major aspect of being in Italy for him. And it did seem that Thaddeus wasn't simply *away* from the City (as he always called it) but had been forcibly parted from it, when his Superior gave him the trip as a gift in honor of his twenty-fifth jubilee as a priest in the order. When one of the younger nuns mentioned that she was from Sioux City, Iowa, he looked at her thoughtfully for a long moment before saying, "I mean, you know people live there—Iowa, Idaho, Michigan. But you don't ever expect to *meet* one."

His love of New York posed a problem. "The thing that bothers me," he said, "Francis is always talking about pilgrims and strangers. You're supposed to be, like, not *attached*. Okay, but they send you to some nowhere place—Buffalo or someplace. How are you going to spiritualize *that*? Like—go to Buffalo. I mean, drop dead." He coughed a mirthless little laugh at the thought.

"I'm a New Yorker," he said emphatically. And then, troubled: "Too much, maybe. That's my problem. I'm attached." Luckily,

in his whole religious life nobody had tried to send him to Buffalo
or anywhere outside Manhattan. "So far, so good," he said.

Maybe it was this worry over his home-boy attachment that
made Thaddeus such an admirer of Sister Bridget, the Irish
missionary who, at seventeen, had left her adored family in Cork
to enter the Franciscan Missionaries of Mary, and had spent the
last thirty-five years in Malaysia. "The FMMs," Thaddeus said.
"They're the Cadillac of the Franciscans." Bridget beamed.

Thaddeus took it upon himself to explain the tangle of orders
and "provinces" that sheltered under the great umbrella "Franciscan." It was as if he were deciphering for me the teams of
the NFL and AFL, sorting out the East and West divisions,
putting the whole thing in shape, setting the odds, working out
the playoff contenders.

It needed explaining. Over the centuries, beginning while
Francis was still alive, the proliferation of offshoots had been—
and continues to be—dizzying. The variety is immense: contemplative orders, active orders, teaching orders, nursing orders, missionary orders, the Friars Minor (which could be either
priests or Brothers, active or contemplative—or both), orders
of Brothers who, like Francis, declined to pursue ordination.

The men who were Brothers were not only the direct imita-
tors of the founder-saint, but in these feminist days, when the
priesthood, reeking and creaking with male privilege, takes its
inevitable hits, the Brothers bear a certain theoretical cachet:
they might have forgone the sacramental powers of priesthood,
but they are therefore automatically aligned with the
powerless—with women, for instance. And in the upside-down
world of spirituality, powerlessness is, in a topsy-turvy way,
ultimate force.

The Franciscans include huge multinational orders and tiny
houses of a few Brothers running a soup kitchen, banded together to say the Divine Office and wearing for their habit blue
jeans and T-shirts. Each order writes its own Rule, the tenets
by which it lives and guides itself. Virtually all such Rules come
from the Benedictine model, but there are different emphases

in each one. A recently formed order of Brothers, for instance, had written into its Rule that no Walkman tape recorders were allowed. "They think," Thaddeus explained, "that having music playing in your head when you're walking around on the streets cuts you off from the people, from experiencing life. They've got a point."

There were groups living monastically based rules (which originally had to do with a property-owning mentality—much against Francis's impulse), and those holding with the older "pilgrims and strangers" vision that encouraged loosely federated groups of hermits. Francis, allergic to all the ecclesiastical complications it involved, had not wanted to found an order, and he lived to see his radical notions about poverty, in particular, watered down. For instance, he did not want the Brothers ever to take money for anything they did; they were to accept only handouts of food and shelter like the beggars they were to align themselves with.

Add to these various types of orders the turns and quirks of nationality and history—the German orders, the Italian orders, the provinces in the United States (themselves often ethnically based—American orders started by German or Italian or Irish foundations), the foundations in Japan, the ones in Latin America where "liberation theology" found perhaps its most legitimate model, after Christ himself, in the example of Francis. It was a global family. "We're everywhere," Thaddeus said happily. "I've got brothers and sisters on every continent. Except Antarctica, I guess."

Donnie had said something similar one day when I expressed surprise that one of the nuns in her monastery was going to a monastery in Poland for six months and another was off to Korea. "Join the cloister," she said, "and see the world."

But the FMMs, a big order of 10,000 nuns with a motherhouse in Rome and a large population from Ireland, were Thaddeus's favorites. "We have it all," Bridget agreed. "Active and contemplative. I would never have joined an order that didn't have the contemplative writ large. I like that perpetual adoration." She

mentioned an FMM convent where, she said, the Blessed Sacrament, behind its eternal flame, had been attended in unbroken
prayer for over two hundred years. "That's wars, famines, rev-
olutions, night, day," she said.

Bridget, however, was "an active," head of the entire Catholic
education system of Malaysia. She had the job of teasing out
delicate contracts and compromises with the Islamic government
of the country. The missionary days were over, that she knew,
but she still believed there was a place for a "Christian presence"
in the country as it returned, sometimes fanatically, she feared,
to its Muslim identity. It was a headache of a job, but she seemed
to have a knack, she said, and nobody would let her step down.
This "knack" amounted simply to charm of the most conquering
sort. Like Francis, who charmed rather than preached people
into conversion, Bridget was someone people liked being
around. Even Francine, patting her own flat midriff unconsciously, admitted "that butterball Bridget" was "a person of
substance."

Bridget had gone to Ireland earlier in the summer on home
leave, which she did once every five years, and had decided to
join the study tour on her way back to Kuala Lumpur. She had
been to Assisi before, and had lived in Rome before her initial
embarkation for Malaysia. She was not one of the jittery nuns,
clutching spasmodically at her pocket to be sure her passport
hadn't been snatched or fuddling over her funny-money lire like
poor Sister Antoinette, who had become so confused trying to
figure out what she had spent in *real money* at a souvenir shop
that she begged Paul to handle her cash for her.

Nothing doing, Paul had said firmly, and sent her away grasping her fistful of bills like so much Monopoly money. Bridget
had the poise and simplicity, amounting to natural elegance, of
one at home anywhere. She wasn't *attached*, but she was at ease.

Nor did Bridget fit into the sporty manner of the younger
nuns in their forties, who had a brisk way about them. Most of
them had entered the convent shortly before or during Vatican
II, had watched their contemporaries depart to marriage or high-

profile careers. They had stayed on to see their way of life change anyway, even though they did not abandon ship. Most of them lived in apartments, worked in hospitals or schools, one at a publishing house. These younger (but no longer young) nuns had none of the eccentric appeal of addled Antoinette or Francine with her unbroken faith in the nineteenth-century novel; they gave off, instead, an almost hygienic aura of good cheer and earnestness.

I had trouble remembering their names or keeping them distinct in my mind. They lacked romance. And this romantic quality—of a life lived from desire, not essentially from effort —was what connected Francine, with her arch opinions and frilly lace collar, to cloddy Thaddeus in his baseball cap. The younger nuns whose names I could never keep straight were problem solvers, on-the-mark analysts about the role of women in the Church (appalling, they thought, and they had the statistics to make their case). But romance, the engine that kept the whole Franciscan machine steaming down the centuries— this was absent from their intelligent, decent faces.

aesthetic
Romance
mission
service

In Rome, when we went to the Vatican for an audience with the Pope (along with about five thousand others herded into a giant, space-age amphitheater constructed for the purpose), Thaddeus had shown up in his habit and cowl, most uncharacteristically. "Sure," he said when some of us exclaimed over the habit. "I wear the habit sometimes. That's my battle dress, my fatigues. That's my uniform." But the younger nuns, although warned that the Holy Father frowned on nuns out of habit, and especially American nuns in casual dress, had shown up in their Reeboks and culottes.

Instead of his usual open-neck shirt, Ray came to the audience wearing a tie that looked as if he'd kept it folded in a drawer since high school graduation. He pointed to the broad swath of creased maroon against which his giant crucifix lay. "I got dressed up," he said.

"I didn't feel like it," one of the nuns in culottes said.

"Don't you like this Pope?" Thaddeus asked.

"I've got some trouble with him," she replied.

"The woman thing," Thaddeus said, nodding sympathetically.

"The woman thing," she said, and then more vehemently, "And this trip to the States a while back. Two million dollars *per day* to guard him. You could feed a lot of poor people for that."

Thaddeus made an unreadable gesture, half shrug, half nod, suggesting that he saw her point and yet couldn't quite keep it in mind. Her reasonable way of looking at things was not a method he had developed—nor, I suspected, had Bridget, who kept her veil at the ready, rolled up in her purse most of the time. She had an on-and-off policy about her veil (off on the way over to the Vatican, on inside the amphitheater), and was showing Antoinette an Irish dance step as we waited to be let into the huge papal hall.

The sensible thinking of the younger nuns muddled Thaddeus and Bridget's whole conception of the religious romance, of why they were living as they did. It obscured why, as Thaddeus put it, they had tossed their lives off in one big free throw when they entered their orders. The habit of judgment was antithetical to the romance they were still thrilled to be living. Donnie was the same way. I had asked her once if she didn't find it difficult to explain her way of life. Didn't she worry that people today must think it was just weird?

"I don't want to explain it," she said, almost coldly. "I just want to live it." It was the rebel's voice, a *young* voice. The voice of a kid taking off on a motorcycle without a helmet, hair free in the wind.

"I wish you could have seen what we looked like," Donnie said, "when I first entered. The light came through the windows at Vespers and filtered down on us as we walked in two long rows—we were wearing the habit, and we were barefoot in those days. The light fell on the dark corridor as we left the chapel singing, and I thought I'd die from the beauty of it."

She was looking back, I realized, on the early days of her romance, as any woman does. She didn't want to *be* that girl again—she simply liked having been her. Yet she, like Bridget, was no ninny (something that could not be claimed for Antoinette, perhaps, but then, as Bridget said, with affection, "Antoinette doesn't live on the same planet, dearie. The Lord takes care of her kind"). Donnie and Bridget weren't defensive about the downside of their way of life, even while they were deeply committed to it. In this, they were like wives who speak of their intimate lives: It's not perfect, but I love him.

Donnie had a keen eye for the negative, too. "Places like this," she once said, meaning women's contemplative monasteries, "were often the worst kind of sweatshops. Spiritual sweatshops. The workday was endless, all unpaid, doing all sorts of menial jobs for a diocese, plus the maintenance of the place itself. And then getting up at all hours to pray and meditate. And everybody sequestered behind the enclosure in a strict cloister. There were a lot of 'actives'—men of course, priests— who wanted those nuns locked up to do their piety for them."

It wasn't her monastery or her life, but she knew it had existed—and still did. Once, when a council of bishops was meeting to draft a letter on the problem of women in the Church, I'd asked her what she thought of it.

"The bishops are wise, gifted problem solvers," she said. She let a beat go by, and added guilelessly, "Of course, that creates a difficulty for them: women aren't a problem."

But this history, whether personal or communal, romantic or pathetic, repressive or transcendent—she treasured it all. It was her life, her romance. Bridget was the greatest romantic of them all. She had about her roly-poly body, afflicted by the remnants of fevers she had picked up from her jungle years, the grace of someone who has lived her life always from the core of her imagination—which must be the heart of integrity. She—like Donnie at home—had a face that could leap from sun to deep shadow in a split second. It was the first thing I noticed about the nuns at Donnie's monastery, in fact: the clean slate of their faces, and how astonishingly vivid the expressions that played across them. They seemed to laugh a bigger, more resonant laugh at a joke, and to telegraph a deeper anguish at bad news.

It is wonderful to look at such a face. Actors must work for years to have that range, the capacity to radiate utter delight and then, on a dime, express the grief of the ages. Bridget had a dumpy little body, and round, deceptively simple features (the eyes were sophisticated and intelligent set in the plain potato of her humorous face). Thaddeus called her Bridget the Magnifico, and she said, "Oh, lad!"

She had the gift of delight, and was always ready to join me for coffee at the Minerva. "And let's just go ahead and have one of those little hazelnut tortes as well," she would say.

We returned late to the dark Casa Papa Giovanni one night (she always wanted to wait until she was sure she had heard all the late-night bell ringing the town had to offer). As we let ourselves into the shadowy front hall, she said, with the same relish she used to allow herself the indulgence of a cream cake, "Let's just nip into the chapel for a moment."

We paused inside for a few moments, Bridget sitting on the cold marble floor in a quasi-lotus position she had picked up in the East. She looked frankly at the tabernacle, as at a person she was giving her entire attention. *The life of the gaze,* Paul had called contemplation. Here it was. *I like that perpetual adoration,* she had said. I was next to her, bumbling through an "Our Father."

Then she was gazing at me, a slight inquiry in her eyes: Ready to go? She was done, and there I was, still *trying.*

Outside in the corridor, on our way to our rooms, she said, "I just like to say good night." She indicated, with a tilt of her head, that she meant the chapel where the small candle in front of the tabernacle would burn all night, as all day, in its red glass, like a stoplight at a deserted intersection.

141

16

The next morning Francine and Bridget and Thaddeus and I were sitting together at breakfast. I was telling them about my visit to the Keats-Shelley house earlier in the tour, when we'd been in Rome.

"I've got to get there," Thaddeus said. "That's the other religion, you know. Those poets." Francine gave him a sharp look, as if he had blundered onto her turf, but as long as he didn't trample the roses, she'd let him stand there gawking a moment. "Didn't Keats have TB?" he asked.

"Yes," Francine said. "He died in Rome, attended by a single loyal friend."

"Just like Mother Seton's husband," Thaddeus said. "Bill."

"It was quite different," Francine said, on guard at the temple of literature.

"I mean the TB," Thaddeus said. "That's what Mother Seton's husband died of. In Rome. Bill."

Francine was ready, I saw, to teach. But before it went any further, Felix, another of the friars on the tour, sat down with us. He had recently been given a new post in Hawaii and was on the study tour in between his old assignment in New Jersey

142

and this new one. "What a deal," he said. "Sun, sea, I've got it all out there."

"What's your job?" I asked.

"Rent-a-priest," he said nonchalantly. A prayer group, apparently with a well-heeled membership, had banded together to hire a chaplain. It wasn't parish work, but he was the priestly presence in their midst that they wanted. "And can afford," he said. "I say the Office looking right out at the waves," he said, as if this were what Hawaii was made for.

Felix did not suffer nunnish foolishness gladly. "See that smile," he said one day when, it was true, Sister Antoinette was beaming around brainlessly for no apparent reason during Paul's lecture. "That idiotic smile was put there by her novice mistress probably forty years ago," he said, "and it hasn't been wiped off since."

Antoinette's perky inquiries about the ways of the world set his teeth on edge. At the Vatican she had almost gotten herself arrested at the security check for saying, "Do they think I have a *gun*? Would I carry a *weapon* and do something horrible to our Holy Father?" She had gone up to Felix (a priest and therefore an authority) and said, "Father, what *was* it they were checking for in my purse?"

He took her in for a moment. Then, in a voice flattened beyond annoyance, he said, "Contraceptives."

Antoinette's birdy face registered vague alarm, but strangely enough, it didn't occur to her to be miffed. She wandered off in her dithery way, wondering how she had given cause to be suspected of carrying a controlled substance on her person. Her innocence was implacable, and in the end, it seemed it was Felix who was afraid of her idiocy, rather than she of his irony. "That woman," he said almost with awe, "positively begs you to be just slightly mean to her."

Nor did Felix encourage the sticky sensitivities of Justine, the ex–Poor Clare, who had tried to engage him one day in Rome by asking if he could explain to her the difference between the orders of the Albertines and the Brigittines. "Beats me," he said, and turned away, leaving Justine wincing, in solid possession of another priestly rebuff.

On the other hand, Felix approved of Bridget. "That's a sophisticated woman," he said. "Not like—" and he gestured toward his nemesis Antoinette, who had come back from an early-morning souvenir-buying trip, her hands full of silver. "I bought two hundred miraculous medals," she said helplessly, to anyone. "Why did I let him sell me two hundred miraculous medals? What am I going to do with them?"

Thaddeus took one from her and inspected it. "They're all made in Brooklyn," he said.

"He gave me the *Pietà* for free," she said, pulling a statuette out of her purse. "He threw in the *Pietà*."

Felix was out the door. Bridget and I would not see him until evening. We had become regular companions at the Minerva, where he and I were in the habit of presenting our observations of the day to Bridget, who howled and said, "Oh, you're wicked, wicked," egging us on for more.

"I suppose," Felix said casually one night as we sat before the former pagan temple where he tilted back in his chair, radiating possession of a delectable morsel he was ready to share, "you've heard the story, Bridget—*secundum traditionem*, of course— about the Holy Family's vacation plans."

"Oh, lad!" Bridget said, almost purring.

"It seems the Holy Family felt it was time to be more egalitarian in decision-making—post-Vatican II, of course. So St. Joseph says, 'Let's each say where we'd like to go for this year's vacation. I'll start: I'd like to visit the relatives in Bethlehem. Jesus?' So Jesus says he'd like to see Egypt again, they were in such a rush the first time. Finally, Joseph turns to Mary and says, 'How about you, Mary?'"

Felix paused, took a sip of his espresso, making Bridget wait. She bit: "Well, where does Mary want to go?"

"So Mary says, 'I want to go to Medjugorje. I've never been there before.'" Bridget howls, and Felix is the cat now, grinning, lapping up the cream of her laughter.

Then, as a kind of spiritual nightcap, Bridget suggested we nip into the chapel for a moment when we got back to the Casa. Which made perfect sense to Felix. I watched them as they sat on the gleaming dark floor, purely attentive, looking up at the tabernacle where the candle behind the red glass cast its trembling light. *watch them*

At first, in Rome, I had thought Felix was a cynic, or had passed beyond whatever bitterness creates cynicism, into a sardonic privacy. Maybe he was one of those Graham Greene priests, I thought, his faith cracked but his life still grinding along the same stony track.

Before long, I found myself looking to see if the seat next to Felix was free on the bus, if there was room at his table at lunch. When I noticed I was doing this, I thought I was seeking out his irony. I trusted his irreverence, I decided. But really, I was intrigued by its flip side. For it also became clear—though how this was revealed remained a mystery—that Felix was one of those who pray without ceasing.

He was so unobtrusive that only our enforced proximity on the tour made his devotion evident, his habit of going off by himself at the caves of La Verna, where Francis had received the Stigmata, his way of using odd moments on the bus to say a Rosary. Even this fact—the rosary in his pocket—cut to my heart strangely: such an old-fashioned, womanish devotion from this Bogart kind of guy.

Felix at such moments was a reprise of the theme stated years ago at St. Luke's when the single lady in her cardigan smiled at me on the way to school, her hand going over the beads as she walked alone down Oxford Street. *She loves me,* I had thought, and was flooded with the sensation not of intimate love but of an embrace even more astonishing—a stranger's which stands for the world's heart beaming at you. It was the love Francis ran naked into the medieval woods for: the love of pilgrims and strangers.

The deepest reassurance, the one sought in religion, is to be loved not personally but because one *is*. The single lady's smile all those years ago had been that smile. It was Donnie's smile, it was Bridget's, and now also Felix's.

He was like one of those pictures in psychology textbooks that appear to be a vase if you look at them one way and two people in profile at another glance. I kept going back, to see which image would materialize: the monk or the imp. He could go either way. In this, he was like Francis. "Don't canonize me too soon," the saint said, "I'm still perfectly capable of making a child."

Felix appeared to be ensnared by the love of God, though he never talked that way, and cringed from Antoinette's scapulars and devotional medals. He was captivated by prayer as Francis had been, simply because it was the best deal around. Period. If there were anything better in this life—hey, he would go for it. "You develop a prayer life over time," he said one day on the bus, "and after a while you can't live without it. You want more and more. Impossible to explain, but if you've ever really been in love, you've had the feeling. Except it's crazier."

As for Francis as founder of the order, well, Felix said, Francis had been a dimwit. "Clare was the brains behind the outfit," he said. "Francis—he was only capable of being a bum." He paused, then said, "Of course, luckily, that was his vocation." Bridget nodded. They left no room to be scandalized. In fact, Felix's irreverence was not cynicism, and it was the opposite of faith broken. It was a while before I realized he reminded me of Donnie.

He was Irish, too, and like Donnie, like Bridget, he glinted with an irreverence which, in any orthodox practice, is not simply irresistibly charming (though it does charm). Such irreverence represents a kind of spiritual stamina, a method of staying-the-course without giving over to the shopworn scruples of religiosity. There was no dogma to Felix, no rigidity, just the constant feints and lunges of a man observing the day tirelessly, and living it absolutely as prayer.

Existence was prayer. The *day* was prayer, and he was in the day, therefore in prayer. That was the feeling he and Donnie and Bridget—and even Thaddeus—all gave off. Prayer was not effort, not just something they *did*. It was something they were *in*, as obviously as they were in the world.

The Church, the order—these constituted the tradition they had inherited, a huge heap of an ancestral home in which they lived rent-free. They stayed in this house because they were born in it, a wreck of a place full of priceless pieces and a lot of junk—but theirs as indelibly as their blood types. The house might be falling down around their ears and have a questionable history, a structure impossible to repair, but it was home, the setting for all they did and all that mattered.

Finally, however, the Church was just a place, not life itself. Life was prayer. And that was to be found in every second of every minute of all the days of their lives. In a sense, they lived in the old beat-up house precisely because it had become automatic, unnoticeable. *The life of the gaze*—that's what they were after, a way of life that trained attention beyond the physical, beyond will and desire. Such a life made possible the concentration that was the real point of their vow of poverty.

They *liked* poverty, not as a condition, but as a dynamic process. It was an art form. "You have to be careful about airplanes," I heard Bridget saying one day to Felix. She had her wise Irish face on, figuring the odds. I listened in, thinking she was going to talk about her fear of flying, a subject near to my heart. But she was explaining "how insidious those wonderful planes can be."

Her point: Flying takes you away from the poor, from the way the poor experience travel. "You think," she said, warming to her subject, happy in her discovery like a technician who has figured out a cunning twist in the software, "you *think* you're saving time, and they need you here, they need you there, and somebody will always get you the ticket. But take the jammed bus, sit on your luggage in the aisle, get the chickens thrust on your lap, hold the baby for the mother who has to change the other one—and get to your meeting late. Get to your meeting

147

and fall asleep in the executive session. You've brought the poor to the meeting."

Felix nodded and frowned, taking it in. They spoke each other's language, and he was absorbing another deft maneuver of a fellow pro who was willing to pass along one of her cool moves.

Felix radiated the confident relish—not simply the steely judgment—of one willing to keep taking note of this endless prayer with its ups and downs, its idiocies and poignancy. The point was never to be caught in the predictable, the ritualistic, to be ever fresh in this ancient business of the spirit. "Beep, beep, beep," he hissed out *sotto voce* whenever a dour group of black habits approached us on the street, "Italian nun alert, Italian nun alert."

"They don't smile," Thaddeus said, exasperated. "Notice that? They never, never smile. What the hell kind of religion is that?" He went on to tell a story about Soeur Dominique, the Belgian nun whose folk singing had made her a sensation briefly in the sixties. "They hounded her," he said bitterly, "her superiors and everybody, when her album made all that money. She left the order, hounded out. They couldn't stand her singing and happy, playing the guitar on TV and smiling. She committed suicide eventually." Another broken romantic for Thaddeus's ledger of poetic losses.

"Poor things," barefoot Bridget in her sandals said, meaning the walking draperies we'd passed or perhaps Soeur Dominique as well. "And that middle one so young."

Yet she and Felix had entered their orders as practically children themselves. "I went through all the growing up already in the convent," Bridget said. "Once I went running to my Superior. I'd fallen in love with a Jesuit, and what was I to do?"

Her Superior took one look at her and said, "Oh now, Bridget, you don't need to go through that song and dance. We all fall in love four or five times in a life."

They all had vocation stories. Felix had started out wanting to go to Annapolis. He was so crazed with the idea that he decided to attend daily Mass in his senior year of high school to pray that he would be admitted to the Naval Academy. The parish priest noticed this unusual behavior and approached him one morning. "You're thinking about your future, aren't you?" the old man asked.

"Not the future you have in mind, you damn fool," Felix had thought—for he was wary of vocation-snaring nuns and priests.

He walked home as usual that morning, and then, just as he reached the railroad tracks, he stopped as if whacked on the head. *This is it*, something inside-yet-outside of him said. He never turned back. From that instant by the tracks, it was decided for him. He never applied to Annapolis.

It was a variation on Donnie's vocation story: She, too, had had no notions of becoming a nun, and certainly not a cloistered contemplative. She was popular, something of a card, always surrounded by friends, and had a nice boyfriend. She went to an open house at the new Poor Clare monastery in the blank Minneapolis suburb in the early fifties, only as part of a courtesy visit organized by her high school. On the way home with her girl friends, someone had said, "I think that would be a beautiful life." Donnie thought the girl was crazy. "You'll never get me back in that place," she remembered saying. Less than a year later she was there, drawn by something she's always felt accurate in calling her vocation.

"I belonged to the generation that knew what it wanted by seventeen," Felix said. "We made life decisions and just kept to them. I've got a nephew thirty-one who doesn't have a clue. Like everybody else these days."

He found himself pursuing the Franciscans, though he had never met one. "It was ridiculous," he said, looking back at this early period. "Silly. Bizarre. But I just couldn't help myself."

He entered the Friars Minor after high school. Five or six months in, he asked his novice master, "When can I say Mass?" That was everything. "No matter how nuts it ever gets," he said, "I could never give that up. Saying the Mass."

"And, Thaddeus," I asked, "how did you become a friar?"

"In my case," he said without hesitation, "it was divine discontent."

"That's a fine phrase, lad," Bridget said.

"Yeah," he said, as if the vocabulary of the mystics were his native tongue. "It was really bugging me. I fought it for three years."

His father warned him he would miss having a woman.

"I told him, 'Pop, God knows what I'd be like with a wife.' " He was convinced by the time the divine discontent set in that all that was not meant for him anyway, was expressly denied him, thanks to the rejection of Molly Malone and her snob of a mother.

"You're kidding," Felix said. "Molly Malone? That was her name?"

"Was she beautiful!" Thaddeus said. "I was collapsing. But my father was a fireman, American-born, and my pal Nicky, his father had been British Army and had a job as a cop. Molly's mother, that's what she wanted for Molly. She shook hands with me, but the curtain went down. Nicky was the one. That was Brooklyn in those days."

So he had entered the Friars Minor. "I can really identify with that St. Agnes of Prague, though," he said, referring to Paul's lecture on a Bohemian princess who had become one of the first of Clare's "Poor Ladies" after her engagement was broken by the Emperor. "How she was jilted. Tough. Like Molly Malone. Boy, did she slay me. She wouldn't even spit on the best part of me." He settled back in his chair, looking glum and hurt in his shaggy-mutt way.

Bridget came from a family full of priests and nuns. One of her brothers was a friar, another had been sent home from the novitiate. "He was delicate," she said. "They had to get up at two in the morning in those days. It was worse than the army, the training."

After the profession of her vows, Bridget had stayed two months in the motherhouse in Rome, peeling potatoes, sweeping floors, waiting for her assignment. "When they said Malaya, I had to run to a map to see where it was. I'd never heard of it," she said.

Her best friend, another young nun, was assigned to Africa.

It was her last link with Cork. "It was, 'We'll meet again in heaven,' in those days. It was goodbye forever. Who would do that today?" she said, shaking her head.

They all had stories from "before." Before Vatican II. The days of the grilles and black curtains in the cloister, the impossible clothes for the women. And the wound that seemed deepest: the cruel division of families. "We all know stories," Bridget said. "One Sister, for instance. Her father was dying. But you weren't allowed to go home in those days. She finagled to walk by the house with another Sister, two by two everybody went then. And somebody props the old man up in the window for a moment so they can wave to each other before he dies. He's dying and they hold up his hand to wave it at her. Things like that. As if that were normal."

One night at dinner at the Casa Papa Giovanni, named for the Pope who convened the council that changed Catholic life forever, Thaddeus had stood up and proposed a toast. "To good John," he said. The glasses were all raised, and a needle of solidarity passed through the room. It was a spontaneous gesture, but the moment was solemn.

"None of us would be here if it wasn't for him," Francine said quietly in the silence that followed. Nobody argued with her. It wasn't clear if she meant none of them would have stayed in religious life or if none of them would be in Assisi, free to travel and pursue their history and heritage as they now were. Perhaps she intended both.

Thaddeus said, "Back then, you'd go out, like, to a lake for a picnic, maybe some softball, a bunch of the guys from a couple of parishes and the teaching nuns brought out by some lay people in the parish. Everybody is calling everybody by name—Philomena, Theophane, Immaculata. One gal, no kidding, named Victima. And I'm thinking, People must think we're crazy, there isn't a normal name in the bunch. These weird names we've all got."

The word—*weird*—touched off a series of stories of the odd ducks they had all encountered in religious life. "There was one old guy," Felix said, "a friar who was retired, living at the no-vitiate when I was still studying. He was gay, but nobody talked that way then. He didn't do anything about it, at least not any-more. But he had this crazy cloak he wore. Half Liberace, half Elton John. He'd wear this thing around the campus, and he told benefactors who came for Mass it was made out of a gown that belonged to St. Elizabeth of Hungary. The money poured in."

"Those days," Bridget said. "In the novitiate, they made us take baths with our chemises on, mopping away at yourself with a sponge, the linen sticking to your body like a big leaf. When it was all wet you could see through anyway."

But now for years in Malaysia she went bare-legged in her short brown-and-white dress, which served as a habit. "I only wear stockings once every five years," she said. "When I come to Europe." She pronounced the word *Europe* as if it were not her native home but some alien place. One hot afternoon, we had walked together toward the Rocca Maggiore, the highest point in Assisi, and the castle ruin of the former barons of the town. We passed a group of tourists coming down. They had Asian faces, and Bridget stopped in her tracks as they passed by and looked at them with a kind of longing.

"Ah, that makes me homesick," she said in her irrepressible brogue. "My people." And no doubt she did belong to them after her thirty-five years in their midst.

Felix, too, had spent a long time away from home, in Latin America. His Portuguese was as good as his English. He used it with the Italians. "It seems to work most of the time," he said. He'd been pastor for eight years in a remote Brazilian jungle village, where the bats sometimes got into the chapel after gorg-ing themselves on a fruit that grew so ripe on the trees it became fermented. The drunken bats bashed against the walls, squeak-ing and diving, as he celebrated Mass. "It was wild," he said, as if it had been fine with him.

It didn't seem odd to him, or to Bridget, that he had spent those years in a jungle, speaking Portuguese, circled by drunken bats, sharing the lives of peasants, and that now he would be saying the Divine Office from the oceanfront condo the Honolulu prayer group had provided for him.

It was all of a piece. It was one room or another in the great ramshackle house they had always lived in and always would, no matter if it sagged and creaked, and looked as if it might collapse around their heads.

17

History, According to Felix

In March 1179, two years before Francesco Bernardone was born in Assisi, Pope Alexander III called the bishops of the Church together. This ecumenical council, called the Third Lateran after its location at the Church of the Lateran in Rome, set the Church's course regarding heresy.

The council branded as heretics the Cathars, a penitential sect active mostly in southern France. But more to the point, it legitimized the use of force against them. Under the council's edict, armed struggle was encouraged against the Cathars, along with confiscation of their property and enslavement of their persons by the princes riding against them in the name of Rome. Furthermore, those knights embarked upon this crusade within Christendom were assured an indulgence of two years off their temporal penance (aka, time in purgatory) and were put under the protection of the papal crown, like Crusaders embarked to the Holy Land. It was a good deal all round for an enterprising knight: crusade work closer to home, and with the same perks.

But it was another edict, considered lesser, of the Third Lateran Council that struck at the heart not of Christendom but of Christianity, and made the conversion of Francis, the rich merchant's playboy son, a necessary redemption for the whole Roman Church. For the Council of 1179 also passed an edict concerning the place of lepers in the Church. Quite simply, the council ruled that lepers should be kept apart from others.

This act, undertaken in desperate response to a hideous, disfiguring disease for which there was no cure, set the Christian world in direct opposition to its central metaphor: the harmonious relation of all Christians as members of the Mystical Body of Christ. And it left these afflicted creatures, already marginalized by society, homeless, wandering about the wildwood in all weathers, their grim clappers sounding the warning of their presence, to feed on whatever parasite-infested vermin they could find. When the Lateran Council cast the lepers of Christendom outside the bounds of Christian life, it effectively took away the only job they could successfully perform within the population: to beg in the midst of the community.

And in the Middle Ages begging was a job, or at least an occupation with social meaning. For in a society where charity is not merely kindness or tenderhearted guilt but an acknowledgment of the giver's even greater need—for salvation—the beggar performs an essential function. He provides a way for the rich man to get to heaven. Beyond that, the beggar is a *memento mori*, and his ravaged face is the Face of God.

It was integral to the fundamental inspiration of Christianity that Jesus was poor, that he was born in a stable, homeless. He was not a prince like the Buddha. He was nothing and nobody, and therefore he could be a metaphor from minute one. He was the Word made flesh, He multiplied the loaves and fishes; He said the flowers and the birds, who neither worked nor fretted, were better off than anyone, and not to worry. He is the poor man's God. But poverty is the big thing Christendom has traditionally held against Christianity. That, no doubt, is why in its fright and in the pseudo-legitimacy that terror gives to institutional bodies, the princes of the Church, gathered in Rome in 1179, amputated their ill brothers and sisters from the Body of Life.

It was an act which also cut away the veil of illusion from the medieval world's best idea of itself: the chivalric ideal of a social order in which everyone was linked to those above and below, wrapped in a web of loyalties, duties, fealties, and secular connections that were made sacred in the transcendent net of relations which was the Mystical Body. This harmony of existence extended to the whole of the created world in the conception known as the Great Chain of Being.

In our own day, the Great Chain is seen as the idea that allowed the West to "tame" nature, to view nature as its pet (or slave) rather than its brother. It is true that the Great Chain was a hierarchical system which saw the whole of creation as related in a rank ordering system that linked clods of earth and stones to reptiles and fishes, and on up to dogs and oxen, passing through the human link to the angelic and, finally, to the Godhead. Humans *are* "above" the rest of the physical world in this system.

But what we tend to miss is that the rest of the Chain—angels and Divinity—were just as real, making decisive claims of their own. In a sense that the modern mind has difficulty seeing (or believing) the medieval Chain was not a straight line. The links made an elastic structure: the Chain was a necklace encircling the whole of Existence—from the Creator all the way through every filament of the created world.

But if those at the bottom of the human heap could in fact be cut off, if certain "members" of the "Body" were dispensable after all—if the Church said so, then the great imaginative act which was the Death and Resurrection ceased to have the metaphoric force to drive an entire society. If the lepers could be detached from the Great Chain, the fluid shape of the perfectly attached links was ruined—never mind that groups like the Jews and the Muslims weren't part of it to begin with. In place of the encircling Chain, the prevailing image at the core of civilization became instead the clanking, unwieldy battle armor of the age.

And *that*, Felix said, was what Francis was all about. He was about saving Christianity from Christendom. About taking the values of chivalry—which included hatred of the rising mercantile element—and putting them to inventive use. It also explained why Francis was so keen on being submissive to "the Lord Pope." And why in his deathbed "Testament," Francis took pains to honor all priests, even "if they were to persecute me," and recommended solemnly that "we should honor and respect all theologians and those who minister the most holy divine words as those who minister spirit and life to us."

He wasn't cringing before the authorities, Felix said. He was shrewdly shifting the focus. Let the princes of the Church fight their theological battles. Let them even define the politics of the situation. He would leap over the whole contentious, murderous business and put his trust in the Word. "The guy was a poet," Felix said. "And uneducated—which is not a bad thing for a poet."

He also proved something, Felix said. "He proved the Gospel works. In a way, nobody since Jesus had done that." And, Felix felt, he did it in a world that even to us still has the glimmers of modernity. The world of Jesus is exotic—in geography, in time. "But Francis was a capitalist's son, and he was a rebel of capitalism of the sort generation after generation of the modern world has given us. He's our kind of person."

Paul listened to all this and said, "Still, ninety years later, and Francis would have been burned as a heretic. He slipped under the wire, before they really clamped down."

Felix didn't argue with him. "I'd like to teach history someday," Felix said.

"Where?" Paul asked. "The Antonionum?" naming the Franciscan university in Rome.

They both laughed.

It was the final day of the study tour. We were walking to Santa Maria degli Angeli to visit the Porziuncula, the Little Portion. Paul had arranged for our last day together to be spent where Francis spent his last day. The bus ferried anyone who didn't want to walk the distance from Assisi to the valley below. But some of us made the hike through the fields of poppies, down the steep slant of the city's hill to the great dome of the church, which was built around the Porziuncula like a voluminous meringue enclosing a nut.

Felix and Paul had been talking Church politics. "He made a big mistake there," Felix said, meaning John Paul II, "when he didn't immediately canonize Romero after he was shot saying Mass in Salvador. Lost a big chance there."

Paul agreed. "There was a big push for it, I think," he said. "But it came—you know—from the wrong quarters."

"The Latin American liberation theologians?" Felix asked.

"The wrong quarters," Paul repeated, apparently not wanting to name names, if he knew them.

Felix was off on his own thought anyway. "They latch on to all the wrong martyrs," he said. "During the Spanish Civil War a whole bunch of monks got machine-gunned. Martyrs of the Faith, Rome calls them. They were a bunch of young monks, just trying to hide, but the fact is, they had some idiot bishop who wouldn't let these guys give up the tonsure. They were marked. They were sitting ducks. Martyred for a holy haircut."

We had reached the Porziuncula. It was a tiny hut of a church given to Francis and his band by the Benedictines of Monte Subasio. In his day, it was enclosed in the dense forest of the valley. It was the place where he had sought refuge early in his conversion, the very place where Clare had joined him on her runaway Palm Sunday night, where he had given her the tonsure. Later he and several of his early followers made their tiny hermit huts, surrounding the little chapel, and began the first days of the new knighthood Francis was determined to live.

In its smallness, its humility and emphasis on contemplation, even its proximity to a hospice for lepers, the Porziuncula was the youngest and most romantic of Franciscan places. San Damiano, nearer Assisi, was where the icon spoke, but it became the cloister of Clare and her Sisters during her long life as a nun. It is a lyric, sunny place, still enclosed by a charming garden and fountain. The Porziuncula, once a dark hut in the wildwood, is dark still, shuttered now inside the colossal dome of the basilica built around it.

"This is great," Felix said, practically smacking his lips over the irony. "There's Christianity," he said, pointing to the hut lost in the middle of the giant marble floor. "And here's Christendom," gesturing to the great billowing cathedral with its side altars, its mammoth main altar, and the grand nave flanked with immense statues.

Thaddeus went over to a tiny structure enclosed behind glass and a metal grate, off to the side of the Porziuncula. The sign said in several languages that here, exactly here, Brother Francis had died, October 3, 1226. All the bells of Assisi began to ring spontaneously. "*Secundum traditionem,*" Thaddeus said. According to tradition. Then softly: "Okay, I'm gonna take a picture of your bedroom." He snapped his Instamatic. A little beetle of a Capuchin came scurrying out of nowhere, scolding furiously, pointing at the camera. Thaddeus backed away, saying from his height to the angry little monk, "Okay, okay, okay, Padre. Hey, *non comprende*, or whatever." I followed Thaddeus to the Porziuncula, just around a mammoth pillar.

To this crude chapel, which was then free in the woods, in the humid summer of 1226, afflicted by the tuberculosis he had contracted as a young Assisi fighting man imprisoned by the victorious forces of Perugia, and suffering even more painfully from the inflammation of his eyes which had rendered him blind yet horribly sensitive to any light, Francis was carried to spend his last days in the place where his dream of love had blossomed.

In this very chapel, years before, he had encountered a weeping monk. "Why are you crying?" the young Francis, seeking his future, had asked.

"Because," the old man said, "love is not loved."

•

Francine's Field Trip

Earlier in the day Francine had convinced Elsie and me to go with her to the Basilica of Santa Chiara, where the body of Clare is enshrined. Even in their sainthood, Francis and Clare are kept separate: his basilica, with his life painted on the walls by Giotto in giant panels, is at one end of the town; Clare's grand church is almost directly at the opposite side of the city. They face each other, but are not visible across the distance.

"I think we should view the body," Francine had said that morning in her take-charge-of-the-class voice. "It's not the sort of thing we're used to, but the Italians look at these things quite differently from us."

"When in Rome," Elsie said gamely, "do as the Romans." Then a moment later: "It can't be any worse than that bone up on the altar in that glass case we saw in Rome."

We had entered the dark basilica, stopping first to inspect the relics on display behind a grille, attended by the spooky presence of a very young nun, her face covered by her veil, even the long drapery of her dark habit rolled down to cover her hands. Elsie leaned close to me and whispered, as Felix had trained us to do, "Beep, beep, beep, Italian nun alert." The young Sister pointed with her spectral sleeve at the habit of Holy Mother Clare—an ancient shapeless gunnysack, but long, suggesting her regal height—and at various other tatters and trinkets.

Then, somehow truly startling, she indicated the hair of the Blessed Foundress. There, tumbling and twining from the enclosure of a gold and glass casket out of a fairy tale, the opulent, shockingly flossy curls of the saint gleamed. It was the platinum hair of Jayne Mansfield, of Madonna, of Marilyn Monroe.

"I can't believe that hair," I said, marveling—and believing.

"Honey," Elsie said as we followed Francine toward the crypt in the lower church, "what that is is another of those *secundum traditionems*. They're nothing but beggars, and here we are paying them and gawking like any freak show. They may be Poor Clares, but I don't call that the contemplative life."

Downstairs, in the crypt, was the real thing. The saint, her head covered by her veil, but the features of the face even more distinct for that, was lying flat, surrounded by candles and flowers behind a glass window. This had been a beautiful woman, lovely and strong. The face was dark brown, the color of old wood, almost black, the grain risen to the surface in minute ridges. The corpse fingers, laid on her stomach in the classic pose, were long and elegant, also black. But beautiful or not, she was mainly dead, dead, dead.

Francine, back in the sunlight, walking toward the Minerva, was all for seeing the thing in context. "It's a cultural value we don't share," she instructed. "But it's the faith of the humble, the poor. We mustn't be repelled."

Elsie wasn't caving in easily to this multicultural view of things. "She looked," Elsie said, "like she was made out of a great big piece of beef jerky."

Francine stopped smack in the middle of the sidewalk, next to a dress shop filled with jewel-colored sand-washed silk blouses and glove-leather skirts no bigger than a large purse. "Elsie," she said sharply, as to one of her charges who had not made profitable use of time out of the classroom, "Clare was a great and beautiful woman. And there she is, for all who have eyes to see."

•

I overslept the next morning, and woke to Bridget calling my name urgently outside the door. Everyone was supposed to be downstairs for breakfast an hour early in order to be ready for the taxis which were to carry us to the charter bus or—several of us—to the train station for other destinations.

Elsie had given over completely to her insomnia and hadn't returned to her bed that night; she had taken her suitcase downstairs to smoke in peace, and wait for someone to show up in the Casa kitchen to make coffee. She hadn't noticed I wasn't up. But Bridget had noticed. She had a farewell gift, a packet of rose petals from the bushes near the Porziuncula where Francis—*secundum traditionem*—rolled in the roses to mortify his flesh, only to discover the roses refused to cause the saint any pain—the thorns had miraculously disappeared.

But now I was seriously late, everyone had finished breakfast, and some of the older Sisters had already left in the taxis. Bridget slapped the packet of rose petals in my purse and began throwing the last of my things in my suitcase. "And your dear notebook," she said, grabbing it from the nightstand. "Don't forget that." I was dressed in three minutes flat, down the stairs, Bridget's sandals tapping behind me after she checked the room to be sure I'd left nothing behind.

The taxi to the train station was already at the door. Three of the younger nuns I hadn't gotten to know were sitting in the back, looking worried. Felix and Thaddeus, Francine, Elsie smoking, Bridget and Paul stood by the Casa door.

"It's best this way," Bridget said, hugging me and laughing, as if it were just so-long-for-a-while. "When you're a missionary, you know all about saying goodbye. It's better faster."

"Not forever, though," I said, alarmed. I felt a strange panic to think I might never see her, never see Felix or any of them again. I'd become *attached*. Where was Malaysia anyway? All I could remember from Sister Julia's third-grade social-studies class was that Bunga of the Jungle lived in Malaysia. "Bunga eats yams," the line under the picture had said. Also: "The people of Malaysia enjoy feasts, and love their children." Bridget was with Bunga already, laughing and pushing me toward the taxi.

"I can't see ever getting to Minnesota," Elsie said shyly, as if it were more remote than Umbria or Malaysia, and at least as problematic. She squeezed my hand and gave me a crocheted coaster that had embroidered on it, *Jesus Loves Me This I Know*. "Our prayer group makes them," she said, a woman who put her trust in the souvenirs she'd brought from home.

Hugs from Paul and Felix. Then Thaddeus who, no surprise, wasn't a hugger. "Put 'er there, Trish," he said, extending his big paw. I grabbed it. "You know where to find me," he said. "Thirty-fourth Street."

Francine asked if I knew where my passport was, and like Bridget, she asked after my notebook. "That's your gold," she said. "The writer's notebook. Henry James . . ."

But Paul was angling me to the front seat. The door was clicked shut, and they became a framed family portrait, standing in the dawn light of Assisi, the streets still innocent of the day's tourism. They were all waving, fixed behind the small glass of the rear window, getting smaller, then very small, gone now, my dear friends.

18

There was an hour's wait at the train station, not far from Santa Maria degli Angeli. I stood on the train platform, drinking coffee from a Styrofoam cup, shivering in the morning damp, looking up at the basilica where the Porziuncula was lodged like a seed inside its monster blossom. At seven, the bells started up, cleaning the mind. That fresh, heart-hitting sound. The prayer gong.

Why does one go to these places, these ancient venues of devotion—or, in the case of Lourdes, my next stop, a manufactured place hardly more than a century old? For in the slow timekeeping of faith, what is a century? Not evidence of conviction, certainly; maybe just the remnants of a craze.

I think it is true that we travel for history, to touch its body. In that sense, to gawk at Santa Chiara's well-smoked face is no more ghoulish than to peer up at a Ghibelline battlement, or to pass through the frigid corridors of the Louvre gazing at great art: it's all moldering body that once was quick.

But Lourdes—am I not going there to see faith, not history? Yet given our world—ours, not Francis and Clare's—isn't to search for faith only to search for a historic shard, a ghost that once did truly walk alive in the land but now is dead beyond desiring? *Why are you crying?* Francis asked the old monk at

the Porziuncula. *Because love is not loved,* the old man said.
Nor belief believed. Still, that is my destination.

Given the to-ing and fro-ing of the train connections that would
bring me to Lourdes, I spent most of the day hopping from one
milk run to another, just to make it to the seedy border town
of Ventimiglia by evening to pick up the night train along the
coast. The day passed in a series of frantic searches for the right
platform for the next train, and then a few torpid hours rolling
along until I dragged my suitcase to the next platform for the
next train. I spoke my ten words of Italian to the others in each
jammed compartment, and then became invisible.

I was reading *God's Fool,* Julien Green's book about Francis,
which is written in brief vignette chapters. I read a chapter,
barely making it to the finish of two pages before my head was
lolling over. I was exhausted, not bored. All day I slept and
woke, slept and woke and ran for the next train, and slept and
woke some more. Once, somewhere past Florence, I jerked
awake to see, directly across from me, the woman who had
greeted me in French in a benign proprietary way when I entered the compartment, serenely pulling a vibrator out of her
purse. She was sitting fleshy and contented in her ropes of
costume jewelry next to her wren of a husband, running her
hand over the little torpedo-shaped plastic contraption. My
groggy eyes sprang open: My God, she's going to use it right
here in front of everybody.

But no, it was a battery-operated fan, and she held it up,
moving it in a steady circular motion around her very bright
face, its tiny Mixmaster engine whirring away. Her pleasure in
the fan was so intense, however, that it did seem somehow
sexual. A young beauty in a tank top, her long legs barely covered
by the suggestion of a skirt, sat on the big woman's other side,
haughty and delicately damp, looking out the window, giving
us her breathtaking profile. The husband gazed at her from time
to time.

The next time I woke, they were gone, and I was looking into the faces of three black-habited nuns who did not flash the Franciscan smile. *Beep beep beep* . . . The day had the unreal, troubled quality of a night full of unfinished dreams.

Finally, Ventimiglia. There, at a sidewalk table outside a crummy café facing the station, I gulped down a patch of lasagna. It was clammy-cold and looked like something that should be bandaged. The town itself had an illicit feeling, feverish, doing deals right to the edge of the border.

Perhaps this is why, exhausted from the fitful day and feeling vaguely threatened, I walked across to the station, paid the extra money, and bought the privacy of a sleeper, taking with me the big rosy smile of a watermelon slice wrapped in waxed paper which I'd bought from a street vendor.

The most beautiful part of the trip, along the Côte d'Azur, went by in the night. But our first French town, before dark, was Menton, another place to pay homage, this time a secular pilgrimage site. Menton: where Katherine Mansfield came early in the century, away from her dank English winters, to soothe her TB and write her stories. Maybe not such a secular site, after all. She was another of the seekers, and ended up sweeping out cowsheds at Fontainebleau for Gurdjieff, the guru of her day. In Menton she had stayed at the heartbreak-hotel pensions of her fiction, the cheap, accepting caves of the sad and betrayed, the genteel lost and lonely. Now the city is packed with highrise condos, their balconies girding the tall façades like bared teeth facing the sea.

Later, in the dark, I stood by the open window, eating watermelon, spitting the black seeds into the night as the train made the generous curve to Monte Carlo, where the lights were thicker than anywhere and the white of the hotels gleamed. Road-toughened young people with bulky camp gear and packs sat on the ground at the station, looking sullen. *Pilgrims and strangers.* Me, fifteen years ago, traveling Europe with a backpack and no credit card. But my real thought, looking at them: Thank God, that's over. I pulled the shade past Nice and crawled under the covers.

And woke to an inland farm landscape whose austere, refined look was somehow Protestant, though this, too, was Catholic territory. But Italy, teasing its spirit along the arc of the Riviera, was gone. This South of France was not the Provence of the troubadours and the chansons Francis loved to sing, but a sterner south, almost Catalan.

There was mist here, but not the haze of Umbria. The air was heavy, dark, and brooding, even menacing, the land itself working its way toward mountains. The stone of the buildings was gray, the Santa Chiara pink of Assisi absent now. And about all of it, less profusion, more care, nothing of the spilled light and sparkle cloaked with the illusion of mist that had been home to me all the weeks before in Assisi.

Here, a greater spareness. No sunflowers. Instead, rows of corn, familiar as Iowa. And of course, the cypresses were long gone, the palm trees just a memory. We arrived in Lourdes not long after I awoke, the streets quite empty, the day not yet open for business.

The hotel manager greeted me over his half-glasses in a courtly way, picking up my suitcase with a flourish, handing it over to a rock-star kid with shaggy hair and an earring who carted it upstairs. "*Et Madame est toute seule?*" And Madame is alone? the manager asked, looking down at his big ledger and making a mark there.

I sensed it was not entirely correct that Madame was alone. Madame was expected to be, if not with Monsieur, at least with *une groupe*. The town was rolling with charter tours. Bundles of pilgrims arrived in the afternoon, in time for the evening procession, then did the Grotte, the baths, and the *prix fixe* lunch the next day, Bernadette's house and the trinket shops the following day, and were bundled back home, or sometimes on to Rome, on the third.

I presented myself at nine that evening, as arranged, at the hotel's dining room, a morose, small chamber burdened with crystal chandeliers smoky with dust. Someone had used a heavy hand with the silk flowers, and the theme color—red—had a depressing rather than enlivening effect on the whole enterprise. People sat at attention, voices low, working their way through the five stages of the *prix fixe* dinner.

The manager was there to greet me, casting his glance over his half-glasses as before, this time turning to inspect the ledger of his dinner reservation book. "Ah," he said loudly, as if in announcement, "the lady who dines alone." Every head in the little dim room turned to regard in the doorway the female person alone in the world, to gaze upon her, to observe her debased passage through the room, as she was led to her rightful place, facing the kitchen and across from the serving station stacked with dirty plates from the previous sitting.

That night I skipped the candlelight procession to the basilica. "I'm not up to it," I told myself, as if something would be demanded of me personally if I went. Yet I had trouble getting to sleep. I could hear the voices of the faithful in the distance, singing over and over the same refrain. What was it? *Allez, allez, allez, Ma-ree-ee-ah.* Was that possible? Go, go, go, Mary. Like a fight song, but sad. The melody was one from childhood, we'd sung it at St. Luke's, but this was France and were they saying, Go, go—go where?

I drifted off to the sound, repeating itself over and over. And must have awakened a few moments later, suddenly getting it right. Of course. It was *Ave, ave, ave, Maria*, the old cry for Mother. How could I have forgotten?

In Lourdes, the hotels seem to divide up the clientele: some cater to the sick, others do not. My hotel, the Imperial, did not. I was given a back room, garbage bins and service entrance for a view, the walls papered manically in blue flowers with yellow centers and dark leaves set against an unhealthy-looking green background. The big mirror mounted on the huge armoire multiplied the floral effect. Yet I was grateful for the room, especially after a few hours on the streets. I even returned to it for an afternoon siesta, staring at the frantic wallpaper as if at a com-

plicated explanation. I lay on the lumpy mattress, adding up
over and over how much of my three days in the town was left,
imagining my way through breakfasts, lunches, through dinners
and evening processions. This is finite time, I reminded myself.
This is three days, two days, one more . . .

It was easy to spot the first-day people. They looked stunned,
wandering down the main street that led to the Grotte. But
wandering is all wrong. Nobody could wander in that dense
mass of people, those walking, those pushing wheelchairs or the
curious rickshaws Lourdes provides for the bedridden. Anyone
who didn't move smartly along, weaving and dodging, was
caught up in the ooze of human traffic, the amoeba movement
of a single primal intelligence, all headed in one direction—until
mealtimes, when the primal drift reversed itself and the ooze
headed away from the Grotte and back to the hotels for its hot
meal.

The streets approaching the Grotte were lined with open
shops and stalls, all selling pretty much the same merchandise
in a *mano-a-mano* competition. The low-key souvenir shops of
Assisi came back as a kind of retail Eden with their flower-painted
Pace e Bene tiles, and the scrolly broadsides of "Canticle of the
Creatures" done in calligraphy, the whole poem decorated with
medieval gilt flourishes.

Here in Lourdes people bought madly, almost savagely,
caught up in a discount-store frenzy as if they had found at last
the K mart of Catholicism, snatching up medals and scapulars,
statuettes of Mary, and tea trays with Bernadette on her knees;
rosaries from the most humble brown bead to glinting lead crystal with 18-carat-gold crucifix; big sacks of paste-white pepper-
mint candies, made with water from the Grotte and stamped
with the image of the Virgin. *Les bonbons sacrés.* Cost comparison was intense, one woman charging back to a vendor with
a bag of the holy candy, slapping the sack on the counter, hurling
abuse at a vacant-faced clerk because just *two stands up the
street* she had found the same bag, *the same, exactly the same
bag* of candy priced at . . .

But all these objects were as nothing compared to the real,

the essential commodity, the object of all purchasing power: the water. Every store, all the hotels, everywhere, everywhere, you could buy the water. And people did. Liter upon liter. All equally holy, all flowing from the same miraculous stream, the water posed certain marketing problems. It was possible to compete in the market only by means of the container. For if you brought your own container, the water was free at the Grotte. The retail water was available in every sort of vessel, from glass decanter to plastic bottle. Most of the bottles were plastic (of varying sizes from tiny to tub) with blue tops. The plastic was molded into the shape of the Virgin, or—more expensive because more artful—into the shape of the Virgin and Bernadette, caught in the apparition moment.

And it was a place of apparitions. The market scene was not exactly repellent—it was too extraordinary for that, a vision of some human marvel at work. I couldn't stay aloof, and got right in there, bought a bag of the candy and a Virgin bottle of the water. And let myself be carried forward to the inevitable destination.

But neither the Grotte, a stone outcropping awash from its streaming fissures, nor the grand basilica farther above it, proved to be the real source. It was the halt, the lame, those sick and suffering from every sort of affliction and ailment, ravaged, eyes fixed or rolling vacantly, mouths babbling or drooling: these composed the vision that we, the amoeba-force surging down the retail alleys, were destined to see materialize before us again and again until we believed.

I don't know why I hadn't thought of this before I came. I was aware, of course, that Lourdes was a place where people came for healing. But Paul's good lectures on Francis and the lepers had not prepared me for this. Nor had my good life, my good health. Perhaps the marketplace, in its crazy chemistry, mixing us all together as we were filtered down to the Grotte and the baths, snatched away the usual tatters of individuality, the veil of separation from Those Others. I could see nothing else.

By the time I had dodged enough wheelchairs and seen—
how many?—children with huge and hideous heads, they were
the obvious and only apparition of the place. There was no
question of disbelief. This dying—this was life. The ranks of
ancient bodies curled in their cribs waiting with their attendants
to be lifted into the baths, next to the bright-faced lifelong in-
valids with their cheerful smiles for their tenders, and the newer
ascetics of illness, the refined bones of those young men, already
bald and gleaming with disease, their wheelchairs pushed along
by other young men, still well, joking to each other and still
hoping.

On the second-floor terrace of the Jeanne d'Arc Café, looking
down on the river Gave, a tidy avenue of water that runs through
the city, the pretty Pont Vieux just below, I sat drinking a
Cinzano *bianco* before going inside for lunch. Off to the left,
very beautiful, the green rise of what I took to be the foothills
of the Pyrenees, or the Pyrenees themselves, rose in velvet
hummocks until they were stopped by the low ceiling of a gray
sky.

Below, from time to time, across the Gave, the sound of
rushing water: the hotels simply dumped sewage raw into the
river. There was a floating mass of junk, mostly Coke cans and
other pilgrim fast-food refuse, hugging the far embankment,
where it was caught in the lovely ivy that covered the stone.

I had discovered a second circle of Lourdes, above the teeming
mass and the market sucking all in its wake to the Grotte. The
town was built in layers, and here, on a loop of the spiral above
the reality below, were the better hotels and the quieter tea-
rooms.

The Irish were present in force, trailing their devotion to
Mary. Some of the hotels were named in their honor: the Tara,
the Hibernia, and a shop called St. Laurence O'Toole. The English were also noted: Hotel Windsor. But most of the hotels
honored the Event and everything related to it. Hotel Madonna,
Le Palais Rosaire, Hôtel La Solitude, the Galilee, and the Hotel

Golgotha, which had a NO VACANCY sign and did not appear to be suffering from an image problem.

I had chosen the Jeanne d'Arc for lunch because the building had three stars on its black medallion, rather than the usual two. I was fleeing the lepers. I wanted to rise above it all—up here with the more expensive *prix fixe* meals, away from the baths and the market crowds—and the perambulators of the suffering. Eat well, be well.

The Jeanne d'Arc seemed taken over by an Irish tour group. Outside the restaurant, near the reception area, a young woman in white shorts and a sleeveless top was being exhorted by her companions to change into a dress because she wouldn't be permitted into the Grotte dressed as she was. Her point—that she was going to the baths, not to church—met with no takers. The receptionist joined in: Absolutely she must change. She shrugged and went off.

Then the receptionist turned to me. Did I really want lunch? *Oui, Madame.* Here? *Oui.* Now? *Bien sûr.* Did I know the cost? I did. She frowned. I frowned. She saw finally there was no getting rid of the woman-who-dines-alone, who would take up an entire table for four during the height of the lunch hour.

"As you see, Madame," she said, speaking English, refusing me the pleasure of responding to my French, "all of our tables are for four. You will be quite alone. Or perhaps I must add strangers to your table."

"Comme vous voulez, Madame."

No strangers joined me. I ate alone, in the grand isolation of white linen and a lot of silverware. Not a very good meal, but I felt cheered by the effort.

The manager, a modish woman in a slick blond blunt-cut bob and an expensive suit of pale blue, very Paris, moved from table to table among the Irish group, who were seated for efficient service at long refectory tables. She touched a shoulder here, bent and smiled into the face of a wheelchair occupant there, reminding everyone that, as overnight guests, they received a discount at the hotel's gift shop.

She assumed at first, when she got to my table, that I was Irish, too, and then apologized as if she had accused me of being illiterate when I corrected her. We spoke in French. I experienced one of my rare attacks of fluency in the language and preened when she complimented me. But the lower town was still roiling inside me, and looking into her canny eyes, I wondered how you say *clip joint* in French.

But she was already drifting away on her rounds, and I was alone again at my big table, having finished the *oeuf en gelée* and awaiting the savory pastry to come. In front of me at the next table a husband and wife sat close to each other; across from them was a boy about nine or ten—their son, no doubt. I was struck by the strong bond between the parents.

Their faces glowed as they turned toward each other; it seemed they were constantly engaged in the low, amused murmurs of lovers. The boy, who seemed lively and happy, was somehow extraneous, though they always paused and gave him their attention when his bright, high voice pitched in.

The husband had broad shoulders, a nice build, and a strikingly handsome face, lean and individual, which I saw in profile when he turned—often—to the wife. The woman was less beautiful, but attractive in a gracious, modest way. I suppose they were about forty. Maybe it was the man's good looks or maybe their happy involvement in each other—but somehow I didn't notice that he was in a wheelchair.

I only saw it—as a shock—when she lifted his wineglass and held it for him to drink. It was done so easily, the way a lover might feed the beloved a grape, that I didn't at first realize that he didn't have the use of his hands.

After that, I could hardly take my eyes off them. They went from jellied egg to *saucissons en croûte*, a greasy, papery affair with a horrid lukewarm finger inside. Slices of pale beef with a salty gravy came next with *frites*, and then salad and fruit. Through it all, the wife fed her husband simply and unobtrusively, all the while the two of them so pleased with each other that it was impossible to feel he was at any disadvantage.

173

I watched them for the whole meal; their interest, their *appreciation*, never flagged. Occasionally, the boy would say something which usually made them smile. When he spoke, they came back to him, included him easily—but always with the sense that they were *coming back*, returning from another, happier sphere just slightly removed from the plane where the rest of us, even their son, resided.

I didn't sense passion so much as delight in each other's presence. The whole thing seemed light. It was impossible to believe the man was really confined to that metal chair, that he wouldn't just laugh and rise up from it at the end of the meal, saying, *Well, wasn't that a curious experience.* And she would laugh and the boy would bound ahead of them out of the bilious dining room into the dark bar, where, the woman indicated to the waiter, they would take their coffee.

But when the time came, the husband remained in his wheelchair, his hands apparently without force in his lap, though during the meal he raised them in a sort of ritualistic performance of holding his glass or touching her, instinctively, on shoulder or cheek or hand, as she went about the easy and graceful feeding that looked so much like a love indulgence.

She deftly turned the chair out between the tables, leaning down slightly to catch something he was saying, their communion still unbroken. The boy did skip on ahead—that part I imagined correctly. And something he said caused them to send up peals of laughter as they disappeared.

The next morning the rock-star waiter at the Imperial struck up a conversation with me over breakfast. I had come down late and was the only one left in the breakfast room while he cleared tables. The usual opening question: Where was I from?

He didn't know Minnesota.

"Do you know the Mississippi River?" I asked. "I live at the top of the Mississippi River."

His eyes widened. Yes, he'd just seen a great movie, *The Mississippi Mermaid.* Did I know it?

As for himself, he was twenty, born in Lourdes. He made a face. "Lourdes is bad. Nothing but commerce. You understand?" he said. "Beez-ness. Bad, everything beez-ness."

But what about the story itself, I asked, what about Bernadette?

He shrugged—*Bien sûr*, it was lovely, the story of the apparition, he was willing to admit, but . . .

Then he looked at me sharply: Was I a believer?

I started up the delicate dialectic between believing in *God* and believing in the whole apparition story. This seemed a strange notion to him, questionable. I found myself not wishing to say, *Yes, I believe*. Repelled by bringing the whole deep question to the surface of an *opinion*. What would Felix say? Or Donnie, mystery-smile playing across her poker face, holding the cards of the spirit close to the vest. Or Thaddeus: *Hey, man, it was a divine discontent got me*.

When I equivocated, he said impatiently, "One or the other, you either believe or you don't."

"God, yes, I believe in God," I said, flustered, as if caving in to an impatient clerk who was fed up with my hesitation and demanded that I either take the goods or quit fingering them. But having said the words, I felt false, ripped off.

The mountains, he said, the Pyrenees—*that* was the real beauty of the place. "You go up the mountains," he said, "it's heaven. Lourdes up there—it's nothing. Nothing. It disappears. That's the only miracle that ever happens here."

His young face was stone. His gold earring flashed, caught in the sunlight coming through the front window. He stepped nearer, leaned against the table. "Are you the Mermaid of the Mississippi?" he said suddenly, grinning, looking right in my eyes.

"I'm old enough to be your mother," I said, startled and caught off guard, still fretting about God.

He grinned, letting his eyes remain all bedroom, and moved away toward the kitchen. "Okay," he said. "But see the movie. It was great; a beautiful girl lives under the water and comes to the surface. The special effects—incredible. Men fall in love with her, but they don't realize she's not human."

I didn't go up the mountain. After lying in my room at the Imperial, hiding from the fright of faith all around me, pleading with time to pass quickly, it seemed there was hardly any time left. No time for a day in the mountains. I discovered, though, an *ascenseur* that went to the upper town, called Centre Ville, the *normal* part of Lourdes, as the boy with the gold earring had explained to me earlier.

There the souvenir stores still abounded, but they were set in between hardware stores, dress shops, groceries, and antiques shops. Normal stores, as he had said. I wandered away from the commercial section, heading in a series of ascending streets into the residential area, where the provincial good housekeeping displayed itself in well-tended stone houses and old gardens with gnarled apple trees, the fruit forming.

I came to the entrance of a cemetery and went in the open gate gratefully, as into a sanctuary. I knew what I wanted, one thing only: quiet. I met no one, and could hear nothing but birds and, somewhere far off, the anonymous *shush* of traffic like an office air conditioner. I stayed a long time, moving slowly along the miniature avenues laid out in graceful curves, pausing often before the civic monuments the dead place in their little walled cities.

Stone lambs, some blackened, their contours softened by time. These were the sign of the child, always inscribed with the heartbroken precision of dates: day, month, year of birth, of death, sometimes only a matter of months between the two. Crosses of all kinds, large and small, with slumped figure or without; one grand marble *Pietà* emblazoned with a proud family name in block letters, surrounded by its satellites: *Père, Mère, Fils*.

Here and there, like rich people on an ordinary block, the domestic fallacy of a mausoleum. But most of all, I paused to read the lives between the lines, the minimalist stories with their bare hint of plot:

MIRACLES

Ici Reposent
Josephine Berdou
épouse François Carraze
décédée à Etamps
le 24 mars 1931
(Catastrophe de Chemin de Fer)

But especially, in this high place, the deaths on the mountains:

Alexandre Berdou
Mort à l'age de 36 ans
Au Pic de Cambales
le 27 fevrier 1936
(Accident de Montagne)

Over and over again the stone slabs of the mountain victims, those, usually young men, who had pursued the heights and been claimed by the one certain miracle, the boy with the earring had said, that this place has to offer the seeker.

I went one last time to the Grotte, just inserted myself in the surging throng and was drawn forward, following a partially paralyzed old man with the beard of Moses. He rode a tricycle mounted with a sign announcing that he was pedaling to Paris and on to Luxembourg. The significance of those two destinations was not spelled out, but there was a bin for donations, and many people greeted him with interest. He had a mimeo flyer which he offered to all donors.

One of the striking props of the Grotte is the thousands of candles, a sort of inverted imagery of the place, opposing with their flames the healing waters. Huge candles, big as fence posts, usually left at the shrine by a group, others tall as a person but slim, scaled down from the great wax pickets. And every other size down to a small taper. People walked along usually with one or two of the tall candles, but sometimes with great bundles tucked under their arms like firewood.

They went to the area at the side of the Grotte where legions

177

of these tall candles burned. There, aides in blue smocks lit their candles, allowing the pilgrims to stand for a few moments in front of the shrine before handing their candles back to the aides, who extinguished them and laid them neatly in great bins. Signs explained in many languages that the volume of candles was so great that pilgrims had to leave their candles. They were put on hold, so to speak, until another candle burned down and a slot was available in the ranks before the shrine.

At the spring, where the healing water rushed free and the lines were always long, another message was mounted in many languages: "Just like Bernadette, wash your face with the water . . . and pray to God to cleanse your heart." Cleanse your heart—not your sins. Okay. I got in line. When I finally was near the spring, I noticed that a very old nun in front of me, a tiny bent thing, was having trouble reaching the water. I moved forward to help her, but she thought I was trying to push ahead and hissed at me furiously, elbowing me back where I belonged.

I spent the rest of the afternoon ambling the grounds of the Grotte, visiting the giant basilica, attaching myself to one or another group for a while, listening to the guides tell the tale. I was waiting for nightfall and the evening procession.

The crowds began gathering early, well before dusk. It was not clear—to me anyway—where the procession began or how to get in it. Most of the crowds seemed to be there to observe, like people lining up early for a parade. Yet when the time came and the thing had begun, the distinction between those processing and those observing was lost. The ooze took over, we were all in this together.

In fact, it wasn't a procession. It was a vast family recitation of the Rosary. For that had been part of the Virgin's message: to say the Rosary. Loudspeakers were set up all over the parklike area of the Grotte, and the people surged together, moving in some unconscious movement which had been choreographed, it seemed, at the level of the chromosome. They called back the Church's mantra-prayer to the series of priestly voices in Italian, English, French, German, Japanese, Spanish, and several other languages I didn't recognize.

The basilica above the Grotte was the destination, and there were dozens of recognizable groups and legions, uniformed and costumed, as well as the little hierarchy of priests and acolytes with banners and special candles to give the affair the look of a procession. But really there were no groups; it was a colossal merging, the ultimate pooling of the pilgrim ooze.

As night truly fell and the Rosary droned on in the endless whirling way it is meant to, losing sense to silence, the candles began to come on, more and more candles, until the whole great public space was a vibrating carpet of light. It was not something to have an opinion about. A shock of reverence passed into me and lodged there.

I understood, vaguely, that the awe was for *all this*, the human *this*, the marvel—not altogether beautiful, but extraordinary—of this communal moment. But that distinction, between the human-this and the divine-that, suddenly struck me as puny, laughable. What had Donnie said when I asked her how she squared divine revelation in the Bible with—well, with reality?

"Oh," she said, as if she'd assumed all along I understood the point of the sacred, "it's the whole intelligence, heart, mind, soul, history, *everything*, of a people." A People, the eternal presence of ourselves—and yet not ourselves, the beyond-ourselves of every urge and hope, every fear and fragment of desire we are destined to live and die. That was what Scripture exposed, she said. The fact that we are a People.

Which this moment also exposed, day ending and each person lost separately in the dark, and then turning to a flame among thousands of other flames, moving in the intricate molecular dance in which all were partnered. The tongues of white light were panting almost imperceptibly, like small animals holding still in the underbrush till danger passes. That faint movement created a single breath, just as the again-and-again Hail Marys took away all words and left what everyone longed to hear: blameless silence.

I turned and noticed a man, a priest about fifty, leaning against a nearby tree. He held a candle—we all did, they had somehow materialized and multiplied—and yet he was slightly apart. The face I'd been looking for: someone observing, taking it in, not taken in. I knew instinctively he was American.

"Is this a special night?" I asked. "A feast day or something?"

He turned. I realized he was coming back a long way to see me. "No," he said. "This happens here every night."

We didn't speak again, just stood there as every person disappeared and the flames made the world before us one harmonious thing, lightly breathing light.

I was at the station the next afternoon well before the train left. I sat in the station café, writing postcards. One to Donnie: "Lourdes . . . I don't know. On to Burgundy and the wine. Then Paris. Then home . . ."

I paused over my next thought, looked up to see the sad-eyed waiter, not young, bringing the paper plate with the slice of quiche and the Styrofoam cup of tea. "You leave?" he asked shyly.

The train north to Dijon, I said.

He seemed sadder still, looked off, and said, "That's too bad."

I didn't want to help him along with this, but something in those loser eyes made me. "Why is that?" I asked.

There was disco that night in town, he said. Long pause. "I wonder if you would like to go to the disco with me?" Before I could reply, he scurried into the conditional mode. "I mean, I *would* ask if you were interested in going to the disco. But I *don't* ask—now that you won't be here."

"No," I said companionably. "Yes."

And he walked away, smiling, relieved as only the truly shy can be that life makes personal contact impossible over and over again.

There was space left on Donnie's postcard. I wanted to describe the man in the wheelchair and his wife who fed him and their happy, extraneous child. I had seen the man again, by chance, on the way to the station. Too long for a postcard, though. I had to wait to *tell* it, sitting again in the little room in the monastery where we met for spiritual direction—"or whatever you want to call it," Donnie would say, sensitive to my overfastidious language habits.

I'd noticed the man in his wheelchair as I left the Imperial. It was that in-between time in Lourdes, late afternoon, when the mass visits to the healing spring were over and the evening procession was not yet drawing crowds.

The street of the vendors was emptying, and I saw his wheelchair, being pushed now by a nurse. The wife was nowhere around, nor the little boy. For an unhinged moment, I thought I'd made them up. They had caused such a strong impression, I could not imagine him without them. The holy family. Not seeing them, I found it hard to believe I was seeing him, there on the street.

He was coming from the direction of the Grotte, one of the stragglers at the end of the steamy returning crowd. He seemed smaller now than the day before in the hotel restaurant, more frail.

His arms with the delicate hands which had moved so gracefully, as if under water, toward the blond hair of his wife as she fed him, were prey, I now saw, to a soft spasmodic tremor. They floated about now, too, just as strangely graceful, but without a destination. The nurse paused to swaddle them in the blanket on his lap. But the hands rose again, full of affectionate longing, it looked like, conducting uncertainly some lost music he was trying to bring into the world.

SILENCE

MONDAY

It happened before—or possibly just after—I drowned. The same trip anyway, the summer I was five, when we went for two weeks to Lake Kabetogama, far up in the Boundary Waters, near Canada. Strange, I think of it that way—the summer I drowned—instead of the obvious—when I almost drowned.

I am standing on the dry, bleached dock. Late in the afternoon, the sun already laying the pine trees down in long black shadows. My mother has been reading Charlotte's Web *to me all week, drawing out the story in slow, delectable segments. But just now she says I must wait: can't I see she is talking to Bernice. This is the wife of Phil, who owns the greenhouse where my father works. We have come here with them, though they have the big house with the stone fireplace. We have the little cabin on stilts, farther from the water. That doesn't matter, my father says. We're lucky to be here.*

Mother and Bernice wear plaid shirts with big shoulders. They are smoking and doing their nails, sitting on a bench, leaning against the gray wood slats of the boathouse. Sally, Bernice's pretty blond daughter my age, is pouring salt on leeches she has speared out of the water and laid on the dock. She likes to see them curl up.

So do I, but not now. Earlier in the day, as we worked together on this project, Sally had said suddenly, "My father owns your father's car. He owns your house and everything you have. Because he's your dad's boss, and he can fire him like that." She snapped her fingers, making a soft thumping sound.

"He cannot," I said.

"Can too," she said, and kept pouring out her pure white stream of salt.

It is possible she speaks truth. I walk past her now.

And continue down the long wooden sidewalk of the dock. Toward the end, I see a small step built onto the side of the dock. People use it to get into their boats. It is awash, satiny with green. A stringer is attached to the dock, right by this step. I want to pull on the stringer to see the fish my father has caught. Either I want to look at them or I want to hold them up to show my mother, who should be giving me her attention. She does not go fishing. She reads to me until her voice goes hoarse, or she reads to herself, two-inch-thick historical novels, about Ireland if possible.

I lower myself, one foot and then the other, to the slimy step just below the dock. I remember seeing the red ovals of my Keds with their rind of white rubber. That happened.

Then, hardly having stepped onto the satin step, and not having touched the metal of the stringer, I am in the water. I am over my head. My eyes are open and everything is gold. I am level with the fish, who are alive but witless, linked like grapes in a cluster. There are more steps below the one I slipped from. Why are there steps into the lake? Who descends? For what purpose?

I realize I will die. I can't swim. Water is rushing around me. It is strong. I can't cry out. No one has seen me disappear. I have been swallowed, accepted, stolen. So easy to be gone.

I realize I must save myself. Although the water swirls and I am panicked and the fish are aloof, I have an overwhelming, heart-bursting sensation that I will live, that I will get out. Panicked—but not afraid. A strange buoyancy: I'm drowning, but I can think about it. *I have never experienced my mind as a thing distinct, as something capable of helping me. And now I realize it is not in my head; my mind resides in my breastbone; it surges with willpower.*

I reach out, I will *the slick mossy step to accept my grasp. It refuses. I reach again and command with the authority of Poseidon. The step obeys.*

And I am on the dock again, in air, dripping like a filled sponge, my red sweater gorgeous with water. I walk toward my mother. She is still sitting by the boathouse with Bernice, working now on her right hand, stroking the thumbnail with the brush. I come nearer; strands of water fall from me. I am from another dimension.

She sees me, jerks up; the little bottle of nail polish tips off the bench. Red spatters on the sand. She is running to me; Bernice jumps up, too, and instinctively runs to Sally. Just as instinctively, Sally clutches her blue Morton box. "You could have died," *she says, and I hear the respect in her voice at last.*

But even more than drowning, that other death, the happy one. The same summer at Kabetogama. It is my mother's birthday, late July. We are standing in the Hudson's Bay Store, across the border in Canada.

My hand is a small wad of moist dough in a dry, warm holder: her hand. Then the little red spade of her polished nail digs at a bolt of brown plaid wool next to us on a table with many other bolts, heaped like logs on top of each other. "Just feel that wool," she says. "That's challis." She lifts the edge of the fabric, flares it out in a dark ripple.

I take my hand out of its holder, reach up to touch the wool. Touch it. And die. Or leave my body. Or fly. Something wonderful is happening that has never happened before. What is it? But there is no question in it, no query. There is just this moment, and it is forever and everything is in it.

My hand, I know, is touching the bolt of brown wool. I am also touching the bone china cup my brother is holding across the store which he is buying for Mother's birthday. Dad has given us each a dollar. I am imprinted on the English downs of the cup's landscape. The floor of the Hudson's Bay store is made of broad wooden planks, scuffed raw of varnish. I am that, too. I am the dollar in my pocket. I am also air and small motes of dust caught in the light.

I have left my body and entered objects. I don't exist anymore. Or I exist everywhere. I no longer stop at my skin. It is the best thing that has ever happened. It is bliss.

Then it is over. I snap back. I am me, I am nothing. I mustn't move from this spot. This is a good spot, and if I don't budge maybe it will come back. Maybe I will die again. But they are calling me. My mother, who has moved to another counter. My brother, who says I can't buy a cup, he's already bought her a cup. My father, who points to a sugar and creamer set painted with cabbage roses: that's what I should use my dollar for.

There is no telling them—it would be a mistake to tell. I don't know why this is, but it is, I know. IT *doesn't want to be told.* IT *doesn't like words, and speaks no language.*

I must move, must remove my hand from the bolt of wool, must return to them. I belong to them and must leave with them. "Come on," my brother calls. "Do you want to be left on this side of the border?"

We are going out to the car. I am with them again. There's no explaining the most important thing that has ever happened to me. But if I tried, I would put my hand back in her hand. I would say: You die, you fly. You don't stop inside, you go everywhere. It's heaven.

Past Mendocino, the fog was thick. The corkscrew road pierced the murk uncertainly, making the highway seem more fragile than the mist that cloaked it. Cars coming from the other direction appeared suddenly, out of nowhere, all going fast, all with a menacing aspect. Semis hurtling north loomed behind the rental car, hugged the bumper, and the drivers seemed to make furious eye contact when I looked into my rearview mirror.

Even the landscape was tricky, a sleight-of-hand act suddenly delivering the apparition of a bright green hill, then snatching it back up a deep milky sleeve. The ocean, the whole point of going this way instead of the quicker inland route, was invisible, out there somewhere beyond the precipice I was steering along in the streaming fog.

My destination, Rosethorn, was a town, or maybe not even a town, past Garberville, in the redwoods near the Lost Coast of Northern California, which sheers off finally into the Pacific Northwest. Not all the maps I'd looked at had Rosethorn marked. The one open next to me on the passenger seat cast a black dot at the end of a frail thread of secondary road. *Rosetorn*, it said in the smallest type the map legend used. Must be the place, I decided.

Another of Donnie's destinations, this small Cistercian women's monastery in the beautiful nowhere. No more pilgrimages, I told her. I just take a billion notes. It's like eating too much. I felt like Elsie, who had washed her hands of Rome, of Assisi, and went back to the Kentucky laundromat to find the Spirit. Maybe Elsie was right. The open road wasn't for pilgrims, it was for tourists. I had been right to mistrust the word—*pilgrimage*. Spiritual life wasn't a quest, it was a disappearing act. I wanted to tell Donnie that I wanted to fade, to vanish. But I was afraid that sounded macabre, though I didn't feel morbid. It was something else: sink, swim, fly, die, that mystic urge from all those years ago, carried at the bottom of my kit bag of religious impulses.

But she guesses everything anyway. "Ready for the cloister?" she said. She suggested a retreat at Rosethorn. It was a year after my trip to Assisi and Lourdes. I'd bought a fancy calligraphy set—not just a pen but an array of nibs and inks, along with a how-to book; I mailed the whole thing off to Soeur Agnès in Assisi, my spooky alter ego. She sent back a brief thank-you note, bearing down heavily on the calligraphy pen, leaving dried-up inky pools at the ends of her few sentences. "We're all so grateful," she wrote. The community "we." She had receded again behind the cloister grille where, I sensed, she wanted an American correspondent no more than she had wanted an American visitor.

Bridget had sent a Christmas card from Malaysia. The political situation was getting rougher; after her decades in the country, she doubted she would be sending next year's Christmas greeting, she said, from Kuala Lumpur. She gave no other address. Paul's news was bad, too: the landlord had evicted him from the decrepit building in the Bronx which he and his cadre of volunteers had rehabilitated for a poor people's retreat center. The landlord wanted to use the place himself now. I had hoped to go there for a retreat, but now that tent had been folded. "I don't know if we'll be able to relocate," he wrote. Also no return address. Even Felix, it seemed, was lost to me: when I called his Hawaiian parish house, a clipped voice said, "Father Felix is no longer with the prayer group. I believe he has returned to his friary." Where was that? The clipped voice had no idea. Thaddeus of course was at the crossroads of the known world, Thirty-fourth Street. But he wasn't a letter writer, and what was there to say, anyway?

No more pilgrimages, I had told Donnie. But I was on the road again, this time to the farthest point, the deepest nowhere she could find for me. I flew to San Francisco, and took two days to make the trip up the coast from Sausalito. The first night, at a restaurant at Little River, I fell in with two women on vacation. I said I'd never seen a redwood and did they really have ones you could drive through? "It's tacky to go to a drive-thru redwood," one of the women said. I pedaled fast backward: just asking.

But of course, now seeing a sign for one, I make a sharp right, away from the foggy coast, into the sun and real weather of the land. I follow the blaring black-and-yellow signs that lead from highway to gravel road, to a trail barely hacked out of the woods. It leads to a small hut, like a kiosk in a parking ramp. I give the attendant my $3 and am handed a ticket, also good for a discount at the gift shop. "Straight ahead," the man says.

There is no straight, but I bump along until I reach a dark clearing. The place is scattered with retirees irritably maneuvering their RVs in the cramped space, regarding a group of bikers with disapproval. The bikers lean on their machines and smoke; they are bearded, helmets off, displaying amiably their greased ponytails, their tattoos, their sullen molls.

And there It is, to the side of the gift shop, with the gaping wound in the middle. A poem has been mounted on a lacquered plaque, reminding the visitor that here the redwoods stand:

> *This is their temple, vaulted high,*
> *And here we pause with reverent eye,*
> *With silent tongue and awestruck soul;*
> *For here we sense life's proper goal.*
>
> *To be like these, straight true and fine,*
> *To make our world, like theirs, a shrine.*
> *Sink down, Oh traveller, on your knees,*
> *God stands before you in these trees.*

I feel a serious reluctance to go through with it, but what with the RVs and the motorcycles parked every which way, I can't figure how else to get out. In my flurry, I gun the engine and terrify a tiny old man trying to tame a huge boat of a trailer who lays on his horn, startling everybody else. I careen through the tree, ashamed to meet it this way, as if it were a being sentient enough to be humiliated, not below us on the Great Chain after all, those of us violating its great gutted bowel.

Wrong, I mutter, trying to erase the moment, unsee this huge scabbed and humiliated elephant in its dirty cage at a bad zoo. I want to un-be myself, ever ready with my endless curiosity and my notebook where—damn it—I pause long enough to get the poem.

Past Garberville, following the directions I'd been given, the little rental car planed along, taking the curves. Inland now.

More than that: enclosed. The big trees, Douglas fir and red-wood, erected their towers, the dense fortress of themselves. The monastery started here—that's how it felt. Before I reached the modest marker for the turnoff, I was inside. Inside what? Within what I am seeking: the silence that speaks.

The gravel road after the turn went past two low buildings, homely like an old-fashioned motel, but without a parking lot. I continued past this clearing, as the instructions I'd been sent indicated, and followed the road to its finish, where several buildings clustered together against a backdrop of the great ancient trees of the place. Straight ahead, the big double doors on a plain gray façade: the chapel. To the left, a low building I later learned was the bakery: the community supported itself, in part, by making communion breads. To the right, a walkway of stones and wooden rounds, leading to the place where I sensed I was to present myself.

A woman in her sixties, wearing a cotton flower-print dress, her bare legs in sandals, was sitting in the shadowy room, a sort of vestibule with several doors and a window offering a view of a small Zen-like garden of stones and succulents.

She came forward and introduced herself: Jeannine, she said, not using the word *Sister*. The community had been founded by a small group of Belgian nuns in 1962. Jeannine was one of these. Her English, fluent and natural, came from a deep voice, as from a cool, still well; the bauble of the Flemish accent was like a soft lowing, nothing of the high French birdsong to it. A voice of bread and butter, honey and rich pasture.

And she did immediately offer me tea and honey and little shortbread cookies. The iced tea was delicious. It proved to be pine-needle tea, made from needles she had gathered. "Rich in vitamin C," she said with satisfaction. One of those people who can make soup and salad out of the back yard. A benign herbal witch, harboring the medieval lore.

Others began arriving for the week-long retreat: a psychology professor from Berkeley, several nuns, a small blond man named Bob, who was retracing all the places Thomas Merton had ever visited: here in 1968, just before his final Asian journey. There were others as well, Jeannine said; they had already gone to their rooms. Everyone was given the iced tea, and we stood around for a while, drinking in the trees Jeannine had distilled, a woodland communion of our first moments on—though no one said it—holy ground.

There were rose petals in the salad that night. "We eat flowers all the time," beautiful Cecile, one of the Sisters, said when I exclaimed, as if she were explaining the menu, one rabbit to another. The petals were splashes of yellow tossed in lettuce from their garden. The roses tasted faintly perfumed; their texture was a skim of cream. Pine-needle tea, rose-petal salad—there was an ambrosial stamp to the food, as if we ate from the still bounteous storehouses of the gods.

The ten visiting retreatants had dinner that first evening with the community, who numbered nine. There was, in addition, André, the elderly Belgian monk who was the community chaplain, and Thomas, the gardener, about sixty, an American monk from an Idaho monastery who spent the growing season at Rosethorn tending the crop that fed the community through the year.

A sociable evening, alive with chatter, introductions, the sketches people exchange when they settle in or set out together. Passionate discussion by several of the nuns about the violence being done to the remaining stands of virgin redwood. "We've become involved," one of them said.

Everyone, even the quiet sorts, was companionable, available, lively. Knowing none of this was *it*. This good cheer was a pastille of sociability we sucked, letting the conversation coat our throats like a gentle anaesthetic. Because we were together to be silent for a week, and soon would say farewell, though we would sit and stand and kneel together every day.

After dinner, I walked back to my room, 6A, in the first of the motel-like string of rooms I'd passed on my way into the property. A monastic cell at last. I lined up my books in a row, toothbrush in the glass by the sink in the corner (toilet and shower in a separate room down the line), the big lug of my New Jerusalem Bible and my square black notebook on the small desk set by the window, which looked out on the field and the rising hill opposite where meadow gave way to woods. Someone had placed a small vase of wildflowers on the desk. Here was my future: this straight chair, this desk, the Word.

To my left, a bare width of sheetrock away, Bob was clearing his throat, encamping his Merton archive, setting up his toothbrush; to the right, Mary, the cheerful retired Dominican biology teacher, soundlessly doing the same. There are only so many choices in space so small. Already we were becoming anonymous: books in a row, pajamas under the pillow, toothbrush, toothbrush, toothbrush.

Then, my house in order, I went back up the gravel road, this time taking the wooded hidden way along the spur trail above the rushing brook, back to the monastery. Vespers. The last canonical hour of the day was to be our first.

The quarter mile back to the chapel was studded by our ragged return, old André in his beret, Thomas biking it, and the new arrivals emerging from the little cells, one by one, everyone headed in the same direction. Everyone walked alone except for Ann, the elderly blind nun with the permanent smile, who had her arm linked in the sturdy arm of Jane, a young nun who had said at dinner she had asked Ann if she could come along. "My buddy," Ann had said. That was their useful fiction: Ann was not in need of a keeper; Jane was the lucky one, allowed to come along. Bob was out ahead with the purposeful gait of a man who knew his turf (he'd ticked off a dozen monasteries, Christian, Buddhist, and a couple of non-denominational retreat centers, where he'd "done some time," as he put it).

The chapel door was big but light; it gave easily and didn't need the heft I put into pulling it open, as if its real purpose were to offer a first lesson in less is more. It closed soundlessly behind me. Once entered, the chapel was a cathedral, or the idea of a cathedral, stripped of every ornament, retaining only that essential quality of the great enclosures of Western worship—the surge of vertical space, the immense upward vault. Architecture as psalm, the soul flung to the rafters in lament, in praise, in its wild reach for its Maker.

Everything was gray, the floor a pearled and polished gray that seemed to have been poured out in one spill and then hardened to a soft glow. Even the raised square dais, at one end, seemed part of this unbroken foundation, merely a natural rise in the organic ground of the place. On the dais, an altar as plain as Stonehenge; at the corner a small vase of flowers, a jot of color like a pulse.

Simple long benches, without backs, faced each other down the sides of the main part of the great chamber: the choir where the psalms and prayers were tossed lightly back and forth between the two sides, as if prayer were a matter of balance, the call-and-reply of singer and song incarnated in the antiphon.

At the far end of the chapel, past the dais and its altar, as if it were the true destination of any possible prayer, a floor-to-ceiling window framed a colossal redwood rooted a few feet on the other side of the glass. Planted in front of the tree and flowering—this is June, still spring in this northern place—a blazing pink scribble of rhododendron. All that rise of trunk, so obviously the *body*, its canopy of leaves way up there. It was a shout in the silent chamber.

I took an empty spot on one bench, next to beautiful Cecile with her long dark hair. At dinner she had been dressed in jeans and a plaid shirt. Now she wore over these the Cistercian cream-colored gown with big cowl and long sleeves, a garment as seamless as the building's poured floor.

The gowns were left on pegs at the back of the chapel behind a partition. As the nuns entered in their work clothes, their jeans or jumpers, through a side door from their quarters (there were enclosure areas, though no grilles or grates, just as at Donnie's monastery), they put on the ritual gowns, slipping them over their heads in a swift gesture, and floated in, suddenly timeless. The wool falling over their bodies behind the partition made the hushed, papery sound of wings suddenly folding.

People filtered in, retreatants from one door, the community from their hermitages scattered on the hills behind the communal part of the monastery, stopping for a moment to put on their cream garments. When everyone had been seated for some time, Cecile rose, walked forward to a candle on the raised dais by the flower, bowed, lit the candle, bowed again from the middle of her body, a full surrender, and returned to her place.

And then, following the sheet which indicated the readings for the day, we sang the ancient farewell to the day, passing the Hour back and forth across the space which I sensed we were meant to understand was our world.

TUESDAY

I woke at 4 a.m., freezing in the little room that had seemed snug and warm when I turned off the light to sleep. The cold was sour and mean, and there was no heater in the place. I slept and woke, off and on until 6:30, when it was time to get up for Morning Praise, the first Hour of the Office.

I piled on several layers of clothes and went out into the foggy night-day of morning. Along the brook trail, the wild iris still bloomed in the late spring of the place, looking chastened in the cold. Before I reached the chapel, my shoes and the cuffs of my corduroys were drenched with a dew so heavy it seemed as if it had rained in the night.

As I opened the chapel door, a low gong sounded, a Zen tone that did not inaugurate something, as a Western church bell does—the monastery had one of these, too, a clanger that sent its sharp metal into the air and brought people, in the medieval way, from work to community prayer. This low gong was different, an *Om* of a bell, and it brought to a close the hour of "sitting," the *zazen* meditation some of the nuns practiced.

The chapel had an area where mats and the hard round meditation pillows favored by Zen monks were laid out. The nuns of Rosethorn and several of the retreatants, including an Amer-

197

ican Buddhist, a man about thirty-five with the lean and smooth aspect of a steady meditator, had begun the day with an hour of *zazen*, before the canonical hour of Lauds—called now by the English term, Morning Praise. It was to this Eastern practice, Bob had told us the night before, that Thomas Merton was devoting himself when, late in 1968, he made his fateful journey to Asia.

"I think we have now reached a stage (long overdue) of religious maturity," Merton wrote at the time of his Asian pilgrimage, "at which it may be possible for someone to remain perfectly faithful to a Christian and Western monastic commitment, and yet to learn in depth from, say, a Buddhist discipline and experience . . . I believe that by openness to Buddhism, to Hinduism and to these great Asian traditions, we stand a wonderful chance of learning more about the potentiality of our own traditions . . . The combination of the natural techniques and the graces and the other things that have been manifested in Asia, and the Christian liberty of the gospel should bring us all at last to that full and transcendent liberty which is beyond mere cultural differences and mere externals."

It was 1968, "the killer year," as Merton called it, not knowing it would claim him, too, in December, electrocuted by a fan with faulty wiring in Bangkok. If religious impulse went anywhere in those years—Vietnam years; Merton was a keen protester of the American war there—it went East. My university friends were reading Alan Watts, Suzuki, digging Ginsberg not only for the psychedelic magic but for the big sustaining *Om* he sounded in the political gloom. Robert Pirsig was living in St. Paul then, and he and his friends started a Zen Center and managed to get a roshi to move to Minneapolis. People didn't argue about whether they believed in God or not—they tabled all that and signed up for meditation classes, loving the plain practice of it, ditching theology as if it were so much excess baggage meant to be dropped from the balloon's gondola as it rose and rose to the transcendent nirvana. People who knew nothing whatever about particle physics liked to say that "even physicists" thought there was something in the far reaches of their abstruse discipline to suggest—perhaps even to *prove* (voodoo word of modern belief)—that they and the saffron-robed monks doing *zazen* were on the same cosmic trail.

I missed all that. My university friends were writers, artists. I saw those from Lutheran and Episcopalian backgrounds go in for Eastern meditation in a big way, finding something genuine in the stripped-down style of Zen, something indisputably better than the Scotch-before-dinner habits of their Episcopal priest or the massive dreariness of the Lutheran Sunday bazaars of their childhoods, which were anything but bizarre. They loved the bare bones of "Zen," and they clawed at their Christian cages, thrusting imitation Basho poems between the bars.

I couldn't seem to get the message. I was still trying to nerve up to tell my dad I wasn't going to Mass on Sunday anymore. It was a James Joyce life all over again, full of rage and impotence at Mother Church. No religion, no meditation for me. My ambition was paganism. I went as far as pantheism, no further, just for the sake of Walt Whitman, my poet, who said you didn't have to go on a pilgrimage—just hit the open road.

But Cecile, my age, with her dark glistening hair and her heroically drawn features meant for the big screen, had told me the night before at dinner that as a graduate student in Southern California she had sought out various Eastern religions. She, too, was a cradle Catholic. "I was getting awfully mixed up with these other traditions. I decided I better stick with what I knew and go deeper." She had no interest in being a nun—someone who taught grade school, in her experience. She wasn't even aware that there were places for women to be this thing she felt herself to be—a monk. And then someone told her about Rosethorn, only a few years old at the time. She arrived the year after Merton had visited.

"In her red Spitfire," one of the older Belgian Sisters said.

"In my Spitfire," she said, smiling. "The car died. Sparkplugs couldn't take the damp up here. But I stayed."

The meditation cushions put away, and everyone now in place,

Cecile rose, as the night before, walked to the altar, the only sound the slight sighing of her cream wool garment as she moved forward. Again she bowed, again approached the candle and lit it—neither for light nor for heat, but for focus. Bowed her deep, sustaining bow to the God-who-is-who-was-and-who-will-be-now-and-forever. And we were together again with the ancient words. Not seizing the day, but something more mysterious: attaining it. The conveyance was praise. I rode it into the gray morning with everyone else.

Breakfast was oatmeal and apples, the beefsteak bread of the place, honey and homemade preserves. Lots of coffee, though some people, I saw, took herbal tea, a purity beyond me. We ate in silence, which Cecile had said the night before makes some people uncomfortable. "Listening to people chew," she said. "It takes some getting used to."

About thirty seconds for me. Immediately I loved sitting at the long tables on my little bench, which I pulled out soundlessly from its place under the table. I loved eating in silence, surrounded by others, but not needing to speak.

I sit across from Cecile: she takes her piece of bread, lays it flat on her plate, and spreads peanut butter and then apple butter across the plane of the slice in a serious, workmanlike way, as if she were organizing the plowing of a field for the morning. Then, with her statue-hands, their long, intelligent fingers moving precisely, without grandeur yet grand, she cuts the square into quads. And eats, attentively, turned slightly toward the big window, where she looks out to the rise of hill and the trees—and to the indication the patch of sky gives as to what the day will be: lovely.

Yet I wasn't looking at her, wasn't staring and figuring Cecile: wasn't taking one of my notes. This was entirely different, this taking-in-of-Cecile. And I didn't, in fact, take her in. It was a matter of being-with. The simple fact of proximity, leading to attention, leading to . . . appreciation. I felt it for Jeannine, too, and for the psychology professor at the next table, even for Bob, who had a too-wet smack and gulp to his chewing. It was fellow feeling so elemental it was experienced as blood tie, but without the emotion associated with *feeling*. Solidarity, then: human beings reduced to the mutual plain of munching. No personality to it, no individual story or quality making an appeal.

Strange how this is revealed: the kernel buried dead center in the black earth of silence and ready to sprout—it's not wisdom after all. It is compassion, that bread-and-butter grace, the communion we must kneel to receive.

Detail again

I stopped at the chapel before returning to my room, drawn to the big shadow of the place. The wall of window framing the basso profundo tree with its scraggle of pink rhododendron made an icon as eloquent as anything I'd stood before in Italy.

Some people speak of prayer as a need to surrender. All that swooning of the mystics, giving over to the Divine Lover. Bernini's St. Teresa in her ecstasy, still scandalizing the rationalists with the orgasmic joy of her prayer. But surrender doesn't *say* it—and even in silence, how I need a thing *said*. What is that impulse that has always been there, refuting logic and requiring song?

It must be the instinct for praise. A ferocious appetite for humility which we intuit is a proper recognition of our truth: We are not simply made, but embraced. Sing a new song to the Lord, for he has made you. Made you to sing. Surrender—surrender even your voice, enter this silence. And become song.

I have always had a powerful sense of something pulsing which I could not name but also could not deny: a dynamic existence beyond me, yet in me. Spirit it is called—and why not? The invisible essence that is everywhere, including within ourselves. It is the glorious impersonality of existence which throbs with the reality of this dream we call our life. It goes where it wills.

This rich experience of life is not personal, though it is interior. It is an aspect of what we know to be the Divine, to be God—who was called in Hebrew, the first language of our tradition, Yahweh. That is, Our Integrity. I wished to find this Integrity.

That is why I took to the pilgrimage trails, why I came here to this silent place near the Lost Coast. On the hunt for Our Integrity. I lived with It as a child. It was not happiness: I have no idea what a happy childhood is—or an unhappy one. As a child, I often felt an oddity inhabit me. It was related to silence, but it was not, as people sometimes speak of religion, a comfort. I was not aware of requiring comfort. This sensation of oddity was pleasure, a spreading delight. I lie on the bed in the flowery room my father has papered for me, and I am enfolded in the booming heart of the world as the chipped blue roller makes its way over the damp clay tennis court. The doves mourn in the morning, and everything is mixed up, and I can hear my mother saying I'm sleeping my life away and I smile.

Is that a happy childhood—the unfettered experience of the strangeness of existence, the pleasure of being caught up in the arms of creation? I stood under the cathedral elms on Linwood Avenue and looked at my arm: Why an arm, why a nose? Why *this* life? It was as if my personality were lodged just slightly askew in my body, and in the inevitable wriggle I made to settle them in correct register, I came upon these epiphanies of strangeness. And experienced this sensation of strangeness as pleasure. Nothing could be taken for granted, nothing was automatic. Yet everything—from my arm that bent in the middle with its small knob of elbow, to the elm's great umbrella of leaves on their splinted branches above me—everything, everything was part of one inseparable thing. It was—It. And It really existed, outside me and inside me. These two facts came together, like cymbals crashing on a downbeat: they hushed me, they gave me that first exquisite taste of silence which was also a draught of awe. Call it surrender. But I always understood it to be song.

I walked back along the brook trail to my room, fell on the narrow bed, and slept past Noon Prayer. Didn't hear Bob bustling out, didn't hear the bell. Slept out the hours I'd lost in the cold night, slept out the lethargy, slept beyond prayers and good intentions, slept away the life I'd brought on my back.

Woke hours later, the natural way: from hunger. And went up to dinner, finally arrived at this hidden place ravenous, my appetite intact.

After evening prayer, it is only 8:30 p.m., still light, but the day is over. And me a night person. But I've given over to the rhythm. I walk slowly back to my room, taking a circuitous route. Hundreds of wild iris, roses, columbine along the road. I look up and see a songbird, very high up, its belly suddenly turned gold by the sun. The rays of the evening sun going down play on the underside of things.

Then, coming onto the county road before turning back to the monastery road, I am looking into the eyes of a doe standing stock-still in an open clearing by a wood. It takes me some moments to comprehend that this is an animal, not a statue. Or, I become a statue myself for a few moments. The arresting sensation of being regarded by a pure wild creature: the mind shuts down.

She looks at me as if I am merely a part of the landscape which has detached itself. I do not feel looked at as myself but as a figment. Disorienting at first, then another pleasure, and somehow droll. I realize I'm smiling, as if the doe has told a good one.

I want it to go on—this moment of being part of the same fabric, the same joke. But of course, at that instant, the deer, whose head is small and narrow as an elegant woman's, turns and canters off in long, refined strides. Not fast, but fluid. She stops for a moment before taking herself more completely away, in a final leap from clearing to woods, where she is lost to me.

That night I dream a ledgerful of dreams. All the people I thought had come to hate me over the years show up. But I've been mistaken: they don't hate me at all. They are simply bored. I sympathize with them: I keep telling the same dull story. We are at a party, after all, and the tale I keep trying to tell is long and complicated and from so long ago they can't be expected to care anymore.

A kind older woman, someone's aunt—the party is in her lovely house—comes up. She has great brown eyes and an ascetic thinness I understand is meant to convey compassion. Her nephew, my date (the word of the dream to describe him), has said his aunt does not believe in God. "Not particularly," she agrees, as if this were a detail. "But I pray without ceasing." She has seen my difficulty, my inability to get my old friends to follow my endless version of how things went wrong. She intercedes. She encourages me to continue speaking, though everything I'm trying to tell happened long ago and is too complicated.

But you must understand, everyone is quite busy. In fact, she says with a smile, *I won't be able to stay myself.* And she turns, taking the air in that fluid stride I recognize, the one I saw earlier in the evening, and is lost to me again in the black-gold twilight.

WEDNESDAY

Summer solstice. Woke to the high whine of chain saws already taking the redwoods on a parcel of land nearby, the sun not yet risen. The loggers get to work even before the contemplatives.

We gathered at 5:30 to walk up to a meadow for Morning Praise, a special outdoor reading of the Office in honor of the solstice. The idea was not only to greet the summer sun on its first morning but to acknowledge the absent trees where the sun would rise.

These were the trees the community had been trying to save, along with a coalition of neighbors and environmental organizations. There were community meetings, negotiations, lawsuits, temporary injunctions, sustaining injunctions, decisions handed down, decisions overturned, judgments pending: struggle. In between courtroom decisions, the logging went on. Right now, this parcel of land was being "harvested," the abbess had told us the evening before, crooking two fingers of each hand to make ironic quotation marks around the word.

The morning was cold. People trailed out of their rooms with several layers of clothes on, still groggy from sleep. Only Mary, the retired biology teacher, emerged looking fresh, ready for the day, in creased black wool trousers, her Hepburn white

turtleneck smooth, a red kerchief knotted at the throat as a stroke of jaunty color. We met the nuns coming from the monastery on the main road; they gave us the readings for the day. The climb to the high meadow was steep, the grasses drenched with dew, and the sky pale and uncertain, the no-weather of pre-dawn. It was the instant before things begin, the most receptive moment of the day, Merton's downbeat stroke when, he said, "the first chirps of the waking day birds make the '*point vierge*' of the dawn under a sky as yet without real light, a moment of awe and inexpressible innocence."

Timeless time, the receptive temporal pivot when *being* hangs suspended, unadorned by will or intention. "For the birds, there is not a time that they tell," Merton wrote of this moment of the day, "but the virgin point between darkness and light, between nonbeing and being . . . when creation in its innocence asks permission to be once again, as it did on the first morning that ever was." The virgin instant. He was writing of the contemplative's signature moment, its icon the virgin, a girl emerging at daybreak. We climbed into the frail light of this instant from the dirt road, up the steep grassy slope. The sun, its great bald head gold with a fontanel of red, was just crowning across the ridge from us eternally innocent, piercing our night eyes.

That old monster, innocence. My ingenue life which had been clutched even more fiercely in the stranglehold of willful Catholic naïveté than James Joyce's furious Irish artist lads—who at least were boys and meant to break the rules. I had done everything I could think of to wrestle free: broke my parents' hearts, hardened my own, mixed it up every way I could, tried to be a furious artist myself. My methods had been many: sex as freedom; books as tactical missles; the outward mobility, away from the soul, of intellectual life; passionate politics; and a string of wrong romances—I suited up in all the knightly armor I could find to ride against the convent school ingenue who refused to convert to the secular faith of the real world.

Or maybe she was simply a failed pagan, incapable of forging a different self. In the end, who have I always been? *You've*

been well trained, Mme X with the gleaming chignon had said in Assisi after taking one look at me, *chez les soeurs*. By the good Sisters.

"You're so . . . wholesome," a man at a cocktail party said when I was past forty. "I hope you don't mind my saying so." I minded. I seethed, but I was crushed by my old convent courtesy and smiled the smile. "I mean," he said, "you have such wonderful enthusiasm." Worse and worse. And how many times, in every sort of social and professional setting, when I have said I felt I really *should* do this or that, has the smooth voice of someone I hardly know, speaking from the authority of a secular background, told me, "Ah, that's your Catholic good-girl background again." And I must smile, must agree to see this not as bigotry but as yet another invitation to sign on with the real world—*as we affectionately call it*, Donnie says, smiling, never offended by anyone, going her way as purely as a cat.

I wanted to betray it all, wanted to join that real world where no good girls are allowed, except as decorative touches here and there. *Catholic? Well, I was brought up Catholic, but of course* . . . I wanted to radiate not this ridiculous girlish light but the dark fire of ordeals and events, episodes and affairs. I was terrified I was missing out on Life, that thing called "experience," all because I'd been held in the cooing Catholic embrace too long and was forever marked. But marked by what? The indelible brand of innocence, which is to be marked by an absence, a vacancy. By nothing at all.

Now, all these years later, to stand on a hill at sunrise with a bunch of nuns who don't look like nuns, everybody wearing sweatshirts and big sweaters, my girlish fury burned, the embers still glowing, joining our light to the new sun of midsummer, mid-life: to find a *use* for innocence, after all. Tears spiked my eyes. *I can't help it, it's how I am.* Like the hot metal of a Linotype, these ordinary words cast themselves across my mind.

The words could have been "Lord, have mercy," or "Forgive me, for I have sinned." They *were* those words, in fact, those prayerful words of old, but neatly camouflaged in my modern *life is the problem* voice that can't resist ripping the religious art off the walls: *I can't help it, it's how I am.* Finally, prayer. After all my running away from it, and then running after it to Assisi and Lourdes.

Standing in a circle of prayer, shivering in the morning cold, with all these strangers. It was another of those moments of oddity carried forward from childhood—the world is so *funny*, I used to think, lying in my flower-papered bedroom. How funny prayer turned out to be. At that moment of saying the words, feeling them course through me like electrical impulses as unbidden as the synapses of my brain, I understood prayer is, after all, a plain statement of fact. An admission of existence. That's all. A surrender of self to the All of history and oblivion. Surrender of intention into the truth of a life. You don't get to live Life—that thing I feared I was missing. You just live a life. This one. Was I crying because the sun was rising? It can't help being innocent either, every day of its life, that old, burning baby born anew.

We had left our cells during the most personal hour of all—the dark night of the soul and all its experience; it gave way at this virginal morning instant to the anonymous presence of being itself. This was the immaculate moment we had climbed into, drenched by the long dewy grasses, achieving the high meadow by 6 a.m., where we turned east, instinctively toward the first rays of summer which we had come to meet. Here I met myself, here I said my first prayer. *I can't help it, it's how I am.*

And, looking up, was greeted by another kind of purity: the perfectly straight lines of the logging operation. For in spite of the high hysterical hiss of the saws, the gouge of land was not a jagged rent. Facing us across the distance of the broad valley where the monastery lay, the ridge seemed to be divided chastely into lots, and the big trees had been taken in a calm, methodical way, as if they saw the logic of it themselves and had lined up helpfully for the operation. This was "clear cutting," the take-no-prisoners form of logging that fells everything before it, chain saws taking down stands of redwood and Douglas fir like a John Deere tractor-mower sweeping a suburban lawn on a lazy Saturday afternoon.

The truth was, when the abbess had explained the night before about the logging and the liturgy of the morning Office, I hadn't cared. Not really. Against cutting the redwoods? Sure. But it was the vacuous, inauthentic sentiment of my knee-jerk liberal soul. Yet now, facing the gap in the ridge, I felt sickened, mortally ashamed. Back at the drive-thru redwood.

It was the amiable presence of a plan that depressed me, more even than the fact of the ugly rupture across the stately eastern ridge. Or maybe it was the *appearance* of a plan that troubled me: those nicely drawn slices bespoke order, care, the tidiness of a mind at work. The blameless tending of the garden.

One of the Sisters read the opening lines of Genesis, and I settled my mind on that earlier moment: the division of light from darkness, before Eden. Before we creatures were given our miserable task and took it up with our ferocious appetite: to rule the garden. When the sun finally winked over the rim of the bald ridge, it hurt my eyes, coming on strong.

"I can't believe how angry that made me," I said softly to Cecile after we finished the Office and were walking back down the steep hill to the monastery for breakfast.

"Seeing it like that," she said. "Yes. It hits you." She paused, and said almost shyly, as if she were afraid I might take it as a correction, "But those are people doing that. We can see the trees—or where the trees were. I think we went up there to see—what we couldn't see."

"The loggers?" I said.

"Human beings," she said, smiling slightly as if she were apologizing for a race of aliens she had come to love. She stuffed her hands in the sleeves of her big lumpy sweater and fell behind, sending me back into silence, where she left me to make my peace with my kind.

Back to the garden then. Where it all began.

Thomas, the gardener Brother, was a man of few words. He didn't actually make an announcement that he needed help in the garden, but somehow the message was conveyed. If you showed up at the gate, a flimsy thing made of grayed wood and

chicken wire near the hut where he kept his tools and his rudimentary greenhouse, he was grateful and always had something that needed doing.

After breakfast, that's where I went. The chicken-wire fence
that enclosed the garden plot was covered with climbing roses,
and there were fruit trees here and there, old and knobbed as
those worker trees often are. Thomas was already busy in his
shed, transplanting seedlings. He was small, but one of those
little men who seem bred so thoroughly of hard labor that the
smallness comes always as a surprise. He seemed not small but
built sensibly close to the earth, his element. He was wiry and
had the face of an elderly angel. Most of the time, except in
chapel, he wore a navy watchman's cap.

His hands, cracked and built on a bigger scale than his slight
frame, were wonderful to look at. He was missing his ring finger
on the right hand, but it wasn't disfiguring. It suited him, as if
to have both hands whole would, in his case, have been the
deformity. A couple of other fingers on that hand were covered
with Band-Aids, suggesting that he was often banged up.

They were hands I knew. The hands of the growers in St. Paul
years ago, in the summers I worked at my father's greenhouse.
Sometimes I was delegated to spend a whole morning inching
my way down one row of flats and up another, pinching back
geraniums. Charlie Metz, the greenhouse foreman, was a big
man, but with these same hands, cracked and much wounded.
His yellowed nails seemed made of horn. Hands I would know
anywhere. And here they were.

Charlie had allowed me to keep the flowers I clipped, and I
left the geranium house with bunches of salmon-colored or
engine-red flowers I needed a wheelbarrow to cart away. But
when I attempted to cram them into my father's Ford at the end
of the day, he frowned. "Take those to the dump," he said. They
were a limp mess by then, but I fought their fate. "All right,
make yourself a bouquet," he said, "but ditch the rest." As I
rolled the wheelbarrow to the dump, he called after me, "Three,
five, seven," which was his artistic reminder: Every bouquet

should be composed of odd numbers. I never questioned the logic of this law. Its rightness was obvious and profound; there was a slight off-kilter quality to life, something perhaps missing but not something mourned for. This imbalance was life's way. In art it was necessary to acknowledge it: three, five, seven.

Now Thomas loaned me a pair of big rubber boots and gave me a tour of his fenced garden. It was a big area, divided like a diminutive neighborhood of several toy blocks, running along streets that intersected, allowing for a place to kneel or crouch down to work on the slightly raised beds.

My assignment was a bed of onions, hardly sprouted. I took the bucket Thomas handed me for the weeds, and two burlap seed sacks to kneel on as I worked my way down the onion street. I had the place to myself, and the day was fresh. "Early is best," Thomas said, looking up and around, as if inspecting the day and finding he could approve. He turned and went back to the shed.

I knelt on the seed sacks and disappeared for three hours. That's how it was. My mind went to the roots. I disentangled, with more patience than I knew I possessed, the fragile onions, which were hardly distinguishable from the weeds. Sometimes I yanked up a few onions by accident. Then I crammed the white wiggles of rootlets back in the crumbly soil madly, as if burying a secret. But even at such a frantic moment, I was gone, absorbed, not thinking. As if I had been gathered into the very psalm of the day, not singing, but song:

> *You keep your pledge with wonders . . .*

> *You care for the earth, give it water;*
> *you fill it with riches.*
> *Your river in heaven brims over*
> *to provide it grain.*

> *You provide for the earth;*
> *you drench its furrows;*

you level it, soften it with showers;
you bless its growth.
You crown the year with your goodness.
Abundance flows in your steps;
in the pastures of the wilderness it flows.

The hills are girded with joy,
the meadows covered with flocks,
the valleys are decked with wheat.
They shout for joy, yes, they sing.

When the bell rang for Noon Prayer, I put the seed sacks away in the shed and left the big boots by Thomas's door. I walked up the brook path to the chapel, took my place next to Cecile, and stood in the softened light of that vaulted chamber. It was all one thing. We passed the day's Word between us on the immaculate trays of chant, me still on my knees with the onions, one choir bowing, offering, to the other.

I called home that night from a telephone in the vestibule room where Jeannine had greeted me with the pine-needle tea, something like a hundred years ago on Monday. Everyone else had gone back to their rooms after Vespers, and I had the place to myself.

My husband answered on the first ring. "I was hoping it would be you!" The familiar voice, eager even over the distance.

I spoke softly. I sounded strange; I sounded slowed down, a record playing at the wrong speed. For the first time in my life: a person of few words.

I had been looking forward to this call all day, but now I heard myself answering his questions in a delayed voice that seemed transmitted from a location farther removed than California. He understood it before I did.

"You're really in there, aren't you?" he said. Fascinated, but a little wistful. "You'll come home, won't you?" It was our joke, after all my shrine-hopping and the visits to Donnie's monastery.

I was looking out at the little Zen garden of stones and succulents. "On Monday," I said. Even to me, this soft voice sounded uncertain.

THURSDAY

I waited, I waited for the Lord
and He stooped down to me;
He heard my cry.

He drew me from the deadly pit,
from the miry clay.
He set my feet upon the rock
and made my footsteps firm.

He put a new song into my mouth,
praise of our God.
Many shall see and fear
and shall trust in the Lord.

You do not ask for sacrifice and offerings,
but an open ear.
You do not ask for holocaust and victim.
Instead, here am I.

Copied from the Psalter. The ancient words, but I write them as if they're off the wire and I'm a journalist taking down the latest, my ballpoint moving fast over the page. News I need.

214

At breakfast, the apple jelly and the honey are so good I eat spoonfuls, like soup. Cecile smiles.

•

The white thumbs of radishes: a bucketful, two hours.

•

Lunch. The retreatants eat separately from the community, except for the serene, silent breakfast. We have an airy room with sliding doors that feels like a porch, and the Sisters bring us our meals there. A portrait of a beautiful woman, framed in severe black, takes up a central position on the wall we face. Who is she, we keep asking each other, but we forget to ask the Sister who brings the food. We forget because it's hard to break the habit of silence, though we've been told we're free to talk at lunch and dinner if we wish.

The woman in the portrait looks a little like the *Casablanca* Ingrid Bergman: that lyric beauty, that ineffable suffering bred of kindness and strength. The image of the Virgin Mary I carry forward from girlhood: not the perfect Catholic wife-and-mother, but the woman who "ponders all these things in her heart." The contemplative face. No one knows who she is, but as the days go by, people give her a story: she's probably the foundress of the community, Bob says. Maybe she's some early twentieth-century saint, someone else suggests. The photograph, greatly enlarged, does seem somehow from an earlier era. Who's a twentieth-century saint? the psychology professor asks. Nobody can think of a twentieth-century saint. "St. Maria Goretti?" Sister Jane suggests. But we all agree she's too old; Maria Goretti was a teenager. This woman is mature; her beauty partakes of wisdom.

Though there's no rule against talking, people fall silent anyway, and conversation starts up slowly, almost regretfully, at each meal. Today at our table the talk, once started, ran almost entirely to animals or flowers people had observed. Human activities have dimmed. We keep meaning to find out who this presiding beauty on the wall is, but the enterprises of other life forms have become significant, worth reporting. The human recedes.

For a moment there at lunch, we were a table of squirrels gathered around our bowls of nuts, telling the day's news. Everyone had something to say, interrupting one another to describe a bird, a cloud, the blue paper of an iris unfurling.

Mass late in the afternoon, just before dinner. At the time given over to personal intercessions, the nuns all praying for the big things: world hunger, El Salvador, the Middle East, the long list that is the contemplative lot. Then Thomas, who never speaks: "I pray for everyone I ever met," he says, head down, "especially those I never think about." One of those sappy remarks that aren't sappy, that capture the evanescence of relationship.

To pray for those we never think about. Especially those. They're all *there*, that crowd of former intimacies, or the potential ones, all the meetings of eyes, the brief lifts of the drapery of indifference. The choral murmur in each life, composed not only of the divas of the family with their grand arias, or the lost loves, the broken friendships with their stuttered refrains. These others are here, too, the people on trains, on airplanes, sitting in restaurants, waiting at the dentist. The pilgrims and strangers, the lost and the luckily forgotten. All the cameos in a life. For them, yes, for those whose names are never spoken. They are not loved: love them.

And Thomas himself, whom I will never see again and will not think of: for him. His clear voice, surprisingly deep for that small, bent body. And the slightly hesitant, searching tone of the voice as he tries to articulate his impulse. He wants to get it right.

> *You have put into my heart a greater joy*
> *than they have from abundance of corn and new wine.*
>
> *I will lie down in peace and sleep comes at once,*
> *for you alone, Lord, make me dwell in safety.*

FRIDAY

What is prayer?
I make a list:

> *Praise*
> *Gratitude*
> *Begging/pleading/cutting deals*
> *Fruitless whining and puling*
> *Focus*

There the list breaks off; I had found my word. Prayer only looks like an act of language; fundamentally it is a position, a placement of oneself. Focus. Get there, and all that's left to say is the words. They come: from ancient times (here, the round of Psalms, wheeling through the seasons endlessly in the Office), from the surprisingly eloquent heart (taciturn Thomas last night with his intercession, precise as a poet), from the gush and chatter of the day's detail longing to be rendered.

So what is silence?

Silence speaks, the contemplatives say. But really, I think, silence sorts. An ordering instinct sends people into the hush where the voice can be heard. This is the sorting intelligence

217

of poetry, marked by the unbroken certainty of rhythm, perfect pitch, the placing of things in right order as in metrical form. Not rigid categories, but the recognition of a shape always there but ordinarily obscured by—what? By noise, which is ourselves trying to do the sorting in an order that may be a heroic effort but is bound to be a fantasy.

Silence, that inspired dealer, takes the day's deck, the life, all in a crazy heap, lays it out, and plays its flawless hand of solitaire, every card in place. Scoops them up, and does it all over again.

And the dark night of the soul?

Is the joker constantly turning up? It's in every hand.

•

Woke stiff as a chair, every muscle creaking. Yesterday I pulled the radishes. Today they're pulling me.

•

"Working in the garden," I said to Thomas, "really focuses the mind."

"Yes," he said, as if this were a new observation, "it frees the mind."

Focus. Freedom. The same thing to him.

And Cecile the other night saying, "Dogma. Always a thorn. Dogma is only the expression of the deeper symbol. If it's treated as the thing that counts, it kills symbol. Just kills it *dead*." The assumption that symbol is alive, not a unit of fantasy. The only absolutely real thing, but frighteningly vulnerable, ever a potential murder victim. A life requiring protection, as any creature does.

And Donnie one time, trying yet again to explain to me: "It's when the Church tries to tame the metaphors that we get in trouble. You can't control the images. That's not what they're for. You have to get *in* there with them."

So that's what this monastic life is, after all, and its core element, prayer, both so devoted to symbol. They aren't "poetic."

They are poetry itself. Not in a decorative sense, not even having to do with an aesthetic experience. Rather, like poetry, monastic life seizes upon daily life and renders it as symbol, attuned to season, to hour, to the cycle on which our lives depend.

The praying monastery as life within poetry. Or say it this way: to become the lines and white space of a poem. That's what the Divine Office is, after all: time reckoned as poetry, hours made into verses, with the white space of silence, work (another kind of silence), and community in between the stanzas.

"They knew what they were doing," Thomas said, looking around the garden, "when they got into agriculture."

Like the Franciscans in Assisi, like Donnie, he speaks of his medieval forebears as of near neighbors. He meant Benedict and the early monastic founders, the ones who took silence out of the desert (a mistake? well, an inevitability) and put it to work in the great monastery hives of what, strangely, we call the Dark Ages. More truly, the Silent Ages. We like to think nothing happened then. Just waiting around in the dark for the Renaissance to screw in the light bulb. Time stopped. Nothing went forward. It went inward. And what was found there, we choose not to know. We leave it buried. It is a poem, and we do not read poetry anymore.

Just like Thaddeus and Francine and all the Franciscans in Assisi, Thomas speaks of that medieval history as *here*, immediate, still warm. Not only because his life here mimics the way of life laid down then, but because he knows, from the literature and *secundum traditionem*, the very people who created or developed the model he lives. He knows them well: there is no person as real as a fictive one, someone made not by the writer finally but the Benedict, the Francis, the Clare created by the humble reader, Thomas, willing to give his full attention. That is, his life, as Donnie was saying.

•

So teach us to number our days,
that we may get us a heart of wisdom.

Noon prayer, Psalm 90. The contemplative point of view: time turned into poetry. The day is a verse, the season a stanza. Number the days: know you will die. Wisdom belongs to the heart, go there.

•

Some years ago, the monastery and the local marijuana growers (this is old hippie country, hereabouts) found themselves united in common cause. Their mutual adversary: the helicopters that the drug enforcement officers use to scan for marijuana fields. The nuns didn't like the noise; the grass farmers—well, obviously. This from Thomas, eyes smiling.

•

After lunch, I went to the grove. Jeannine had told us about it the first day, part of the monastery property just off the county road where a great stand of redwoods endures from—who knows—well before the time of Benedict.

I found the place easily, just off the road behind a fence I had no trouble clambering over. Another sensation of enclosure, once over the fence: I was *in*. All around the gathering of the chiefs, great redwoods established like feudal lords on their mounds of earth surrounded by a spongy field of pine needles.

Wild iris bloomed everywhere in clumps, along with early wild roses and violets, and (Jeannine had taught us to recognize it) poison oak. I wandered on, drawn forward from one lordly redwood estate to another. Maidenhair fern filtered the light that reached the ground from the thick leaf cover above. Below was the same brook that cuts through the property nearer the monastery, the one I walk by to get to the chapel. Dappled light from the redwood leaf canopy above, birdsong, the cathedral of the trees. Dreamy.

Suddenly my heart seized up in terror. In a panic, I realized I didn't know which way was out. I had just ambled in, wandered any which way. The panic of adrenaline coursed through me, as primitive as if I were a rabbit sniffing a predator. Prickles of fright froze on the back of my neck, ran down my arms.

I did what I've read that people—foolish people—do lost in the wilderness: started to run. But just as I began to bolt, I remembered that no matter where I was I couldn't be far from the road, from the known world. Furthermore, the brook was down there. The brook, if need be, could lead me back.

But then the feeling of dislocation came back even stronger, crazier. I couldn't tell which way the brook was going, which way was *back*. And *was* it the same brook? Maybe it was another thing altogether. The urge to bolt, to run screaming, was intense. I forced myself to stop, sheerly out of the even deeper panic that once I started running I would truly be lost. A heap of bones a hunter finds ten years later. I'd been in the grove only ten minutes, and yet I was grisly with terror, lost in the fairy-tale woods no innocent wayfarer escapes from alive.

I stood there panting.

Then, almost casually, the path leading to the wooden fence I'd climbed over presented itself. And I was out, safe, my heart still pounding.

It had been a forest-primeval fright, something far older than I. The redwoods seemed at that moment of terror not sacred (as everyone has been saying of the grove) but sinister. My fright was not simply a fear of being confined, not just claustrophobia (though that was part of it). It was an awful dread of the great beasts who seemed capable of seizing me . . . and having their way with me. A virginal terror of being laid hold of, violated. The sacred was phallic there, and meant no good to a girl. Something like that, a crazy sensation.

Walking back to the monastery on the county road, I realized I'd picked up a sliver in my palm. In my initial hysterical bolt, I must have somehow hit against a tree. Then a brief snapshot flashed from the nightmare: I'd hurled myself at one of the redwoods. I'd scraped my hand against the bark. What had I been doing? Taking up arms against the feudal lord of the place? Begging for mercy? There were no lepers in the grove, but I had leapt from my terror-heart, wanting out, the opposite of Francis, who ran madly to get into the dark of the scary wildwood.

Back in my room, I managed to get the sliver out with a tweezer, a bare figment of the tree, long and clearly russet. It came out smoothly, in a single piece. I swabbed the palm with alcohol. It stung briefly, but there was no blood, no wound at all.

SATURDAY

The last full day. The social urge reasserts itself, people talking more, the temporary hermits molting back to type. Bob ticks off the places he's gone for retreats, rank-orders them as if he's working for Frommer. New Camaldelese at Big Sur: bigger rooms, your own full bathroom, plus a patio with a view of ocean; tea and coffee available all the time. Tassajara, where there's a sauna, and families and couples can go together (nude beach—you have to go Zen for that). A place on the Oregon coast, very wild—for hermits. And Taizé in France, his farthest foray: go there just for the music; the food and the amenities are the pits.

The Berkeley psychology professor has been reading *The Medieval Imagination* by Le Goff. The point, according to Le Goff, he says, is not that Christianity is dead or even moribund, but since about 1850 it has not enjoyed the "near monopoly" it once held "in the realm of ideology." Like Cecile and Donnie, trying to turn off the cold shower of dogma. *You have to get* in *there.* The Berkeley professor has thought it over: now, he says, is the time to be a Christian, now that Christianity isn't the ruling social system of the West. He makes the same distinction Felix

223

made in Assisi, though he uses different words: he's here, he says, to find a contemplative path within his own tradition, not a catechism, not even a moral code. "Secular humanism does morality just fine," he says. "It does a lot just fine. It just doesn't give you prayer."

Felix said St. Francis was trying to save Christianity from Christendom. But Felix is tougher than this psychology professor, whose reasoning reminds me, I must admit, of my own; Felix sees that Christendom is ever with us. You can't just think it off the map, out of history. Felix, Donnie, Bridget—they refuse the temptation to divide their religion into categories. No good faith/bad faith for them. *You have to get in there*—with all of it. No innocence, no virgin faith for those old veterans. *Hi, troops*, Thaddeus had said, falling naturally into military jargon, the language of Christendom, anointed knights riding against the Other in the name not of the Poor Man but of the Lord Pope.

"She's a whore," Felix said one day, quoting one of the Berrigan brothers as we sat with our coffee at the Minerva in Assisi, "our Mother Church." And Bridget did not laugh and cry, "Oh, lad!"; her eyes went sad. But the Church is their Mother all the same. Perhaps in the end Felix stays not only for Christianity but for Christendom, too. He is a contemplative and maybe stays for the *drama* of Christendom, which is an astonishing replica of the brute habits of power which history restages age after age. If contemplatives live the life of the gaze which is the deepest prayer, then they must try to see it all. Prayer as focus is not a way of limiting what can be seen; it is a habit of attention brought to bear on all that is. And who is it we pray to here in the great gray chapel: *the God who is, who was, and who will be for ages unending. Amen.* The God inside and outside history.

Merton had thoughts on the question of focus in prayer and how prayer fits with the reality of history and politics, Bob says, a quote from his man at the ready in his notebook: "The contemplative life must provide an area, a space of liberty, of silence, in which possibilities are allowed to surface and new choices—

beyond routine choice—become manifest. It should create a new experience of time, not as stopgap stillness, but as *'temps vierge'*—not a blank to be filled or an untouched space to be conquered and violated, but a space which can enjoy its own potentialities and hopes—and its own presence to itself. One's *own* time. But not dominated by one's own ego and its demands. Hence open to others—*compassionate* time, rooted in the sense of common illusion and in criticism of it."

The lean Buddhist says that sounds like the Dalai Lama's point about Buddhist practice: "Know the sufferings although there is nothing to know; relinquish the causes of misery although there is nothing to relinquish; be earnest in cessation although there is nothing to cease; practice the means of cessation though there is nothing to practice."

"In other words," Ann, the elderly blind nun, says, her airy voice cheerful and deadpan, "pray the Rosary." It takes the Buddhist a moment; then he grins. Big Dalai Lama grin.

After lunch, several of us decide to drive to the ocean, the wilderness parkland of the Lost Coast, where Merton went to look for a possible hermitage site. Bob is a-twitter, has his camera, his books in a backpack: his pilgrimage. The rest of us, I suspect, are looking for some action, some excuse. I am. It isn't boredom. Nobody seems bored: there is already a lot of talk about not wanting to leave tomorrow. But some sort of finale, an *act* amid all the lush inaction of the unbroken week, seems called for.

I look at my notebook, the stranded sentences marooned on blank pages: prayer has done this. Prayer and time. Strange time. In fact, this week is a blip, barely long enough to shed the world's clock. But the very sameness of each day has rendered an eternity: if Monday is Tuesday is Wednesday is day after day to ages unending, then maybe we have pulled a thread of timelessness from the giant weave of the world. *Won't the time just drag?* a friend asked me when I left home. *I'd be bored out of my mind.* But the days have soaked me up like a blotter.

"I think," I told Cecile at dinner the night before, "if I had entered here, thirty years would have gone by before I decided whether it was for me."

"Something like that," she said.

Elaine, a financial planner from Los Angeles (she handed out her business card at lunch, not to drum up business, but because people wanted to exchange addresses, though everyone suddenly had money questions for her), has offered her Volvo station wagon for the trip to the coast. We pile in: in the back seat Mary, the spry retired biology teacher who reminds me not only of Katharine Hepburn but of Lollie on "The Road to Assisi," her wiry persistence, stopping to inspect the wildflowers; next to her in the middle, Jean, the Sister who teaches grade school in Oakland, frowning from sheer seriousness; me with watercolors and notebook behind Elaine. In the front, Edwina, the Corondolet Sister who introduced herself the first day as "a language monster": she works as an interpreter. Unlike Jean, who frowns all the time, Edwina frowns only, it seems, when Bob is speaking.

Bob takes the front passenger seat, reads relevant passages from Merton, shows us a picture of the tree under which Merton meditated: the Merton Tree. We're going to see the tree for ourselves in less than an hour, but we all grab for the book, stare at the bare bones of the leafless tree as if we mustn't miss the opportunity.

The power of the image. Or maybe, the authority of the frame: there it is, the Merton Tree, caught and contained on the glossy page of the book. An example of what Merton and his Buddhist teachers would call "the common illusion." We reach for it, an apple in Eden. More essential to us than the tree we're driving to.

We arrive finally, after the slow ride on the rugged dirt road: a contemplative's stripped locale, all vista, windswept as Monte Subasio above Assisi. And there's the Tree, across from the ranger's house, a Medusa of driftwood. Beyond it, the great confusion of sea and sky. The beach is far below, an impossible destination.

We leave the car by the ranger's house. The road leads farther along the Lost Coast, a jagged crown running high above the black beach and the crashing steel water. But the road is badly rutted, too much for the Volvo. It's a hiker's trail now. Any farther, you go on your own steam. Bob is out ahead, hot-footing it to a place he's sure, from his texts, Merton got to. He has been breathlessly recounting the Merton life. "I'm a convert," he has confessed, "solely because of Merton." He has much lore. Merton had a passionate affair toward the end of his life with a gorgeous woman. It was real love, but in the end he decided he was a monk. It broke the woman's heart. "I heard that," Edwina says.

Bob has more. Tells us that John Howard Griffin, Merton's friend, died as a result of the injections he took to make him look black so he could write *Black Like Me*. "He knew when he took those injections," Bob says, eyes saucering wide, "that he was done for. I call that social action."

Edwina watches him go up the trail alone. "That boy's a talker," she says, and walks firmly in the opposite direction. She stands now by herself, advertising solitude, arms crossed tightly in front of her, hugging her sweater, at the edge of land, staring out at the refreshing abstraction of sea and sky.

Elaine and Mary settle in together at a picnic table with a thermos of coffee. Elaine says she is taking time off from her financial planning job and is going to Medjugorje. Mary, very Katharine Hepburn, says, "You know, I've never had a taste for that sort of thing." And then, wiry being with a keen, sharp voice, "I want to get to Salvador."

That leaves Jean and me. We begin walking up the trail, Bob already far ahead. "We'll just go till we want to stop," Jean says. "Just to see what the view is farther on. Do you think that's a good idea?"

It's been a strange week for her, she says. So peaceful. Unreal. She teaches at a parish in Oakland where it's impossible, "I mean absolutely impossible," to imagine the kids not getting into drugs. They come out of school, out of their houses, anywhere they go, and there are the dealers or the addicts, everywhere. "It's their childhood," she says.

She has a wildflower book. "I don't know any of the names," she says. "I grew up in the city. You know, I can't seem to match anything up with the pictures in the book. They're drawings. Photographs would be better, maybe. Take out the guesswork." This seriously troubles her. The frown deepens.

Rosethorn, she says, the life there, it's so peaceful, it's an apparition, too lovely to wholly believe in. "I guess I'm suffering from what they call burnout," she says.

But what's really troubling her, she says, has to do with her younger sister in San Francisco. "My married sister," she says. When their mother died, it was left to Jean to sell her house in the Sunset district. Her sister got involved, brought in a real estate agent, set the price.

But Jean already had someone in mind. "I didn't need the agent," she says. "I even convinced her to come down on the price." While she was cleaning out her mother's house, she'd fallen into conversation with the man across the street. "Chinese," she says. "They like the Sunset. A lot of them are there now."

The man had a brother who wanted the house, would be perfect for it. The children of the two families could play together, grow up together. "My sister and I never had cousins," she says, as if this lack makes everything clear. In the end, she got rid of the agent, came down on the price, practically gave the place to the man's brother.

That was over two years ago. The brother has never lived in the house. He uses it as income property. He never comes by; who knows if he even has any children. "They're good at business, I guess," she says—that's what her sister has told her; her sister, who is furious and says Jean made a mess of the whole thing. "She says business is all they care about."

Jean sees it differently, but she can't get her point across.

She's been taken advantage of—"I know that"—but her sister won't budge an inch. "There's more to it." But she hasn't figured out how to explain the bigger picture so her sister will listen.

"She thinks I threw it all away years ago," she says, a ghost of an expression that might be a smile if she let go but is instead a painful grimace. "My vocation."

What's left after thirty years is the exhausted frown, the raw nerves, and absolutely no confidence in herself, even to know a daisy when she sees one without a clear photograph to prove it. A life of too much giving, too much trying to make it right for everybody. Love as a form of fret.

"Do you think that's true," she asks me, her terrible frown as deep as it was for the drugged childhoods, the lost sister, the unidentified wildflower, the whole world of woe, "what Bob said about John Howard Griffin, how he died? How does he know? Was it in one of his books? Could that really happen? Isn't it awful? Or is that a martyr in our times? Is that what it is? What do you think?"

Our last dinner together. We eat with the community, as we did our first night. Though I've hardly spoken to any of these people, I feel I know them. And I feel known. Not *known*, but taken in. What you're supposed to do with pilgrims and strangers: they've done it here. I felt it at Donnie's monastery, too: the intimacy, which is not intrusive, of standing in a circle around the altar.

Again, the mysterious ambrosial food. Vegetarian, but half the time I haven't known what we're eating. Tonight, for instance, a tofu-like substance, cubed, in a creamy sauce. Yet it didn't have the rubbery texture of tofu. It was satiny, the unctuous sauce as finely draped as the Cistercian chapel gown, fresh marjoram worked into the cream like a subtle tweed. Roasted potatoes, charred slightly. And steamed kale, a dark hillock of softened forest, taken this morning from the garden. Nothing here has a crude taste. There's an elusive quality, almost a tease to the palate: guess what *this* is. The entire effect is light, fresh.

No one talks about weight, diets, all that. Thinness is gone, so is fat.

Tonight there were rose petals again—deep red this time—in the salad. "I think I like the yellow ones better," Mary, who was sitting next to me, said.

"A more delicate perfume," I agreed, nodding. Two feasting beings, discussing our native foods the way we understood others speak of theirs: peas and carrots, cabbage and corn, whatever it is that mortals eat.

Coming out of the community dining room after dinner, I happened to meet André, the chaplain, leaving the kitchen, where he had taken his meal. "Too much yak-yak-yak," he said, indicating the dining room. He likes to eat in silence. He wore his beret, and his voice had a rasp that seemed to augment his Belgian accent. From a distance, he didn't seem so very old, but near him like this I realized he must be well over eighty.

"I have a question to ask you," he said, without preamble. "You have this streak of white hair at the front of your head. Is this natural or do you put it there with dye?" A question a child would ask, direct, without judgment, but insistent with that purest instinct, curiosity.

"Natural," I said.

"Ah," he said—disappointed, I thought.

"It turned gray several years ago like that," I added.

"No!" he said vehemently. "Not gray. It is white." As if, had it been gray, *obviously* it would have been of no interest to him. It was a little like talking to the Mad Hatter, yet he wasn't crazy, just himself.

By this time we were headed in the same direction, clearly going to walk back to the guest area together. He didn't seem to want to elude me in order to avoid the yak-yak-yak. In fact, he was doing most of the talking, in the rasped, heavily accented voice that kept me leaning toward him in an effort to grasp what he was saying.

"The English language," he said, "true, it has become an

international language, but it does not have the range or depth, not the subtlety of the Flemish." For example, he said, all the need these days to pray to "Our Father and Mother," to make awkward reference to his/her—none of this was necessary in Flemish, he said, where one neutral word included both genders. These matters were important. The mystics, he pointed out, were the first writers to use the vernacular. As for the word itself—*vernacular*—did I know that it was derived, ironically enough, from the Latin? The root was *verna*, a word denoting a house-born slave. The people's native tongue given a word meaning home-grown slave: significant, he was sure. Latin was the language of the Church, but not of mystical experience. "Home words, simple words," he said. "That's what they use. Down the ages. Watch for this."

This led him to other dualities, as we walked along the gravel road. He didn't turn off for the brook path, my favored scenic route. But then, he had his mind on things other than wild iris. By the time we reached the bend in the road, he was distinguishing between two different kinds of mystical experience in the word *ecstasy* (another example of the poverty of English, he noted in passing, where the word means only one thing: "gone away" with the experience of joy).

One mystical ecstasy, he said, was the experience of visions, the other an experience of God. This latter—impossible to describe. Not Latin or English, not even that most subtle of languages, his own Flemish, could say it. Neither case of ecstasy had any relation to personal will. "If someone tells you he can do this, can have visions or experience God, don't believe him." He said it as if the claim of mystical union with the Divine were a known scam running its course in the neighborhood.

We had arrived at the first of the two motel-like structures: his. He invited me into his room. Or rather, he kept talking, opened the door, and when I didn't at first enter, he turned around, frowned, and said impatiently, "Come in, come in, and close the door."

Actually, he had two rooms, divided by a bath, but I saw only the first, because the bath formed a barrier between the two. "More books," he said, when I asked what was in the other room. We had stepped into a European room: map of fifteenth-century Ghent on the wall, back-to-back desks piled high with his notes. Against another wall, a daybed covered with dark blankets, a lamp rigged up from a bookcase, the light directed toward the head of the bed—clearly where he slept, though it had the look of a dog bed, small and denlike.

The walls were books, floor to ceiling. He had four thousand, he said, all catalogued, with an index file for retrieval (yellow for Western religions, green for Eastern, blue for mysticism, as if on this aspect of spirituality alone the two concurred and merged into the celestial color).

Mounted on one side of the desk, tabernacle-style, was an IBM XT computer and printer. He complained about his word-processing program: "I'm not entirely satisfied with ZyWrite," he said. No television, but there was a tape deck and a sophisticated radio, perhaps shortwave. Aerials and wires trailed from their sources and were laid out like a cross, perhaps just coincidentally, on the ceiling, linking him up, up, and away.

It was a monk's *scriptorium*, a scholar's den, a lair of language, a mind externalized into a room. Out the window, from his crammed desk, he had a view of Thomas's garden and the tumbling roses on the chicken-wire fence. "I've been working in the garden for Thomas," I said, looking out.

"He's a good gardener," André said, as if he'd looked into the matter closely, had referenced the relevant texts, and could now speak to the issue with some modicum of authority. "He knows his work." Then, more severely, "But he has no organization. No organization!" Repeated with genuine, though fleeting, anger, as though the word had a meaning to him that it lacked for others.

The smell of pipe, more than of smoke, a kind of woody, pulpy, male-book-leather-sludge-and-smudge elixir had worked its way into the place. Every surface and crevice seemed varnished with it until, having married with these hosts of books, blankets, and surfaces of any kind, the scent re-entered the airstream as the living and breathing, rooty soul of the place.

I found myself telling him my Hudson Bay store experience. I don't know why. Some rudimentary form of confession, that sacrament of my childhood never returned to? Or did I want to be told by the student of ancient mysticism that I, former virgin of the twentieth century, had had a mystical experience: I had met God.

I reach up to touch the wool. Do touch it. And die. Or leave my body. Or fly. Something wonderful is happening. What is it? I am also imprinted on the English downs of the bone-china cup my brother is holding. I am the scuffed wood-plank floor. I am the dollar in my pocket. I have left my body. I no longer stop at my skin. It is the best thing that has ever happened.

He listened attentively, smiled slightly. I took this as a good sign. Seemed intrigued in a wise-old-man way, lying in the weeds. Perhaps I am giving him material, a new monograph? Contemporary mystics, a series of biographical portraits? My old screenwriter scrolled up: *And finally*, he would write in his last chapter, *I turn to a most unusual case. A woman, quite worldly in many ways, but who* . . .

I continued my own recitation, giving him the experience, still so vivid after all these years, of that moment of fearless flight into the world beyond me. *Then it is over. I snap back. I am me, I am nothing. We are going out to the car. I am with them again. There's no explaining the most important thing that has ever happened to me. But if I tried, I would say: You fly, you die. You don't stop inside, you go everywhere. It's heaven.*

"So?" he said, gesturing slightly with his hands open, ready for more, if more I had.

"So." I repeated the word a little impatiently—I'd given him the whole thing, what more did he need?

He said nothing, seemed not to need to say anything. Thinking it over, pondering the imponderable, the ineffable I'd laid before him?

Finally, I said, "What was it? What happened to me then?"

"You maybe had an experience of feeling at one with the universe," he said, shrugging a bit. "You maybe felt at one with the universe in that one place. So you remember it."

"The universe?" I said. "Not God?"

"Well," he said, throwing me a bone, "God made the universe."

We paused for a moment. He saw this wasn't going to do. "It's not a mystical experience," he said flatly. "You feel at one with the universe—the cup, the wool, the planks of the floor, that place. It makes a strong impression on the child, so the child remembers it. These things happen."

"Has it ever happened to you?" I said coldly, picking up my marbles, ready to go.

But he didn't take offense. "Rarely," he said. "I've never had a mystical experience either."

He once had a friend, now dead, a monk who told him thirty years ago (the man was already very old at the time) that he had experienced God. "He got up from his desk, and he went— please, you will excuse me—he went to pee. At that instant, on the way to pee, he has—but only so briefly—this experience of God. He never gets it again. He cannot explain it. And this is not something he can use in a homily, you understand. That is the thing with such mystical experience. They write in the vernacular—the *verna*, you remember, this home-grown language slave every culture puts to hard labor. They try to express it. But there's nothing to be said." He looked right at me, reaching out his hand to indicate the walls of books that hemmed us in.

SUNDAY

*At the end of what seems a longer, more complicated journey
(where?—lost, impossible to retrieve that part), I find myself in
a place like the river crossings I saw in El Paso when I visited
there several years ago. That camel color, dust, and the coffee-
and-cream river. Holy Land colors. People swimming across the
Rio Grande, but not to escape. They are wetbacks, going to
work, cleaning somebody's house. Then they risk swimming back
again. They could drown just going to a job. "Why do they do
that?" I ask.*

*"They need the work," a dark man says evenly. He knows I
am a fool.*

*But in the dream this place also at times seems lush, more
fertile, and even like a rain forest. Anyway, I've been having a
good time in this area, have treated it, as white people do, as a
vacation. Maybe it was all constructed for the tourists (there
was a waterslide I went down, splashing and laughing).*

*Then I look up. There's Donnie approaching. She's on a don-
key. She is somehow smaller or maybe younger than in real life.
"Real life," she says, laughing, "as we affectionately call it." She
and I have been together on this trip, but she has gone off on*

235

her own without my realizing it. She has gone deeper into the territory all by herself on this donkey. Now she is back. Streaked with dirt, I see—especially her forehead.

And ecstatic. I suddenly understand: she has gone on the real part of the trip. I've been hanging around the theme park. She is exultant from her trek to—but it isn't clear where she's been. It isn't some Franciscan place. Somewhere else. I don't understand the word she uses.

I say I want to go.

No, she says. You're too late—or maybe she says, You don't have a donkey. Some such response. The idea is that there's no chance of going now. I'm very upset by this.

It's not fatal, she says.

But she won't get off the donkey. The donkey is real, and it's laughing. Animals do laugh, she says. She's laughing, too.

Hair washed, bag packed, sitting in the beach chair in the meadow near my room, letting my hair dry in the sun before I take off. It's cold here at night, full of damp. But in the midmorning sun, everything dries fast. Yesterday I draped my wet towels over the wild-rose bushes behind the building. In the afternoon, when I collected them, they smelled faintly of roses, as if I'd packed them in sachet.

A letter arrived from Donnie on Thursday, but I decided not to open it until now, wanting to be entirely *here* during the week, not even her good voice from Out There drawing me away. She turned up in my dreams anyway. The envelope is fat, and I slice it open neatly with my nail file. Lots of news, as it turns out. "You've gone into the cloister," she writes, "and I've finally passed my driving test! I flunked parallel parking and almost put the examiner through the windshield on the quick stop—but I got an 87." Another cloister grille goes down. And where will she go? "I'm already planning a trip—a real hermit experience—to a cabin way up north somebody says I can have for two weeks. No plumbing! Haul your own water! Soup out of a can! Silent prayer, visualization prayer, walking meditation!"

She has other news. Soeur Agnès has left the Assisi monastery after all. She's Patricia again, back in Detroit, looking for a job. Two different versions of her departure: She couldn't take the summer heat or she couldn't take praying in a foreign language. Another seeker back on the road.

More: a group of nuns from my old convent school has formed a contemplative community in the roughest neighborhood they could find on the North Side of Minneapolis. The French finishing school brought upriver in the nineteenth century from St. Louis to educate the daughters of the Catholic middle class has sent its next expedition around the corner "from that street they call Crack Avenue," Donnie writes. She says they're making friends with the neighbors. People stop in for Morning Praise before they go to their jobs. "Not just Catholics, just people who like the life. Want to check it out? I'll drive."

I said goodbye to the Rosethorn community after breakfast. I finally remembered to ask about the portrait of the beautiful woman. Who was she, the beauty who presided over our meals?

"We don't know," Cecile said. The picture had come in a mailing from Amnesty International, the photograph of one of "the disappeared" in Argentina. "We thought she would keep us in mind of the struggle," she said. "People get interested in the face. They make up a story about her, and then they finally ask who she is. It's a jolt—which it should be."

After the farewells, I stopped at the chapel for a moment. The rhododendron had finished blooming, the big window was given over wholly to the abiding colors of the lordly tree. Dark green and the scabbed bark of deep russet, unperturbed now by that brief scribble of pink. No longer springtime, but suddenly midsummer. Along the brookside path that I took for the final time on my way back to my room, the wild iris, too, were finished, their deep purple turned to pale onionskin; even the blady stalks were frayed, becoming the color of old corn husks. It's been a long spring, but it's finally summer, even here, so far north.

I put Donnie's letter back in the envelope, leaned back, and

237

closed my eyes in the sun. And instantly blinked open, laughing. That donkey Donnie was riding: I knew where it had come from. I had been thinking maybe it had something to do with the deer I saw the first night here at Rosethorn, that serious, lyrical doe. Glimpsed that fleeting instant, pausing on the edge of twilight, a girl poised at womanhood, regarding the world.

None of that. It was the donkey in that Piero della Francesca painting. I have a postcard of it, from the National Gallery in London, over my desk at home. It's been there so long I don't even see it anymore. But I put it there originally for the donkey. He's laughing, howling really. He's in the stable. Everyone is there, the usual positions in the stylized manger. The donkey is to the right, head thrown back, big teeth exposed, guffawing. The picture is called *The Nativity*. It's an icon of the Word made flesh, which is the opposite trick literature keeps trying to do: making flesh into word.

But even in the vernacular, André's faithful home slave, it can't be done, he said; the deepest experience of being alive, the mystical one, cannot be told. Is it the same heartbreaking failure of every story, every person who leans forward and tries to tell her tale, as Alma did that night in Spello, the goddess glowing in the dark? The story of mystical life or our stories from real life, *as we affectionately call it*, the dream-Donnie had said, laughing. We're all trying to say our truth, bringing forward our oddly shaped piece of the puzzle. But don't believe them, old André had said in his room full of texts. Even in the vernacular, the most important experience—he was firm about this, speaking walled in by books—cannot be told.

Edwina has just come over to say goodbye, her car all packed. She is taking Mary and Bob back to San Francisco, returning her rental car at the airport, and then she's off to a conference in Rome, where she will translate from Italian into English— "or French, if that's what they need," tossing her languages lightly like balls she keeps easily in the air.

"Good luck flying," I said cheerfully. I who have just clawed into my jacket pocket, to be sure my gold airplane brooch is at the ready for my own flight home.

"Oh, I'm not afraid of flying," she said coldly. "That's not the way heights affect me."

My fault. I shouldn't have brought it up, I suppose. I thought she was afraid of all heights.

Yesterday, at the ocean, after Jean and I turned back from the trail, we returned to the area around the Merton Tree. "I'm going to sit right under that tree," Jean said. "And I'm going to meditate. Do you think that's all right? Is that allowed—to go out there?"

I gave my permission and off she went.

No one else was around, except for Edwina, still standing as we'd left her, a statue with crossed arms at the edge of the precipice, looking out sternly at the swarm of pastel light.

I got my backpack from the car—watercolors, notebook, Hershey bar, book of Psalms. Bob had said there was a way to get down to the beach. I went over to Edwina, looking for the path. To my surprise, it was right there at her side, clearly posted.

"I'm going down," I said when she turned, hearing me approach. "Do you want to come, too?"

A look of panic crossed her face—that sophisticated face. "We're the women's version of the Jesuits," she had said earlier in the week to explain her order of college teachers. "The intellectuals." She was the daughter of a physicist who spent his life in Europe, mostly in Vienna. Her parents had provided her with an education, she said, that was meant to give her "sparkle, polish—and depth." She spoke five languages effortlessly.

Her parents, both worldly people, but without a stroke of interest in religion of any kind, had been unable to comprehend her conversion. Her entrance into the convent drove them wild. That was over thirty years ago. Her satisfaction in breaking their glossy veneer was still evident, though it was the milder pleasure of a harmless vindication now: she'd stuck it out, she liked the life. "Mama is dead," she said. "Papa accepts the situation. He is taken care of by my brother. He's a physicist, too. He goes all over the world."

This was her story. But her face, turned from the ocean to me, lacked defiance of any kind. She looked frightened.

"I'd love to go down," she said shyly, almost pitifully—this commanding woman who suffered fools not at all and gave short shrift to Bob's moist Merton sentiments. "I'd love to, but I'm afraid of heights."

I looked down. It was a dizzying drop, the path barely zig-zagged; it seemed to shimmy down the sheer face to a low bulkhead of boulders, giving out finally to the rare black sand of the beach and the steady beat of the sea. Easy to imagine your broken body rolling from boulder to boulder, landing in a crushed heap on the smooth washed sand.

Still, there were, at least at the top, some handholds, and the Park Service had hacked out rudimentary steps. And way down, you could see pin-people who had gotten to the beach somehow and were playing tag now with the incoming breakers.

"I just can't," she said miserably. "I get terrible vertigo."

"I'll go first," I said. "You keep right behind me. It's looking down that causes the problem. If you just keep looking at my back, you'll be okay. I'll help you." For some reason, the more terrified she seemed, the easier the way down looked to me. Airplanes leave you no illusions. But here at least, both feet were on the ground. I could afford to display courage.

But there was no convincing her. I saw that it was impossible. "You go on," she said at last, the way in the movies a wounded soldier tells his comrades to leave him behind, he's done for.

It wasn't a bad climb down. Steep, but there was more stairway than had been obvious at the top. I lowered myself, careful step by careful step, sometimes grabbing an outcropping of bramble, just as I'd done coming down Monte Subasio, skidding on white stones into Assisi.

Edwina was still there at the top, very small now, face impossible to read, waving. I turned and walked toward the sea.

A skull floated on the water, its black eye holes staring right at me. *Memento mori.* It clutched me. *Number your days: know that you will die.*

I stared back at it for what felt like a long minute, weirdly mesmerized by this living skull with its intelligent bead on me. Then it dipped under the water, or was washed over by the heave of a wave, I couldn't tell which.

When it resurfaced, I saw clearly it was a seal, its head turned now slightly away, showing a bit of body. But it had looked alarmingly like a skull, a gray skull with large, very black eye holes and nose, the jaw stuck at the waterline, lying there in wait, as omens do.

The rest of the afternoon was a beauty. I settled in with my watercolors, measuring out the hours with bits of Hershey bar. I dipped my brush in a tidepool, tried to get the big boulder and the waves smashing against it, smashing for a million years plus this minute.

But waves were beyond me. The drawing was a mess, it was nothing at all. The Assisi magic was gone. I needed a bell tower, a fountain, a dribbling bas-relief lion, stone gentled by the monastic grasp. Nature was beyond me, and I knew it—it was too much *the real world as we affectionately call it.* I put my paints away and walked along the black sand beach, stopping to shout the day's Psalms to the waves, which roared back.

When I returned finally to the base of the path to begin the climb up again, I tilted my head far back to take in my destination. There was Edwina, still standing, though now not like a statue but bending ever so slightly, looking down. Then jerking back, before she attempted this act of daring again.

"Want to try it now?" I yelled up at her. "It's gorgeous here. There's nothing to be afraid of." Brave me, rooted at sea level, speaking from the floor of the world as if I were calling from the clouds, flying free and undaunted.

"Wha—a—?" Her word got lost coming down.

"There's nothing to be afraid of!"

She stepped back. It was impossible to read her expression so far away, but she shook her head vehemently.

I realized, finally, I was being cruel. And who was I to make claims about scaling the heights?

"Never mind," I hollered, though she probably didn't hear me. The waves were taking my message, throwing it away. "I'll tell you all about it," I called to her, as if I could beam myself up, a fearless flyer at last. "I'm coming right up."